INTERMARKET ANALYSIS AND INVESTING

INTERMARKET ANALYSIS AND INVESTING

Integrating Economic, Fundamental, and Technical Trends

Michael E. S. Gayed

, New York Institute of Finance

New York   London   Toronto   Sydney   Tokyo   Singapore

Library of Congress Cataloging-in-Publication Data

Gayed, Michael
   Intermarket analysis and investing : integrating economic,
fundamental, and technical trends / Michael E. S. Gayed.
    p. cm.
   Includes index.
   ISBN 0-13-929225-X
   1. Investment analysis. I. Title.
HG4529.G39 1990
332.6—dc20   90-6321
                                          CIP

The following companies' charts have been used or adapted with permission: Bank Credit Analyst, Knight Ridder—Trade Center, Ned Davis Research, Securities Research Company, and Standard & Poor's.

This publication is designed to provide accurate and authoritative information in regard to the subject matter covered. It is sold with the understanding that the publisher is not engaged in rendering legal, accounting, or other professional service. If legal advice or other expert assistance is required, the services of a competent professional person should be sought.

From a Declaration of Principles Jointly Adopted by a Committee of the American Bar Association and a Committee of Publishers and Associations

Printed in the United States of America

10 9 8 7 6 5 4 3 2 1

New York Institute of Finance
2 Broadway
New York, New York 10004-2207
A Division of Simon & Schuster
A Paramount Communications Company

To Nadia and Michael, my precious loves,
to Ester and Shaker, who gave me birth,
and to Mary and Dr. Albert who blessed me with the
greatest gift of my life.

Perseverance has been the hidden force behind every success story in the history of mankind and will continue to be the source of progress for the remainder of man's life on earth. No matter how bad things get, if you persevere, chances are that you will conquer all adversities and prevail.

—The Author

Contents

☐ **3**

Part Two: Economic Analysis

☐ **4**

☐ **5**

Part Three: Fundamental Analysis

☐ 6

The Fundamental Catalyst, 161

☐ 7

Industry Group Analysis, 187

☐ 8

Fundamental Investment Dynamics, 221

Part Five: Investment Strategies

☐ **12**

Tops . . . Bottoms . . . and Trends, 381

☐ **13**

Portfolio Management Dynamics, 411

Preface

Today's world is fast-changing and complex. Each day, investors, brokers, economists, money managers, and financial advisors are deluged with tons of statistics that cover almost every aspect of the business world. This abundance of information often obscures what is meaningful and what is not and makes it easy to lose sight of what the prevailing trend may be leading to.

Successful investing depends on the ability of investors to determine the market trend and the direction of future price movement. This book reviews some of the most effective market analysis techniques and integrates the economic, fundamental, and quantitative (or market-timing) methods into a unified approach with which to forecast market trends. By using this multidisciplinary concept, the reader will gain a better perspective of market mechanics; once aware of the intricacies of market mechanics, the reader can then hope to sharpen his or her forecast of future trends.

There are three schools of stock market analysis: economic, fundamental, and quantitative. Each advocates a unique methodology devised to help anticipate, and capitalize on, potential profit opportunities. In large research firms, there are three distinct groups of analysts that perform elaborate studies based on these dominant disciplines. Yet, very few books have tried to integrate the three approaches into a unified methodology that deals effectively with risk in financial markets. This book probes into the basics of these three techniques and makes an effort at presenting a coherent method to use the best they can offer. *Intermarket Analysis and Investing* focuses on explaining these methodologies and the factors that influence prices of stocks and bonds. The ultimate goal of these techniques is to manage the risks associated with the investment process.

Economists are concerned with the business outlook, inflation, employment, and the economy at large. They study the statistics published by the Department of Commerce, the Department of Labor, the Federal Reserve Board (Fed), and the Bureau of Census, among others. Economists analyze carefully the Fed's monetary policy to project the future course of business activities. By analyzing the economic indicators, economists can forecast inflation, the housing market, the rate of unemployment, the household savings rate, corporate profits, and the economic cycle.

At times, the Fed may have several concurrent objectives: stable growth, low inflation, expanding employment, and the maintenance of a healthy dollar. In order to achieve these goals simultaneously, the Fed may experience a policy conflict. On the one hand, inflation is undesirable, and the Fed may choose to tighten the monetary reins. On the other hand, the control of inflation is often attained at the expense of rising unemployment, which is politically and socially unacceptable. The Fed's practice of using the accessibility of money to balance the economy results in wide swings in business activities.

These phases of economic expansion followed by periods of contraction are known as the business cycle. Economic fluctuations, in turn, have a direct impact on corporate earnings, cash flow, sales, profit margins, market share, and dividends. Studying the cyclical behavior of the economic indicators can help investors anticipate major turning points in business and in financial markets. Geoffrey Moore authored a number of books that examined economic indicators and their value in timing important junctures of the business cycle. John Samuelson, John Kenneth Galbraith, Milton Friedman, Wesley C. Mitchell, Arthur F. Burns, Joseph Schumpeter and other well-known economists have also contributed to the wealth of economic and business cycle studies.

Careful analysis of the economic aggregates can enhance investors' understanding of the impact of the business cycle on the stock and bond markets. This, in turn, can lead to improved awareness of the risks and rewards associated with the different stages of the cycle. This book studies the relationship between the economic indicators and the stock market and how they have behaved relative to each other over the past several decades. It also examines how these indicators can be used to forecast the long-term trend of equities and fixed-income securities.

Analysis of fundamentals, is, by far, the discipline most widely followed by professionals in the investment community. Benjamin Graham and David Dodd are the godfathers of the fundamental school. By performing an in-depth analysis of the balance sheet, they claim, investors can assess the financial health of a corporation and its long-term potential. Fundamentalists' techniques are considered of great value in forecasting earnings, dividends, and sales growth. By analyzing financial statements, they identify liquidity, profitability, leverage, and market-related ratios as key to ascertaining a solid financial position. Their book, *Security Analysis,* is considered by many analysts to be the ultimate authority in the field. The book focuses on the careful analysis of financial statements in order to uncover the intrinsic value of the corporation and determine its investment worth. Fundamental analysis is an effective way to deal with security risk and helps ensure the soundness of the overall investment decision. Fisher, Bellmore, Cohen, and Zeikel have also written extensively on the fundamental aspects of security analysis.

Fundamentals serve as the catalyst that propels the trend of stock prices. Rising earnings and growing sales of a particular company should lead to financial growth. When investors are alerted to those improving fundamentals, buying demand for stocks expands, which pushes prices upward.

Fundamental analysis of industry groups is also important for the asset allocation process and active money management. Awareness of the groups' characteristics and typical behavior during the different phases of the business cycle helps identify leadership and avoid poor performers.

The quantitative, or market-timing, method utilizes stud-

ies of the internal market dynamics. It is helpful in measuring
the relative performance among the various market sectors.
Quantitative analysts (market timers) rely on statistical analysis
to assess the prevailing trend. This method's thrust is based on
comparative studies of the price momentum that propels
strength or weakness in the broad market as well as on comparative studies of different industry groups and individual
stocks. One of this method's greatest strengths is its ability to
track the flow of money that results from the continuous shift
in the supply-and-demand forces characterizing intermediate
and long-term market dynamics. By analyzing the industry
groups' price momentum and the market averages, the quantitative method helps investors detect the changes in the market trend. Such analysis uses concepts of rate of change, momentum oscillators, and investors' psychology to determine
evolving strength or weakness in financial markets. It is, indeed, the school that concerns itself with market trend perspectives; it relies heavily on comparative techniques to uncover the
internal dynamics that help propel prices along a well-defined
course. In addition, quantitative, or market-timing, techniques
can help detect major turning points in the general market,
industry groups, and individual stocks.

At the turn of the twentieth century, Charles H. Dow and
Edward Jones pioneered the research effort that led to the
proliferation of the quantitative approach: They devised the
famous Dow Jones Industrial Averages and introduced Wall
Street to the world of charts. By constructing the most widely
followed index, they helped to quantify the amount of advance
or decline in prices and to measure the intensity of such
changes. Their work was later expanded on by such quantitative analysts as William Hamilton, Robert Rhea, Richard Schab-
aker, Robert Edwards, John Magee, Harold Gartley, Garfield
Drew, Richard Russel, and many others. Today, the market-
timing school uses such sophisticated techniques and computerized methods that only state-of-the-art technology can make
possible.

Quantitative analysts pay little attention to the prevailing
economic or fundamental background. However, they respect
the signals of the market indicators. Market timing has a com-

pelling value for the savvy investor who has made a thorough economic and fundamental analysis. By fine tuning the timing of buying and selling decisions, investment results can be enhanced. This book covers the most important market-timing methods used to analyze current trends and the long-term direction of price movements.

All of these disciplines of market analysis have one goal in common: This is to identify the market trend and anticipate important turning points. Yet all of these methods have been addressed in isolation from one another. No effort has been spent toward integrating them in a unified approach. The objective here is to examine the interaction of the underlying economic, fundamental, and quantitative dynamics and analyze their predictive value for securities market trends.

This study encompasses the analysis of the equities and fixed-income markets in response to a continuously changing economic and fundamental background. It will probe deeply into markets' interrelationships and illustrate the influence of financial markets on each other. For example, what is the economic impact of rising oil prices? How is such a development likely to affect the monetary policy? . . . interest rates? . . . the bond market? . . . the stock market? If the price of aluminum rises in the futures markets, what impact could that have on aluminum companies? Is there a relationship between gold and interest rates? What is the relationship between commodity prices and the bond market? Which stocks or industry groups are likely to benefit from a weak dollar? There are many economic, fundamental, and market-related dynamics that have an impact on the trend of securities, and this book examines a large number of them. It tries to fill the gap that has long existed between the dominant schools of market analysis to help the reader identify evolving trends in financial markets.

The focus here is on trends: how to detect them, follow them, and forecast their likely future course. The thrust is to study the economic and fundamental factors that are constantly at work in the marketplace and that propel trends of stock and bond prices. *Intermarket Analysis and Investing* reviews a large number of techniques that can help identify trends and provide insights into their behavior.

The book consists of five parts: concepts of trend analysis, economic analysis, fundamental analysis, quantitative market analysis, and investment strategies.

Part One lays the foundation for this study by introducing some important concepts that are used throughout the book. This section briefly reviews the tenets of the three main schools of market analysis and familiarizes the reader with their methodology. It studies the components of risk in the investment process and identifies ways to control it. It reviews the early theories of trend analysis and market averages and introduces some generic market analysis techniques that are applicable to a large number of situations.

Parts Two, Three, and Four deal with the most widely known schools of market analysis techniques: economic, fundamental, and quantitative. Each part starts with an explanation of the basics to help the reader understand the underlying concepts of each of these schools of market analysis. After establishing the basics, the book proceeds with more advanced concepts.

In Part Two, the focus is on the most important economic indicators and their typical behavior during the business cycle. In addition, it reviews the impact of the economic policy on the housing market, household consumption, capital spending, the job market, corporate earnings, consumers and corporate debt, and many other key sectors of the economy. The leading, lagging, and coincident indicators and their components are fully studied. This section of the book looks into their value in timing long-term bull and bear markets and probes into the relationship between the economic indicators and the stock market. I then demonstrate how the stock market behaved at major turning points of the business cycle and what the position of these economic indicators was at that time.

Part Three explores the fundamental method of security analysis. Using financial statements as the basis of this study, this part examines in detail the components of the balance sheet and income statements. The key financial ratios used to analyze liquidity, profitability, asset utilization, and leverage are then fully discussed. Some case studies of several stocks and industry group behaviors are examined in light of their prevailing fundamentals. An overview of several fundamental investment theories and strategies is then provided. Comprehensive analyses of industry groups' characteristics are fully explained to illustrate their behavior during the different stages of the business cycle. Their earnings behaviors under different economic and fundamental conditions are also examined.

In order to explain the basic concepts of trend analysis techniques, I rely heavily on graphs to illustrate past behavior during the different phases of the business cycle. The graphs stress the relationships between the stock and bond markets and economic and fundamental developments. They show what happened in real life, not what we like to see happening or what our opinion is. This is a study from the files of history. The graphs powerfully demonstrate the impact of the fundamental and economic forces on price trends.

In Part Four, the tenets of the quantitative school of market analysis are reviewed. This discipline is thought to be the most instrumental methodology for determining when to buy and when to sell. The Dow Jones Industrial Average opened the doors for many studies of the forces at work in the marketplace. At times, these internal dynamics cannot be explained by either the economic or the fundamental method. Yet, they are powerful and govern the price action of securities in financial markets. Our study begins with a review of the statistical tools used in analyzing the price behavior of the market, its industry groups, and individual stocks. The construction and characteristics of a large number of market-timing indicators are explained. These techniques are then integrated with what has been learned from the economic and fundamental studies. This part of the book covers the most important trend indicators and illustrates the market behavior during the different stages of the business cycle. Following a thorough analysis of their characteristics, the internal dynamics of industry groups are focused on. This part demonstrates how momentum and sentiment concepts are used to time buy and sell decisions for both the intermediate and long-term horizons. Some key intermarket relationships are explained to illustrate the complex interaction of financial markets in the real world. The element of constant change during the investment process compels us to make timely decisions and to react to evolving trends. At this stage of the book, the influence of commodity prices on industry groups and the fixed-income market is addressed. The subtle relationships between the different industry groups and the correlation between their trends are explained.

Part Five explores investment strategies and trading techniques. It examines methods of constructing a diversified portfolio to serve specific investment objectives. In addition, it expounds on the asset allocation process, portfolio structuring, money management, and the timing of investment decisions. Trading techniques for intermediate-term investment objectives are briefly reviewed. All of the indicators covered in the book are then assembled into a unified line of thinking. Characteristics of market tops and bottoms are discussed in light of typical economic and fundamental environments. The difference between positioning and trading is addressed, with some thoughts on applicable strategies that enable their proper utilization.

Investing in the stock market is a humbling experience. I felt that my work would not be complete without emphasizing the flaws and pitfalls of the disciplines and strategies described in the book. I do not have any preference for any single technique; I also believe that no one single market analysis discipline is superior to all the others. It is also important to emphasize that trading systems may work for awhile, and then fail to deliver profits. Nothing is infallible on Wall Street. The best companies with the best fundamentals at the best of economic times may suddenly reverse their upward trend and go into a tailspin. The reason for the decline may not be known for a long while, but the market has often been correct in anticipating bankruptcies and future crises. Constant monitoring and management of one's own investment is crucial; overconfidence is the seed of all failures.

The concepts explained in the book are not complex. Money managers, analysts, brokers, financial planners, trust officers, corporate treasurers, and investors with basic knowledge of stock market operations will benefit tremendously from many of the techniques explained. Trading strategies can be applied to many investment profiles and can help enhance the decision-making process for specific portfolio objectives. Many of the philosophies covered in this book can find solid applications in the business world outside the investment arena.

Trends develop in practically every kind of social, economic, or political activity. Some of these trends are temporary, while others are long lasting. Yet, in every endeavor, success is highly dependent on recognition of the trend and its future direction. With hindsight, events are easily explained, yet real gains are only possible if we apply reason and an orderly methodology in advance to reach sound conclusions.

In every field of human endeavor, success depends upon careful analysis, identifying objectives, mapping appropriate strategies, and modifying action in light of obtained results. Yet, the element of luck, especially on Wall Street, is an integral part of the whole effort. The word luck represents the ingredient that will take care of all the unknown and enable the work to be fruitful. Recognizing that the stock market is a difficult game to play, and admitting that investing in securities is an art, we can only preface the book with

.... Good Luck ....

PART ONE

Introduction

❑1

The Investment Process

An investment in knowledge always pays the best interest.

Benjamin Franklin

The investment process is no more than an ongoing effort to control the risk associated with a portfolio of assets. Although this books's focus is on analyzing securities market trends, the techniques used are applicable to a large number of investment vehicles. It is only by assessing the risk associated with an investment that an informed decision that meets objectives can be formulated.

Before exploring the subject of risk analysis, some basic concepts thought to be helpful in the investment process should be reviewed. First, we have to understand the difference between investing and speculating. Speculation is a fine art in which the gambling instinct, the will to survive, and a little bit of luck may be all an investor needs in order to achieve his or her financial goals. Investment, on the other hand, is more like a science aimed at directing and managing investors' hard-earned savings to capitalize on opportunities in the marketplace. Investment strategies supported by extensive research are the ultimate defense against financial risk.

Successful investing is a journey of consistency. Stating the objectives at an early stage, revising those objectives in light of the prevailing and anticipated business environment, and actively researching the economic, fundamental, and quantitative dynamics of the marketplace are key ingredients in achieving high returns. Investing is a process, not an event.

Wealth and fortune can be attained over many years of careful crafting of strategies and continuous assessment of investment alternatives.

Gèrmane to successful investing are five main topics that investors should be aware of: financial planning, investment analysis, risk assessment, portfolio structuring, and performance evaluation. Each of these subjects has been addressed in many books. Yet they are brought together here because of the importance of integrating them into the final decision. Without a financial plan there is no necessity for either market analysis or risk assessment. The investment process, then, approximates a random walk of trial and error.

Investment analysis is the ultimate defense against the many unknowns that influence prices in the marketplace. Without both macro and micro consideration of the impact of the dynamic economic and fundamental environment, investors are at the mercy of a multitude of unknown factors that can adversely influence their investments. Risk assessment is a core ingredient in determining reasonable objectives. In the absence of a thorough risk assessment plan, structuring a portfolio becomes an exercise in futility. Portfolio structuring is the first step toward executing carefully thought out financial plans. Finally, constantly reviewing investment results, then matching them to stated objectives, is the final checkpoint that keeps a plan on target. If the rate of return does not meet desired objectives, then perhaps the whole process should be examined to uncover where things went wrong and adapt the plan to achieve the investor's goals. The success or failure of the plan often depends on the feedback provided by the performance evaluation.

FINANCIAL PLANNING

You can develop your financial plan at any stage of life. Before drawing the plan, however, a personal balance sheet and income statement should be set up. Financial planners spend a long time profiling their clients in order to determine what portfolio of assets suits their needs best.

The plan should be designed to achieve a certain level of security while meeting financial obligations at different stages of life. Careful assessment of our current and future earning power as well as other financial resources is at the heart of formulating realistic objectives. Cash flow analysis is an important step toward tailoring the plan to suit our risk tolerance. Potential future increases or decreases of income are key considerations in determining the risk threshold factor. Your age may mandate a menu of investment vehicles that are geared to minimizing risk exposure. What is suitable for one person or household may not be suitable for another in a different age group. The younger the investor, the more risk he or she can take and, hence, the more growth oriented his or her portfolio should be. The older the investor is, the more conservative his growth expectations should be and the more income oriented the portfolio has to be. The portfolio should be structured based on your age and your current and anticipated future financial position. Younger people should strive at accumulating assets; but safety of capital is of prime importance as retirement approaches. The wealthier the investor becomes and the older he grows, the more conservative a risk taker he should be. Old age is the stage at which preservation of capital supersedes in importance any other consideration. However, safety has consistently proven to be the ultimate winner. Conservative financial planning should always strive at preserving wealth for young families and even more so for older individuals.

Aside from age and earnings potential, there are other important factors in choosing the type of investments suitable for specific objectives. Insurance, for example, is an important pillar of a carefully designed plan. Real estate and other tax shelter vehicles are also needed for both accumulation and preservation of capital. Liquidity often proves to be handy during emergencies. The children's education is a "must" consideration for any family. One may choose to manage part or all of the plan or one may delegate it to a professional manager. There are many considerations that have to be thought out during the early stages of the financial planning process that go beyond the scope of this book. The focus of this book is on the most important component of any financial plan—how to analyze the financial markets in order to invest in promising securities and realize investment goals.

Investment Analysis

Once a financial plan is in place, the investment vehicles with the best potential and most appropriate level of risk should be chosen. The process of selecting from among investment alternatives involves a great deal of analysis. Trend analysis techniques are applicable to all types of investments. Real estate, collectibles, stocks, and fixed income securities can all be analyzed in light of their underlying fundamentals, their liquidity, and trend perspectives.

A thorough analysis of the risk associated with each type of investment should be done before any other consideration. As is well known, commodities trading and land speculation are considered the riskiest of all investment vehicles. High yield securities also rank high on the risk spectrum. Options and futures carry an excessively high risk premium; very few speculators in those markets can demonstrate consistent success over time. As a matter of fact, any investment that is limited by time is considered risky—investing in stocks is riskier than investing in bonds; the safest investment of all is in three-month Treasury bills (T-bills).

Following the risk assessment process, investors should try to find out as much as they can about the nature and behavior of their investment choices. A variety of techniques used to analyze the risk and potential reward in the securities markets are discussed here. The concepts discussed are not infallible, but they are considered to be good tools for identifying the trends in stock and bond prices.

The economic environment and the cyclical nature of business in a free enterprise system have an important impact on trends of stocks and bonds. Periods of economic expansion lead to rising corporate earnings, increasing sales, and improving profit margins for most industries. Understanding the relationship between economic fluctuations and the price behavior of securities markets is vital for making well-informed investment decisions. The influence of the business cycle on financial markets cannot be ignored and should be well understood in order to win at investing.

During recessions, companies stand the risk of losing market share, realizing lower earnings, suffering from shrinking margins and eroding profits, failing to service their debts, and, in rare cases, being totally ruined. The financial risk associated with periods of economic slowdown often hamper growth potential. Long after a business recovery is well under way, many companies and industry groups continue to suffer deteriorating financial strength and to struggle for mere survival.

Once the stage of the business cycle is determined, fundamental factors pertinent to specific industry groups and stocks are analyzed. The modern valuation theory is a study of the firm's fundamental foundation and an in-depth analysis of its financial position. The purpose of the analysis is to uncover the intrinsic worth of individual stocks and to assess their future earnings potential. Sales growth, profit margins, and asset valuation are key factors to consider. Financial ratios are derived from companies' financial statements. They can be used to assess liquidity, profitability, leverage, and potential future growth possibilities. The fundamental approach is long-term oriented by nature and is not necessarily concerned with investment timing. It is an important step toward ensuring a sound financial position and is an effort to evaluate future growth prospects. Fundamental analysis, based on well-accepted principles, is the rational way of uncovering values in the marketplace. Fundamental assessment of a company's financial position goes hand in hand with analyzing the economic cycle. Such analysis is one of the most important steps toward dealing with security risk.

Thus, the economic analysis helps uncover the likely long-term direction of interest rates, production and consumption demand, and the outlook for corporate profits. Fundamental analysis enables discernment of the underlying value of the company you wish to invest in and assures you of its financial soundness. The only questions then remaining are: When to buy? And when to sell? That is the juncture at which you have to examine the internal dynamics of the market and to fine tune the analysis with some market-timing techniques.

Stock prices are often governed by waves of optimism and pessimism. Investors' expectations and perceptions of value shape the trend in prices. Psychology plays an important role in financial markets, one that can hardly be ignored. Those waves of optimism and pessimism influence the actual value reflected in the securities markets. Such expectations often lead to periods of overvaluation during bull markets and periods of undervaluation during panics and bear markets. Timing buying and selling decisions accordingly can help improve performance and enhance final returns.

Also, supply-and-demand factors play an important role in determining securities prices on Wall Street. The value of a stock from day to day reflects all the known and unknown factors relevant to it. There are hundreds of smart individuals and mammoth institutions that make their living predicting trends and investing in the market, using extensive research. Their buy-and-sell decisions are often based on sophisticated models that incorporate advanced valuation techniques. The sum of all those investment activities is reflected in the daily and weekly price and volume behavior. Those internal forces, which may not be readily apparent in the published and known fundamentals about a company or an industry group, cannot be ignored. Such forces have a tremendous impact on the value of securities in the marketplace.

Thorough analysis is crucial in order to meet investment objectives and to deal effectively with risk. Consistency is of prime importance for both capital appreciation and preservation. While the buy-and-hold investment strategy has been considered supreme, a portfolio stands to lose substantially if the economic, fundamental, and quantitative dynamics are ignored. For instance, several decades ago, the steel industry had its heyday. Then, during the late 1960s, steel companies encountered financial difficulties, eroding market share, and deteriorating fundamentals. Investors who had been holding these stocks for the long haul discovered, to their dismay, that it would have been better to have sold. A similar scenario occurred involving the mobile home companies, which witnessed a gigantic rise in their stock price in the early 1960s. When the trend reversed, the firms were never again able to duplicate that impressive performance.

Risk Assessment

Risk is the possibility of suffering losses of your principal investment capital. Most people, sophisticated as well as novice, tend to take the issue of risk lightly. Over the years, the stock market has attracted brilliant individuals from all walks of life. Some brought with them the savvy, a desire to win, and the readiness to learn and pay the price of earning an above-average rate of return on their investments. Others approached the investment process ill-prepared and soon discovered that their early successes were followed by painful losses. No one has the ultimate formula for success, yet there are facts you should know before entering the financial market arena. In addition, there are also techniques to help you control the risk. Money managers have as their most important fiduciary duty the use of methodical strategies with which to control the element of risk.

Risk varies, from the probability of losing the total amount invested, to the possibility of losing only partially. There are different degrees of risk associated with different kinds of markets. Even within the same market, there are some investments that are considered to be "blue chip" and others that are considered speculative. For example, pink-sheet stocks that have little fundamental credibility have a higher risk than those of the financially strong and well-known companies. Everyone hopes to find that young and promising company that will become the Xerox or IBM of tomorrow; yet, the fact is that startup companies stand a slim chance of making it to the blue-chip rank. Similarly, small companies with unproven track records in managing growth are riskier than those of high quality that have been around for decades and have survived good and bad times.

When addressing the subject of risk, two important factors must be stressed. The first is the time risk, and the second is the inflation risk. Investment trends are continuously changing with time. First are the early stages of growth, usually followed by accelerating upward momentum, and finally reaching a stage of maturity that often leads to reversal of that trend. This concept is applicable to almost all known investments, from real estate to bonds.

The second factor, inflation, has more to do with the redirection of purchasing power than the tangible risk of losing the principal. The inflation risk is a comparative risk, as it brings the investment decision closer to the "opportunity cost" issue. That is, when assessing the reward associated with a particular type of investment, one has to compare it with all other available opportunities to reach a desired rate of return. Investment in a particular security that yields a specified rate of return may be chosen, but when adjusted for inflation, it may perform less well than other investment choices at the same level of risk. The reduction of purchasing power and the opportunity cost of an investment are two considerations that have to be factored into risk assessment and the choice of investment vehicles to achieve desired returns.

TYPES OF RISKS

Always bear in mind that the higher the desired return, the higher the risk involved. There is a tendency to look at the optimistic side of the equation without fully digesting the negative possibilities. This book is concerned specifically with two main types of stock market risks: systematic, or market risk, and unsystematic, or security risk.

Systematic or Market Risk

The market risk accounts for the cyclical nature of the economy. Also known as the systematic risk, it is assumed the moment capital is invested in the marketplace. The stock market is a discounting mechanism and has been acknowledged by the nation's monetary authority, the Fed, as a fairly reliable leading indicator. In the past, bull markets led periods of broad business expansion, and bear markets started before downturns in real economic conditions. It is quite difficult amidst a boom to detect the end of an uptrend in stocks and the onset of a major market decline. The risk of being fully invested in the stock market around cyclical peaks can result in substantial losses. Typically, during major bear markets, all equities suffer a large setback. When a primary downtrend starts, stock prices come tumbling down independent of their size, quality, financial position, or even their future prospects. That is why the systematic or market risk cannot be controlled by diversification; such risk can only be reduced by proper economic analysis, or, perhaps, by global diversification.

   The market risk may vary from one country to another. The possibility of a synchronized global recession whereby all economies and securities markets decline concurrently is unlikely. The U.S. economy, for example, may enter a recession, while European economies may be stagnant without necessarily following the contraction pattern of the United States. The lead and lag and different performance of Western economies at any point in time conceivably can reduce the market, or systematic, risk of a global portfolio. The chances that all securities will decline around the world with the same magnitude in response to their local economic conditions are small. Figure 1-1 illustrates the two components of risk for a globally diversified portfolio.

Figure 1-1. Risk Components of a Globally Diversified Portfolio

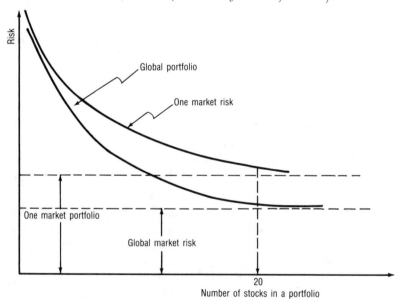

Risk

Global portfolio

One market risk

One market portfolio

Global market risk

20
Number of stocks in a portfolio

Unsystematic or Security Risk

In the marketplace, the long-term trend of stock prices is governed by their underlying fundamentals and the potential of their industry group. The unsystematic risk is dependent on the financial health of the company. The key factors that influence earnings, sales, profitability, return on equity, and growth prospects of a firm or an industry group change during the different stages of the business cycle. Also, these factors may improve or deteriorate in response to new emerging trends or to persistent mismanagement of resources.

Sometimes a lucrative market becomes crowded by too many companies. In their effort to gain market share, their management may decide to sell products at big discount. Price competition often puts a squeeze on profit margins, and all companies in such an industry end up suffering great losses. Even the well-established members of the group feel the impact of eroding profits and declining earnings as a result of industry overcrowding. Often, the stock prices of the members of this industry group decline. Balance sheets are further weakened as leverage increases. Usually this leads to some bankruptcy among the marginal companies in this industry group. Once the balances are worked out, the industry becomes profitable again. It is important to note that the poor fundamental position of a single industry group does not necessarily mean that the broad market has to be affected, since other stocks and industry groups may be doing well.

Other types of unsystematic risk are the risk of holding a stock that is caught in a price war or, more generally, deteriorating fundamentals peculiar to the stock's industry group. The market under such circumstances may be a raging bull, but such stocks will continue to decline in price.

For example, in the 1970s, the oil companies gained substantially in the wake of the fast-rising oil prices mandated by OPEC (Organization of Petroleum Exporting Countries) and by the runaway inflation that characterized the decade. During the 1980s, however, the oil group suffered eroding prices, and the closely related oil services group experienced a semidepression. The risk level of the same industry group was totally different during these two periods of major change.

The unsystematic, or company risk, however, may not have to result from the deteriorating fundamentals of a whole industry group. A particular company may be ill managed and be suffering from excessive debt services charges that cannot be covered by its generated cash flow. The company's marketing plan may be weak, and its distribution channels may be ineffective. The best defense against unsystematic or security risk is diversification. The logic here is that, barring a nationwide depression, it is highly unlikely that all stocks would have such precipitous deterioration in their fundamentals at the same time.

In the 1950s, while experimenting with computerized portfolio models, Dr. Harry Markowitz discovered that the unsystematic portion of risk could be eliminated by proper diversification. It was found that a portfolio consisting of 20 stocks or more has a minimal and negligible amount of unsystematic or security risk. Figure 1-2 illustrates the two com-

Figure 1-2. *Systematic and Unsystematic Risk Components of a Portfolio*

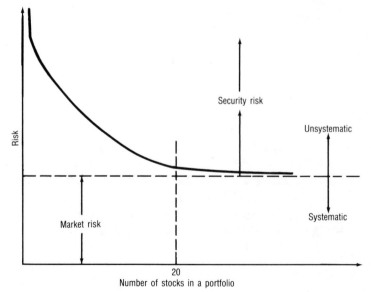

ponents of risk for a portfolio with varying numbers of securities. Note that the unsystematic risk is almost eliminated when the number of stocks in the portfolio exceeds 20.

The Beta and Alpha factors

The study of security risk and return relative to market performance has brought investors closer to understanding the concepts of risk. When the return of a stock is plotted against the S&P (Standard and Poor's) 500 rate of return, the relationship is likely to take different forms. Figure 1-3 illustrates such correlation, from which we can define the beta and alpha of a stock.

Beta, or the security risk, represents the return of a stock relative to the market and is the slope of the line delineating the relationship. If the line is a 45 degree line or the relationship is one, it means that the stock appreciates at the same rate as the market. If the slope is less than 1, that is, beta less than 1, it means that the stock will have less appreciation than the market. A slope that is greater than 1 means that the stock produces a rate of return superior to the broad market. The point at which the line intercepts the vertical axis is known as the alpha of the stock and represents the return on the stock independent of the market.

In practice, however, the relationship between the return on a stock versus the market return can take other forms, depending on the trend of the security itself and the type of industry under consideration. The slope of beta, for one, may be negative or positive. If the stock is in a long-term downtrend when the market is on a bullish course, beta could be negative, as the return on the security is negative. Examples of such conditions would be the performance of Wang Laboratories or Advanced Micro Devices in the 1983–89 period, when the market was a raging bull and those securities were in a long-term downtrend on their own. Another situation may be that of a fast-growing stock whose price is outperforming the broad market and its own industry groups. In such a case, the slope of beta is expected to be positive. For example, the return for L.A. Gear in 1988–89 by far outperformed the rest of the footwear market at that time.

Figure 1-3. Stock versus Market Returns

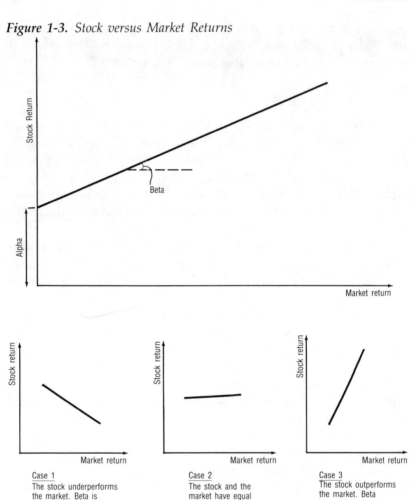

Case 1
The stock underperforms
the market. Beta is
negative.

Case 2
The stock and the
market have equal
returns. Beta is
zero indicating
flat performance.

Case 3
The stock outperforms
the market. Beta
is positive.

Compaq is another example of an explosive growth situation whose stock return has way outpaced the market or any other technology stock from 1986–89. As to alpha, it is natural to expect it to be high for utilities stocks. On the other hand, emerging growth stocks with a steep beta may have a smaller alpha.

Figure 1-4 illustrates the monthly charts of Wang Laboratories and Compaq Computer as examples of stocks that

Figure 1-4. *Wang Laboratories and Compaq Monthly Charts and Examples of Steep Positive and Negative Slopes*

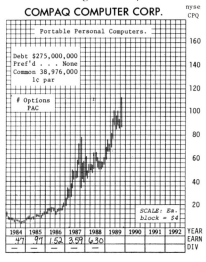

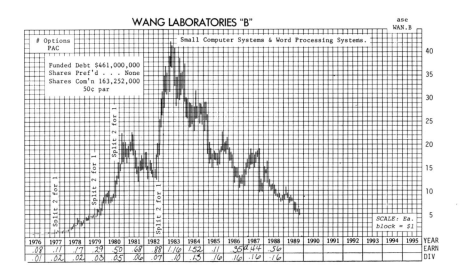

have either severely underperformed or sharply outperformed the broad market in the 1980s. In the case of Wang Laboratories, the beta coefficient had a negative slope for 1983–89. For Compaq Computers, however, the beta slope was positive for 1985–89 as the stock rose at a faster rate relative to the market.

REFLECTION ON RISK

Dr. Markowitz's discovery is a revelation highly regarded by academicians and practitioners of money management. From a practical standpoint, however, the concept of elimination of the unsystematic or security risk through portfolio diversification has not been thoroughly resolved.

The market is the best discounting mechanism of fundamental factors that govern the price of a security. The trend of the stock, however, may reverse, and the stock may decline before it becomes clear that earnings have peaked. Diversification may help avert the risk in a specific security. But what if the choice of security has been concentrated in stocks that have a negative beta relative to the market? The Markowitz findings have not touched on many issues, such as the choice of securities, their liquidity, their historical relative performance in relationship to the market, and the industry group they are in. Consider the different nature, for example, of gold stocks, which are beneficiaries of inflationary pressures, versus electric utilities stocks, which are inversely related and severely affected by rising interest rates. Moreover, can the same conclusions be drawn for a portfolio consisting of secondary stocks or another consisting only of blue-chip Dow companies? Liquidity of a stock is another issue that should always be taken into consideration. Illiquid stocks tend to be more volatile than those that command wide ownership and big capitalization. As to the beta factor assigned to a security, it may vary over a period of time as a super flying stock may undergo periods of dormancy and underperform the broad market.

The stock market is not a scientific game. It often responds to psychological considerations of the investing public more than to computer models and well-conceived equations. In spite of all we know, investing in securities remains risky and warrents a high level of knowledge and intense analysis. Things change and industries rise and fall. It is good to be aware of all kinds of theoretical discoveries, yet it is even more important to invest in research and knowledge when dealing with risk.

Portfolio Structuring

Structuring a portfolio of assets depends on the objectives set up in the financial plan. Those stated goals are functions of the individual's age, financial position, and anticipated future income. Translating financial objectives into a structured portfolio of stocks and bonds is by far the most important step towards achieving desired results.

In its simplest form, a portfolio consists mainly of three components: cash, income-yielding securities, and common stocks. The portion of each of these components in an investment portfolio will differ throughout the span of the business cycle in light of individual risk tolerance and specific financial objectives.

Cash should earn interest in a risk-free, liquid type of investment. Three- and six-month T-Bills are considered the safest among all fixed-income securities. The amount of cash in an investment portfolio is different from the cash reserves to be used in an emergency. The liquid components of the portfolio should rise during times of economic uncertainty to capitalize on emerging opportunities.

The income-yielding portion of the portfolio can be invested in government securities with different maturity dates, in corporate bonds, or in utility stocks. Government securities, depending on their maturity, are more prone to suffer from rising inflationary trends and secular rises in interest rates. The longer the maturity, the higher the inflation risk. As to default risk, government securities are relatively immune to it unless the U.S. government fails to honor its obligations, which is highly unlikely. Another factor that adversely impacts the appeal of government securities is the callability feature attached to them.

As to corporate bonds, investors can encounter both kinds of risk: inflation risk and credit risk. Corporate bonds are rated depending on the financial position of their issuers. Because of their potential credit risk, they have a higher coupon rate than government securities with the same maturity date. During periods of credit crunch and high interest rates, corporate bonds' value can decline substantially, depending on their rating. They tend to have higher volatility than the relatively more secure government obligations.

Utilities stocks may also be chosen as a vehicle for conservative, income-yielding investment. They have a much higher risk level than bonds. In the past, many utilities stocks suffered substantial losses in the wake of nuclear mishaps. Although they are riskier than bonds, utilities offer increasing dividends over the years plus the potential of capital appreciation.

The third part of the portfolio can be positioned in stocks. Here, many economic, fundamental, and quantitative factors enter into the selection process. The rest of this book presents a variety of techniques and strategies that help control the risk element. At this stage, however, it is worth noting that sector analysis and diversification of investment in different industry groups should be at the heart of structuring an investment portfolio.

Asset allocation differs during the different stages of the business cycle. There are so many choices that can be made here. There are cyclical stocks and defensive stocks. There are industry groups that have good growth potential. Yet, other groups, while growing at a slower rate, may command a steady flow of revenues and a remarkable market position.

Structuring an investment portfolio constitutes the first step toward translating financial objectives into action. There are two aspects to the portfolio structuring process: the asset allocation and the dynamic management of the portfolio.

Dynamic portfolio management entails the repositioning of the investments depending on the stage of the business cycle. During the late stage of a bull market, cash should be raised, and liquidity becomes of prime importance. Stocks of questionable earnings outlook should be sold. The fixed-income portion of the portfolio should also be trimmed. At that juncture of the economic cycle, interest rates are likely to be rising as the Fed is tightening money to fight inflation. As equities trend lower and bonds decline in the face of rising interest rates, liquidity will help investors to preserve capital and to capitalize on evolving market opportunities. When the economy starts showing signs of a slowdown, the Fed is likely to ease the monetary rein and allow interest rates to decline. Gradually, as this process continues, cash can be invested in select fixed-income securities, because they stand to benefit from the long-term decline in interest rates. Stocks may also be selectively purchased during such a time, because valuation and intrinsic values ensure future profits. Then, as a new bull market starts in earnest, common stocks should become an increasing portion of the portfolio.

Dynamic management of investment portfolios requires a high level of expertise and professional attention. A variety of techniques and strategies that may help control both the systematic and unsystematic risks is presented later.

PERFORMANCE EVALUATION

Whether actively or passively managed, portfolios should be reviewed periodically and repositioned to respond to changing financial objectives. Age, income level, and financial status affect the financial plan throughout the lifetime of the investor. Levels of risks must also be adjusted as the makeup or profile of the investor changes. Even if the investor decides on delegating the management of his assets to a private money manager or a mutual fund, periodic performance valuation of where the portfolio stands is of major importance if desired objectives were to be realized.

CONCEPTS OF TREND ANALYSIS

Market analysis is the first step toward controlling the inherent risk in the securities market. This necessitates the review of a large number of economic, fundamental, and quantitative data in order to project the overall trend. If the market is heading higher, then stocks are likely to follow the prevailing momentum and go up. If the market is going down, then the stocks held in the portfolio may suffer a setback. Trend analysis

is probably the most important ingredient of successful investing. In order to understand the concept of trends and its importance during the investment process, the price behavior of
some securities relative to the market must be examined. The
correct identification of trends can be rewarding, and recognizing them is probably the most important factor that the investor
should be concerned with. The rule is to stay with an uptrend
until it exhausts itself. Signs that are consistently found during
the early stages of uptrends can be identified with careful
analysis. Moreover, junctures of major trend reversals have
common recognizable characteristics, to be examined in later
chapters.

Before introducing concepts of trend analysis and market
forecasting, it should be emphasized that stock market movements are not scientifically founded phenomena. One is constantly dealing with the unknown. The best one can do is to
use all the knowledge available in the arsenal of Wall Street
research to enhance the chances of winning. Trends, at times,
exacerbate one way or the other. Like the pendulum that
swings to one extreme and then heads back to the other extreme, markets deal with excesses all the time. The gyration of
investors' expectations and the unpredictable psychological behavior of masses during crises make the process of investing a
game of informed guessing, with the odds tilted in investors'
favor if the choice of specific investments is thoroughly re-
searched.

❏ 2

Schools of Market Analysis

Since we are the prisoners of what we know, often we are unable even to imagine what we don't know. . . . Man, given the proper initiative and freedom to act, has repeatedly found alternatives to ambiguity and doom.

Walter Wriston
(Former Chairman of Citicorp)

At times, the market demonstrates a well-defined trend. At others, the cross-currents of events make it difficult to judge the future direction of prices. Often there are periods during which the market is trendless, because the forces influencing it are in equilibrium. Most investors would like to be on top of new developments. Yet, not every piece of news is meaningful. As a matter of fact, the abundance of financial news often leads to confusion and blurs the picture.

Market analysis is a step closer to reducing the risk inherent in financial assets. By identifying the internal and external forces at work, the future direction of securities prices can be anticipated and better investment decisions can be formulated. But analyzing the anticipated trend is not as simple as it may seem. Scientific projection of the factors affecting securities prices is not sufficient to correctly determine their future direction. Trend analysis is a combination of art and science. Common sense also plays an important role in the analysis process.

There are three main schools of market analysis: economic, fundamental, and quantitative. They are all used to serve one purpose: to identify profitable investment opportunities and to avoid staggering losses. No matter which method is used, the objective is to determine the direction of future prices and to forecast the trend. Savvy economists, fundamentalists, and market timers go a long way to promote the superiority of their disciplines. Yet, when it comes to investing in the stock market, one should not be biased to any particular method of analysis. All of the tools that could help predict the trend should be used. Each method has its own merits and its drawbacks. The focus in this chapter is to discuss the tenets of these schools of market analysis and to identify their strong and weak points. Later they will be integrated into a unified approach that is more powerful than any method used alone.

ECONOMIC ANALYSIS

The economic school of market analysis concerns itself with the state of business in order to anticipate phases of expansion and contraction of the economy. During periods of economic slowdown, corporate earnings suffer, dividends may be curtailed, profit margins decline, and sales revenues sag. Economic recessions adversely affect the rate of growth of many corporations and may lead to deterioration in their overall financial position. In rare instances, recession can bring about total ruin and bankruptcy. However, during phases of economic expansion, corporate sales and earnings tend to grow. Profit margins expand. Dividends are not only relatively secure, they may even increase. Over all, in a healthy business environment, the financial position of most companies is enhanced.

The state of the economy is an important determinant of the fundamentals upon which investment decisions are based. The stock market is a discounting mechanism that anticipates those periods of expansion or contraction in the economy before they become apparent in the published statistics.

Bull and Bear Markets

In the past, bull markets were born during the latter stages of a recession. During those periods, corporate earnings for most companies were doubtful, yet the market anticipated their rebound. The outlook for dividends was shaky, but the market foresaw an end to the cyclical credit risk. While sales levels were down, the market expected their renewed expansion. In short, the market anticipated correctly the economic recoveries amid an overwhelmingly sceptical mood among investors. The market discounted the improving fundamentals that characterized the onset of an economic expansion.

Bear markets often started amid an environment of unbounded optimism. The economy at those junctures was growing at a fast pace, and corporate earnings were rising. Dividends were increasing rapidly and sales were expanding. Here, again, the market correctly anticipated the beginning of the slowdown before it actually materialized. The stock market proved time and again its ability to forecast accurately the future state of the economy. Over the years, the stock market established itself as a reliable leading indicator of the economy—that is why its activities are widely monitored by the highest monetary authorities around the world.

Economic Indicators

The economic school of market analysis is based on measuring key business activities and examining their typical behavior during the different stages of the business cycle. In late 1937, the Secretary of the Treasury requested guidance from the National Bureau of Economic Research as to when the sharp recession of 1937–38 would end. This triggered the early work on a set of leading, coinciding, and lagging indicators. The initial task of preparing a comprehensive list of reliable indicators was carried on by Wesley Mitchell, Arthur Burns, and Simon Kuznets. After extensive revisions and modifications, the Department of Commerce began publishing on a monthly basis a number of vital economic indicators. Since 1961, the *Business Conditions Digest* has provided economists as well as investors with a wealth of economic statistics in a graphic form. The value of this information cannot be understated for anyone who is looking for a viable source with which to determine the pulse of business. The figures throughout this book illustrate the typical behavior of a number of economic indicators during the full span of the business cycle.

Followers of the economic school of market analysis study

the position of the aggregates at any point in time in order to tell what is likely to happen next to stock and bond prices. The economic indicators can help anticipate major turning points in the business cycle. Once such indicators' typical behavior at the different stages of the cycle is well understood, long-term investment decisions can be formulated accordingly. Accurate forecasting of the future course of business is a step forward toward taming the systematic or market risk in the financial markets. By carefully assessing the message that these indicators deliver, a better feel of the outlook for the economy can be gained. By understanding the behavior of stocks and bonds during the different stages of the cycle, investment timing can be enhanced.

The economic indicators are designed to measure the state of the economy. There are many factors that are vital to the study of business cycles, such as: inflation, capital spending, unemployment, household savings and credits outstanding, level of disposable income, the money supply, the trade balance, interest rates, the activities in the housing market, and the dollar's strength or weakness in the foreign currency markets. The interaction of all these aggregates over the span of the business cycle drives the primary waves of economic expansion or contraction. There is a close relationship between the Gross National Product (GNP) and sales. This, in turn, has an impact on corporate profits. Dividends are also tied to earnings and profits. Stock trends are sensitive to fluctuations in earnings, dividends, and the overall risk attached to the corporation's financial position.

Over the years, in current dollars, the GNP has continued to grow. One would expect the total value of stock prices to grow at about the same rate. Yet the economic school addresses the macro or long-term trends of fundamental developments. This school's forecasting capability is limited by its inability to project the intermediate-term corrections that are often accompanied by changes in market leadership. Moreover, the economic indicators can tell you when the momentum of economic expansion or contraction is slowing down—but the market may have sensed this loss of momentum and may have already reversed its trend. The delay associated with the process of

gathering the economic aggregates and adjusting them for seasonal factors is long. Because the stock market is a reliable
leading indicator, it discounts future economic developments
before they are factually known. By the time the economic
statistics are released, the market has already adjusted itself to
discount their impact on the future earnings of stocks.

Used in isolation from any other market analysis discipline, the economic school of market analysis fails to account
for the wide difference in capitalization among industry groups
and stocks. The business environment may at times be on a
well-defined recovery course, yet other sectors of the economy
may be undergoing a severe adjustment.

The economic indicators display the aggregate activities
without giving any clues as to which industry group or sector
of business is likely to outperform the rest. Furthermore, the
study of economic statistics gives only a broad perspective of
anticipated future business activities without much focus on
emerging stocks or industry groups. The economic school also
fails to warn of the deteriorating infrastructure in the fundamentals of particular industry groups or individual companies.
For all these reasons the economic analysis school is superior
only at calling major turns in the business cycle and, hence, at
taming the systematic risk portion of the investment process.

Figure 2-1 illustrates the leading characteristics of the stock
market. First notice the cyclical nature of the industrial production index, which represents the national output of manufactured goods. The Standard & Poor's 500 Stock Index has led
periods of expansion and contraction in the industrial production during previous business cycles. Also notice that industrial
production has kept growing over the years. The stock market
too has advanced to increasingly higher levels despite recessions and economic slowdowns.

Analyzing the economic indicators is useful in timing
long-term investment commitments, but it is of no help in
trading. Yet, because such analysis is vital in order to identify
major turning points in the business cycle, the economic indicators must be integrated with the assessment of equities
trends. Fundamental and quantitative analysis can then be
used to fine-tune stock selection and portfolio structuring decisions.

Figure 2–1. *Industrial Production vs. the Stock Market*

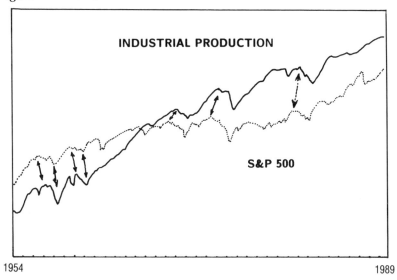

INDUSTRIAL PRODUCTION

S&P 500

1954   1989

The market risk can be partially controlled by recognizing important economic peaks and troughs. The assumption here is that as the stock market is a leading indicator, it can be expected to decline ahead of an economic slowdown in anticipation of sagging earnings or to advance when an economic recovery is about to start. However, forecasting the outlook for the economy can only help time primary bull or bear markets and does not enable the selection either of promising stocks or of industry groups.

A case in point is illustrated in Figure 2-2, wherein the monthly price record of four stocks in four different industry groups is displayed. Of the four stocks, Armco Steel and Black & Decker missed the roaring bull market of the 1980s; meanwhile the other two stocks, the Coca-Cola Company and Campbell Soup Company have outperformed it.

Economic School Shortcomings

Armco, which is a steel company, had advanced considerably during the 1970s. It emerged strong from the 1974–75 economic recession. Early in 1981, the stock achieved a high of some $40 per share. It was normal to expect the stock to decline

Figure 2–2. *Some Stocks Outperform the Market While Others Underperform It*

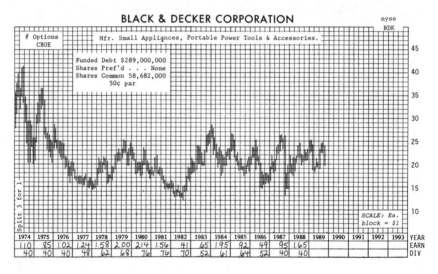

during the bear market of 1981–82—but the economic recovery that started in 1982 did not help Armco. The stock, after a brief advance in 1983–84, proceeded on a downtrend, ignoring one of the strongest bull markets in history and one of the longest economic expansions in the century. It goes to show that the analysis of the general economic conditions may be of no help in assessing the performance of specific stocks. Black and Deck-

Figure 2–2. *(continued)*

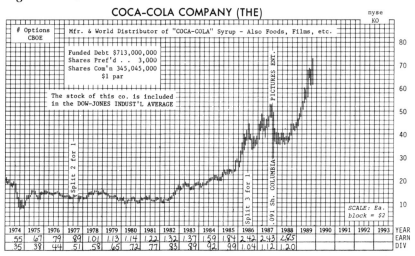

COCA-COLA COMPANY (THE)

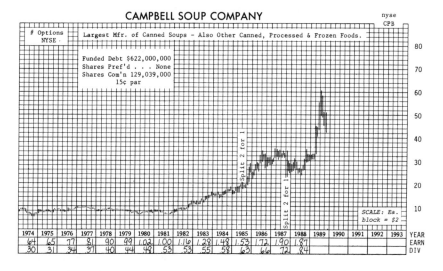

CAMPBELL SOUP COMPANY

er is another example of a stock that, during the 1980s, failed to benefit from the powerful economic expansion and the terrific bull market. The stock remained locked in a trading range completely ignoring the favorable economic background. The Coca-Cola Company, however, was rediscovered in the 1980s. The stock outperformed the broad market and also became a Dow component. This is an example of a stock that benefited substantially from the economic boom. Wang Laboratories is an example of a stock in a fast-growing industry that has done very well in the late 1970s, was hardly scathed by the 1981–82 deep recession, and emerged strong in the early phase of the bull market that followed. In 1984, however, the stock reversed its trend and proceeded on a downtrend, ignoring the great bull market of the 1980s and the decade's phenomenal economic strength.

Hundreds of stocks that peaked long before the economic cycle can probably be found. Hundreds of examples of stocks that did not participate during past economic recoveries or bull markets can also be found. This shows that the economic school of market analysis leaves a lot to be desired when it comes to anticipating stock trends. All economic analysis can show is the potential for improvement or deterioration in the economic outlook, which may or may not imply a favorable investment environment. Similarly, many cases can be cited in which a bear market hardly affected the price of a stock or industry group. In the examples shown, a study of the economic indicators might not have helped an investor who held either one of these stocks. That is why economic analysis should only be considered for timing primary bull or bear markets. The selection of individual stocks of a given portfolio should be based on extensive fundamental and quantitative analysis.

Another criticism of the economic school of market analysis is its inability to give a warning signal ahead of the 1987 crash. A follower of economic analysis would have been able, at best, to recognize the signs of a maturing business cycle, but not a meltdown. A study of the economic indicators only gave a broad sense of the state of business. The lag and lead in the buy and sell signals make them unsuitable for either the short- or intermediate-term trading activities. The economic indicators should serve more as a confirmation for other, quantitative and fundamental, factors.

FUNDAMENTAL ANALYSIS

The fundamental school is by far the most widely followed and practiced discipline of analysis in the investment community. It studies the accounting and financial position of the company under consideration and strives to evaluate the company's intrinsic worth. By appraising the sales, revenues, financial ratios, and earnings, practitioners of fundamental analysis can discover whether a stock is overvalued or undervalued. Moreover, assessing the growth potential of an industry or a particular stock allows investors to attach a value to the investment under consideration. The underlying assumption is that an undervalued stock should yield to the investor a handsome rate of return when the market finally recognizes its true worth. The valuation process is based on rate of growth of revenues and earnings. The price-earnings multiples, the method says, expand or contract based on investors' perceptions of their future earnings potential. Fundamentals experts prefer to increase stock holdings during periods of undervaluation. However, unless their investment commitments are timed in sync with major economic turns and with attention to the supply-demand balance suggested by quantitative techniques, this becomes an illusive task.

The most dominant factors that fundamentalists are concerned with are the rate and duration of growth and the capitalization rate applied to the future stream of earnings. In real life, however, the interaction of these variables is difficult to measure. Many Wall Street analysts know that future cash flow is hard to estimate. A company that has a solid financial position and healthy growth may be adversely affected by a recession more than the other members of its own industry group. The reason may be excessive inventory accumulation and slower-than-expected sales. By the time the economy is about to recover, technological obsolescence may have rendered the company's products of little value.

Another development that challenges the fundamental camp is the evolution and demise of industries because of social, political, or demographic factors. The steel industry is a good example. In a world faced with ever-growing needs for lighter and increasingly energy-efficient material, the steel industry weakened substantially over the decades. Aluminum, plastic, and light alloys robbed the steel industry of many of its applications. Combined with this was the intense foreign competition that the industry then faced. In addition, the cost structure of the industry in the United States remained high relative to imports, as management failed to modernize. All these factors slowly but surely hampered profits for the whole industry and adversely affected the financial position of steel companies.

Fundamental analysis may also fail to detect excessive capacity and crowding factors in a given industry. The oil services group is an example of such a situation. After expanding rapidly in the late 1970s, and in the face of declining oil prices in the 1980s, oil service companies were hard hit, sustaining staggering losses and facing shrinking demand. Excessive capacity and deteriorating fundamentals did not help. That industry group actually declined precipitously when the great bull market of the 1980s charged. Even the most established and well-run companies in the industry, such as Schlumberger and Halliburton, did not escape the primary downtrend that hit the stock prices of this group.

The brokerage business is a third example of an industry that faced fundamental changes in the late 1980s. After the excesses of the decade's great bull market, the time came for retrenchment. The scepticism that dominated the investing public, the decline in investment banking activities, the potentially, fierce competition from banks and insurance companies in the wake of the deregulation of the financial services industry, and the collapse of the junk bond market all contributed to bring about severe dislocation that prompted an adjustment.

Fundamental analysis, however, tries to identify the factors that affect the future price level. Such analysis suggests what ought to happen in the market. It is based on rational expectations, ignoring to a large extent the psychological make-up of the market participants. Fundamentalists tend to project earnings based on past records and to assume that sales growth will continue to expand in the future. During good times, their forecast may be on target, but when a slowdown in economic activities materializes as part of the cyclical nature of business, they must revise their optimistic projection downward. If the fundamental approach were to be synchronized with knowledge of the economic indicators and their behavior at major cyclical turns, the results of fundamental analysis could be enhanced. Yet the tendency of most analysts on Wall Street is to concentrate on the individual security they are studying or on its industry group in isolation from economic developments. That is why most of the surprises occur during major bear markets, when the ardent fundamentalist is still living with past earnings records, unwary of the potential deterioration that may result from an economic contraction.

While fundamentals may work out slowly, they are more reliable than any other approach to stock market investing. They are tangible and logical. They are particularly useful during major price swings. The long-term investor is in no hurry to reap the profits that sound fundamentals promise to deliver eventually. It is much more important to be confident about the financial strength of a company than to base investment decisions on temporary price strength that may lead to false expectations.

Some Fundamental School Shortcomings

One difficulty with the application of this school of market analysis is the tendency of fundamentals to lag behind the price action. The discounting mechanism of the market often senses evolving financial problems before they are actually disclosed by the company. Negative earnings surprises are anticipated and sales declines are also accounted for. Because the price of a security reflects people's expectations, and because the market attracts sharp and knowledgeable individuals as well as institutions that have massive research resources, it is no surprise that the shadow of earnings disappointment is immediately reflected in the stock price. The process usually starts with what looks like a normal intermediate-term correction. The difference is that investment commitments by those in the know stop, and the stock becomes driven by the emotional considerations of some of the weak hands. When demand is satisfied, the stock may continue to trade in a narrow trading range as more optimistic, yet unfounded, buying continues for a while. As the date of earnings announcement approaches, the outcome becomes clearer and the market may decline some more. When the lower earnings are finally announced, the stock declines further. At that moment, the downtrend has started, as the disclosed fundamentals confirm the price weakness. The worst thing that can happen to a stock is that its rise reaches euphoric dimensions. In such circumstances, no matter how appealing the fundamentals are, the trend tends to reverse and contrarian thinking prevails.

Because the deterioration of the financial position of a firm often lags the price action, it is often hard to judge a trend reversal using the fundamental analysis method. When a stock that has good earnings prospects is about to reverse its trend, the initial reaction of the fundamentalists is likely to suspect that this is a temporary decline and that the trend will soon continue. When the unexpected happens, the stock proceeds to tumble without giving analysts enough time to reassess the situation in light of the new developments. That is why proper analysis of the financial health of a stock or an industry group should be based on the assessment of future fundamentals rather than on prior performance.

Government policies can affect the fundamentals driving stock prices on Wall Street. Take, for example, the case of a tax increase or a tax cut on a certain product and think about all the positive and negative implications that such taxes may have on companies producing this product. Sometimes quotas are imposed to protect domestic industries from unfair foreign competition. Here again think about the impact such an action may have on a certain industry or the group of stocks in this industry.

The intrinsic value may change over time. It may improve or may deteriorate. Fundamentalists tend to focus their analysis on promising securities. But, at times, a stock that has been underperforming for a long time because of poor management may develop excellent fundamentals. It may be that a new management took control and aggressively decided to seek new business opportunities. Typically such a process may involve a hefty write-off of the nonperforming segments of the business and large investment in profitable or new promising ones. When this happens, the market will sense those favorable developments, yet fundamentalists may ignore the new developments for a while. Only when earnings start to grow rapidly and sales increase manyfold will the stock begin attracting investors' and analysts' attentions. By that time, the stock may have already advanced and be selling at a premium.

When all is considered, a sound financial position eventually leads to reappraisal of values and higher prices in favor of the patient and informed investor. Fundamental analysis of stocks and industry groups is the ultimate hedge against the unsystematic or securities risk. If proper fundamental analysis is performed on a stock it adds to the advantage gained by diversification, further reducing the overall portfolio's risk level.

QUANTITATIVE OR MARKET-TIMING SCHOOL

The market-timing school of securities analysis is based on the study of the internal dynamics that cause the price of a stock or the market as a whole to fluctuate. In the marketplace, there are the average investor and the professional trader, the corporate executive and the market maker, the pension fund manager and the aggressive speculator. There are also the scientist, the chemist, the lawyer, the accountant, and the broker. Their collective view of the intrinsic value of a security is represented in the price displayed on the ticker tape. Their hopes, emotions, desires, and judgments are all reflected in those digits that follow the stock symbol. That is all the market timer is concerned about: price and volume. But out of this data, he can create wonder, theorize the world, and determine the direction of the trend.

Once known as statisticians in the 1920s, market timers spend their days analyzing charts of stock prices, volume, moving averages, oscillators, the rate of change of prices, money flow, and the like. They respect the prevailing momentum of stock prices and abide by buy-and-sell, short- and intermediate-term signals. They focus on market psychology and believe in the supremacy of trend analysis. They study relative performance and search constantly for group leadership. They deal with the irrational side of the market and adhere to the ticker tape message.

Borrowing from the third chapter of Ecclesiastes: "To everything there is a season. . . ." In the investment arena, there is a time to buy General Electric and there is a time to sell General Motors. During the course of a year, a stock has a high and a low. A quick review of the financial section of any newspaper will indicate a certain range between the yearly high and low prices of any security. Money is made if a stock is bought when it is selling close to its yearly low. Even better than that, stick to stocks that are moving in an established uptrend rather than bargain hunting for those that have declined. Sometimes if you ask people why they are buying a stock the answer is: because it is cheap. Yet the reality is that a cheap stock could get even cheaper. It does not serve investors well to be the proud owner of a major corporation if they buy it around the high for the year. Although over the years the stock may come back or even surpass the price at which it was bought, in the interim it may decline and take a long time to recover before breaking even. Market timing is most helpful in allowing investors to buy or sell a security at the most opportune price.

Market timing strives at finding the answer to the two eternal question: *When* and *When?*—*When* to buy and *When* to sell. The methodology circles around determining the overall market trend. If the weight of the evidence indicates a bull market in progress, the relative performance of the different industry groups is then compared to the broad market. Once strength and leadership have been detected in one or more of the industry groups, the practitioner can focus on the stock selection process, which is usually confined to picking the strongest stocks in the strongest groups.

Quantitative Method Shortcomings

Since the early 1970s, as market volatility increased, the market-timing school gained popularity. The pressure on money managers to perform in the face of a market susceptible to erratic buy-and-sell programs compelled them to incorporate this method in their portfolio strategies. Yet, at the academic level, the market-timing school has found little if any support. The methodology is considered empirical at best and lacking any systematic value to its reasoning. Market timers themselves are unable to explain the reason behind any major advance or decline. When their predictions fail they hide behind stop losses.

Market-timing techniques are suitable for traders. They lack the fundamental value of patience that goes along with investing. For the average investor and the out-of-town speculator, applying market-timing principles is very difficult. Costly chart books, inefficient execution at times, and the transaction costs can quickly erode any short-term profits. Its real danger, however, is in getting carried away in a frenzy of speculation, overtrading, and eventually becoming a gambler. In many cases, investors end up by churning their own accounts. The result is often substantial losses.

Some Conclusions

While none of the market analysis schools is always right, each has its merits in helping decipher the likely future developments in the economy as well as in securities prices. Being biased toward any discipline does not serve a purpose and takes away from the available tools that investors can use to formulate improved decisions. Applying economic concepts alone leaves a lot to be desired at the selection level of individual securities or industry groups. Strictly following the fundamental analysis methods could lead to costly errors when the economic scene or the market-timing dynamics are delivering a different message. Blindly applying the concepts of market timing can result in staggering losses and over-speculation. It can also prompt a fast turnover of the portfolio at great cost to the investor. A well-balanced multidisciplinary methodology, using the wisdom of all three approaches, is the most efficient way of controlling the risks involved in the selection process. Strategies and techniques then enhance performance results and lead to healthy capital appreciation.

CONTRARIAN INVESTING

At this early stage, we would like to also introduce the contrarian methodology of operating in the marketplace. While it is not considered a market analysis method that can compare with the thoroughness of the other, more powerful disciplines, it does serve in deciding the appropriate course of action at critical market junctures.

The contrarian approach to investing is based on analyzing the psychological environment as demonstrated by investors' sentiment. The philosophy of that school preaches taking a contrary investment position to the consensus opinion. When the market environment is gloomy, and there has been a substantial market decline for a long period of time, followers of this method suggest initiating long-term buy positions. By the same token, when the market has been rising for a while and seems to be invincible, contrarians will sell into market rallies and raise cash in expectation of a downtrend.

The contrarian method is the best antidote to markets' extremes. It works best at market junctures when investors' expectations are excessively optimistic or pessimistic. It calls for establishing positions opposite to the prevailing trend. The rationale behind the method stems from the belief that the market never accommodates the masses. The method assumes that the crowd is always wrong.

The wave of rampant inflation in the 1970s is a good example of contrarian investing. Gold soared to over $800 an ounce, which prompted some financial advisors to expect the trend to continue and projected gold to reach $1600 per ounce. That was the time for a contrarian to reason that real interest rates were high and that the rush to invest in gold had reached euphoric proportions. It was time to expect a reversal and, indeed, one occurred shortly thereafter. The same line of reasoning can be applied to the spiraling oil prices of the same decade. The world was at the mercy of a cartel that cornered the market. Energy shortages and long lines at the gasoline stations reminded us of our vulnerability to the whims of OPEC. Things reached crisis proportions. That was the time for contrarian thinking to prevail and project hope amidst despair. A rise in interest rates, a war between two OPEC members, and some measures of conservation on behalf of conscientious citizens made the price of oil come tumbling down.

Contrarian Method Shortcomings

The only correct application of the contrarian approach occurs when the market psychology reaches unanimity in either direction. Beware of being a contrarian all the time, since this attitude violates the well-established norms of trend following. The crowd is *not* wrong at all market junctures. Operating as a contrarian all the time could lead to disastrous consequences.

To operate contrary to a well-established trend often means to ignore the economic and fundamental perspectives. The contrarian method is most powerful only when the market is very active and the stock market is all over the news. A classic example of its legitimacy was the Crash of 1987. At that time, the summer months saw ample rewards provided to all investors. It was like a candy store in which investors did not have to know about any discipline of market analysis in order to score hefty gains. The media had it that the market was well on its way to breaking through the Dow Jones Average's 3000 mark. The economic and fundamental background was healthy. The real estate market was buoyant and foreign securities markets around the world were charging to new all-time highs. Analysts were unanimously bullish. Even the bearish ones were afraid to declare their bearishness, as they did not dare sacrifice their reputation. Then came October 1987—the market declined almost 20 percent in two weeks. Even the bears thought that this was as far down as the market would go—and then there was the shocking meltdown. An economist could not have expected it, a fundamentalist would certainly have doubted it, market timers were surprised by its intensity, and there was no discipline that could have prevailed at such a juncture except that of a contrarian.

The economic, fundamental, and quantitative schools are well-structured disciplines of analysis. The contrarian philosophy is more a method of investing than of analysis. It could be combined with any of the other methods to enhance projections. The "what if . . ." tactic is well advised in every kind of investment.

TOP-DOWN AND BOTTOM-UP MARKET ANALYSIS

The process of market analysis can be lumped under two main categories: top-down and bottom-up. On the one hand the focus of the top-down style of market analysis is to determine the direction of the broad market. The assumption is made that stock trends closely follow the direction of the general market. The focus of the bottom-up approach, on the other hand, is to assess the potential of individual securities and industry groups. The reason is that stocks may behave completely differently from the broad market.

The top-down philosophy believes that if the market is bullish, all stocks are likely to advance. And vice versa, if the market is bearish, all stocks are likely to decline. While there is some truth to this assumption, not all stocks or industry groups advance or decline at the same rate even during the strongest of bull markets or the most intense bear markets. Stocks as well as industry groups are constantly switching roles as leaders and laggards. There are those that outperform the broad market action and advance at a faster rate than the broad market during major primary uptrends. Also, there are stocks that may not participate during bull trends and severely underperform the general market during long-term advances.

The bottom-up philosophy, however, believes that the market trend is not as important as the direction of prices of individual securities and industry groups. Industry groups tend to lead or lag the market at the different phases of the bull cycle. There are those that come out very strong from a major cyclical low and greatly outperform the market during the first stage of a primary advance. Those same industry groups, however, may not be able to sustain their stellar performance as the bull market continues. Some new leaders may emerge and outperform the general market while the old leaders remain subdued. Stocks, too, may behave differently from their own industry group. Some stocks may even decline precipitously during major bull markets and others advance during bear markets.

Which approach is better? A combination of the two styles is probably the most effective way to dealing with the market risk. Investors cannot ignore the powerful upward momentum generated by most bull markets, yet they cannot close their eyes to the possibility that a company may go bankrupt in the best of times. Also, bear markets should be respected, but that does not mean that some stocks may not buck the broad trend and outperform the market.

COMPARATIVE MARKET ANALYSIS

Whether an investor is an economist, a fundamentalist, or a market timer, he is betting on the trend. The careful fundamentalist, who spends hours of intensive analysis of the financial position of a company, is trying to support the evidence for a prospective appreciation, or simply an *uptrend*. By going over the piles of fundamental information, the analyst is constantly assessing the potential of continuing or accelerating earnings growth based on sales and revenue growth rates. The underlying assumption is that as earnings keep rising, the market will soon recognize the intrinsic worth of the stock and the price will move up accordingly.

The dedicated economist, on the other hand, is constantly reviewing the outlook for business. He or she constantly monitors the housing starts, consumer spending, interest rates, inflation, and the Federal Reserve Board's policy in order to forecast the future course of the economy. By interpreting the statistics, he forecasts the likely course of business upon which depends future earnings potential and dividend growth. The assumption here is that an expanding economy will help companies flourish, and, hence, their stock prices will rise in the open market. And vice versa, a slowdown of the economy could heighten the credit risk and impair chances for future earnings and sales growth.

The market timer is constantly looking for profitable trends by examining the pattern of price movements of the broad market, the different industry groups, and individual stocks. By doing so, he is ignoring the economic and fundamental underpinning and is hoping that his signals will afford a quick exit when the trend reverses.

And then there is the contrarian, who is brooding on the news. Good news and euphoric optimism would indicate a fragile investment environment and warrant initiating a position in the opposite direction in anticipation of a sharp correction. Bad news and pessimistic forecasts are often the reasons for buying for the long haul. When the future looks bleak, they buy, and when euphoria sets in, they sell. The astute investor, in their opinion, is the one who would constantly operate contrary to the opinion of the majority.

The two basic investment risks, as is well known, are the systematic or market risk, and the unsystematic or security risk. Economic and market-timing methods are vital in assessing the long-term environment. The stock market has proven to be an excellent indicator of future business conditions. The economic indicators can be used to predict the likely outlook for vital sectors of business. These indicators can alert investors to an impending economic slowdown or to a strong recovery in the making. Given that bull markets start before an economic trough is reached, the position of the aggregates can help investors buy securities close to cyclical lows. Such indicators could also warn of a weakening business outlook, signalling a need to raise cash and sell securities.

Economic analysis is a great tool to control some of the market, or systematic, risks. Another important tool in controlling the systematic risk is offered by several of the techniques used by market timers. For example, the trend interrelationship between bonds and stocks could indicate the potential of a strong rally or a correction. The moving average direction of the averages, industry group trends, the annual rate of change of the S&P 500, the percentage of stocks above their 200-day moving average and other internal dynamics can help identify the trend and detect the weakening or strengthening of the price momentum in the marketplace.

As to the unsystematic or security risk, thorough fundamental and quantitative analysis are of great use to determine the potential rewards or the extent of risk in investing in an industry group or an individual stock. Fundamental analysis is like an X-ray of the pertinent forces that govern the long-term value of a stock. Financial ratios uncover sources of intrinsic strength or weakness in a security. Deteriorating fundamentals can only lead to a long-term price decline as the risk of bankruptcy rises. However, sound fundamentals are bound to be reflected eventually in earnings and dividend growth and to command a higher valuation when investors realize the true value of the stock.

The fundamental domain is based on the firm-foundation theory. Its predictive power is derived from correctly projecting the stream of earnings that the company will be able to make over the long run. Another assumption that goes hand in hand with this theory is that those earnings will be translated into a growing distribution of those earnings in the form of dividends. The major drawback in the theory is that future earnings themselves are variable. In reality, however, they are closely dependent on the continuation of strong demand for the company products and on management's ability to diversify its portfolio of businesses in promising industries. Also crucial is that the firm's executives and decision makers be capable of managing those new businesses profitably. The different growth rates of the new endeavors can command different valuations. The end result is that the market's perception of the company's future prospects will determine the number of multiples that the price may command in the marketplace. During periods of sweeping optimism, the valuation may differ from that assigned to the stock during times of economic slowdown. This may lead to relative valuation rather than absolute worth.

Market-timing techniques can also support the fundamental catalyst and provide a guide to potential rising demand for a security. Here again, the moving average system, industry group relative performance, strength of the stock itself relative to the broad market as well as its own industry group, and so forth can help determine the internal dynamics supporting the prevailing trend. The contrarian style can be used in conjunction with any of these schools of market analysis to enhance the outcome. For the economist, contrarianism may raise questions that may not be apparent in the statistics at any given time. For the fundamentalist, contrarianism may question some of the information provided by the company's management or the disclosed results. Moreover, it may also question the durability of strength or weakness in the financial position.

COMMON-SENSE TREND ANALYSIS

History shows that trends sooner or later come to an end. The pendulum swings to extremes and so do the trends. They always deal with excesses and almost always appear invincible, when, instead, they are vulnerable to reversals. Economic, fundamental, or even market-timing techniques may not be able to warn of an impending trend change or to pinpoint the peak of a move, although a contrarian may stand a chance against all odds.

Trends at times last for a decade or more. A bull market that spans several business cycles is called a secular bull market. During those periods the economy is typically characterized by real growth and cumulative wealth. But companies and industries go through their own growth cycles. The mortality rate is very high at early stages. Small, promising companies face a myriad of hurdles as they grow. Managing growth is itself a difficult process at which only a few companies succeed. After the early stages, a company may go through a period of accelerated earnings and sales. During infancy and fast growing stages, a company should not be expected to pay dividends. Past that time, a company matures and management of its resources becomes more important than the ability to continue to grow at a fast pace. Dividend payout should then become a vital factor in the valuation process. In most cases, the entrepreneurs who have started the company are replaced by professional management, which may or may not be able to take the firm to new shores of growth that match previous records. A growth stock is not to be expected to grow forever, and dividends are not to be anticipated to rise forever. New emerging industries are constantly replacing old ones. The key to survival is often the ability of the company's management to explore new ideas, beef up its research and development, and diversify its portfolio of businesses to seize new opportunities.

Investors should not try to forecast the trend but to follow it as long as it exists and to recognize unemotionally when the weight of the evidence points to a change in course. When the price stops going up, and hesitates, then the possibility of a trend reversal should be contemplated. At such times, investors should reassess the long-term outlook for the stock or industry group they are holding. Careful analysis of future potential and reappraisal of the underlying fundamentals should be done independently of any emotional attachment to the type of investment committed. Stocks should be bought if they are to yield a healthy rate of return, otherwise they should be sold. In addition, if in the course of a downtrend, prices resist declining on bad news, then watch for the signs of a possible recovery. Here again, careful analysis is warranted. A fundamental catalyst has to exist in order for the stock to advance. This catalyst could be the resumption of earnings growth when the economy is ready to expand again. It could also be that the company is paying a high dividend that is expected to be secure even during difficult times. Another catalyst could be an explosive demand for the firm's products. In the absence of any solid catalyst, it is ill advised to buy a company for the sole reason that it has declined to a relatively low level. Some companies spend many years after a bear market is over selling at a price that is far below the peaks reached during previous business cycles.

The Long-Term View

Take a long-term view of the trend. Ask: How did it start? How long can it continue? How bad did it get? Watch for changes in demographics, new technologies, and the political environment and think about how these changes are likely to affect the specific trend. We live in a dynamic world where things change and trends evolve. Watch for evolving trends, because if an investor happens to detect one at an early stage, he can benefit substantially from it.

Back in the early 1980s, video games were very popular. It was a fad. Coleco Industries Inc. was one of its beneficiaries. They had the hottest video game in the industry, and their computer "Adam" held a great deal of promise. The price of the stock shot from $3 to $65 per share in less than two years. Fads are trends that exhaust themselves fast. They die silently after a short while. Investors can benefit from them provided they move quickly and recognize that the trend will not continue forever. Indeed, amidst the great bull market of the 1980s, Coleco declined from its highs, until it eventually sold below $1 per share and filed for protection from its creditors. "Adam" was not destined to succeed—"Nintendo" soon dominated the video game market.

Long-term trends are more profitable because they give investors time to position themselves as such trends progress. Moreover, they take a long time to mature and to reverse their direction. Secular bull trends are often the result of major discoveries. The automobile, the airplane, and the personal computer are examples of such breakthroughs that over time became part of civilization.

Changes in the way things are done sometimes led to the birth of new trends. Just consider the impact of the video recorders on the movie industry and family entertainment. The Walkman is having a major effect on reading and listening habits, and on educational resources.

Trends that evolve out of infrastructural changes have a long-lasting effect on people's lives. The baby boomers of the post-World War II period will become senior citizens in the early part of the next century. Nursing homes will probably be one of the best growth industries of the future. The market may not account for it now but as this bulge of the population keeps moving through the different stages of life, it will impose its will and patterns of consumption on the rest of society and on the different industries.

Long-term trends can also have varied patterns of growth. First there was the change from an agricultural to an industrial society. Since the early 1960s, the embryonic evolution of the service society has slowly gained momentum. Simultaneously, strides in robotics and automation have accelerated at a fast pace. Investors should investigate the fundamentals of those emerging growth companies that stand to benefit from evolutionary trends.

CONCLUSION

In a free enterprise system, financial markets are constantly discounting future fundamental developments, both domestically and internationally. Political and social changes are assessed and often translated into major secular trends before their impact is fully digested by observers. For example, one would have expected the market to react negatively to World War II. The fact was that the market ignored the disastrous consequence of the war and proceeded to discount the aftermath. The message was decisive as the stock market predicted the victory of the allies and the rebuilding of Europe. Even more important, the market embarked on a major secular uptrend that lasted for two decades. The great economic growth around the world prompted the celebration that the invisible hand accurately foretold.

☐ 3

Markets and Averages

The passionless barometer is disinterested because every sale and purchase which goes to make up its findings is interested. Its verdict is the balance of all the desires, compulsions, and hopes of those who buy and sell stocks. The whole business of the country must necessarily be reflected correctly in the meeting of all these minds, not as an irresponsible debating society, but as a listing jury whose members, together, bring more than the counsel or the judge can ever tell them in finding what has been "the bloodless verdict of the market place."

William Hamilton, 1926

"Where is the Dow going?" is probably the most often asked question on Wall Street. The moment you inquire about the market direction, you are effectively searching for the trend. At the close of the nineteenth century, Charles H. Dow and Edward C. Jones were searching for a method to identify the market trend. These two pioneers' early studies have left their mark on Wall Street and on the art of market analysis forever. The Dow Jones Averages (the Dow) were named after these two great men, who paved the way for the field of investment research to reach today's level of sophistication. Not only was their effort the first attempt ever to identify the trend, it was also the first try at quantifying and measuring the trend's amplitude. Just imagine the media reporting on market activities without referring to the Dow-Jones Averages.

The origin of trend analysis forms the background to any study of the economic and fundamental schools. It is also important to introduce some statistical methods that can be applied to a large number of situations. In order to identify the market's trend, it helps to be aware of the Dow theory, the market averages, group indexes, relative strength, moving averages, and so forth. Later, more advanced techniques that are vital to investment decisions will be elaborated.

TREND ANALYSIS AND THE DOW THEORY

The concept of indexing was born thanks to the insight of Charles Dow, who was searching for a way to analyze the market trend. Today, the same principles of indexing, with minor variations, are used in all endeavors of business. The consumer and the wholesale price indexes, the leading, lagging, and coincident indicators are also indexes calculated by averaging the data of many aggregates in order to measure the performance of the economy.

Trends may be better understood when compared to the ocean's tides: Rising tides lift all ships. When a trend is strong but is of short-term duration, it represents temporary imbalances in the supply-demand equation. Long-term trends in business, politics, or social structure affect the fortunes of corporations, their earnings, and their growth potential.

Trends are cyclical: a bull market, a topping process, a bear market, and a bottoming process. The most widely advertised business cycle is the four-year presidential election cycle. There is also the decennial pattern, which lasts for a whole decade. During such periods of long-term expansion the market continues to rise for about ten years. Finally, secular trends that bring about major economic and social changes tend to persist for several decades. Secular trends can bring new lifeblood to emerging industries or announce the demise of some of the well-established businesses. Figure 3-1 illustrates the stages of a typical stock market cycle. Figure 3-2 illustrates the concept of cyclical behavior in the context of the secular multiyear trend.

Born in Sterling, Connecticut, on November 6, 1851, Charles H. Dow is credited with opening the door to all of the great discoveries in the area of trend analysis on Wall Street. In 1879, Dow arrived in New York City to pursue a career in financial reporting. Between 1885 and 1891, he was a partner in a member firm of the New York Stock Exchange (NYSE), where he executed trades. Dow teamed up with Edward C. Jones and founded Dow, Jones & Company, Inc., which published the first edition of *The Wall Street Journal* on July 8, 1889. Dow edited it until his death in 1902. During the last three years of his life, he wrote a few editorials dealing with stock speculation. Dow never knew that his faithful followers would develop his few remarks into a full-fledged theory that has earned its place at the top of all market analysis research.

Thanks to his friend, Samuel Nelson, the world became aware of Dow's wisdom. The Dow theory was introduced in

Figure 3–1. *The Market Cycle*

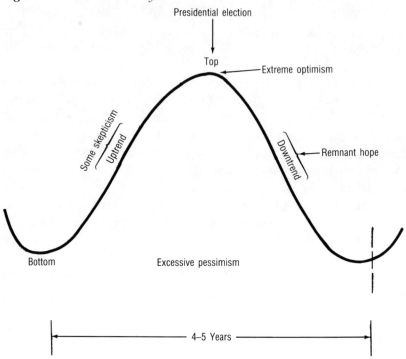

the book, *The ABCs of Stock Speculation*, that Nelson authored in 1902 and that explored the tenets of Dow's philosophy. William Peter Hamilton succeeded Dow as the editor of *The Wall Street Journal* and remained in that position for over twenty-five years. The credit for developing the Dow theory should go to Hamilton, who applied its postulates to stock market forecasting. His observations and analyses proved to be accurate and soon became one of the most popular features of *The Wall Street Journal*. Hamilton also wrote *The Stock Market Barometer* (1926), a book in which he explored trend analysis methods based on the Dow theory. The legacy of Hamilton's theories were proven shortly before he died, when he correctly predicted the 1929 bear market that led to the Great Depression.

Dow himself may have never guessed that his name would live as long as the Dow Jones Averages will. His remarks were not intended for the stock market, but for business. Hav-

Figure 3–2. *Decennial Patterns and Secular Trends*

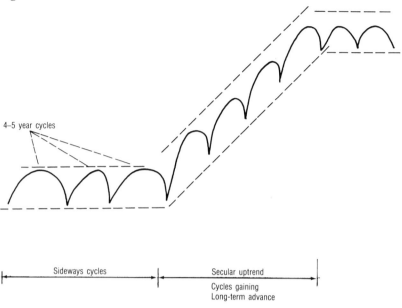

ing been a trader on the floor of the Exchange, he noticed that stocks moved up or down in unison during periods of broad advances and declines. He compared it to the wave rhythms of the sea. Dow's spark of ingenuity was that of constructing an index by averaging the prices of 20 stocks. A few years later, this average became known as the Dow Jones Industrial Average and consisted of 30 stocks. Moreover, Dow devised a transportation average, which consisted of railroad stocks. He compared the movement of these averages and formulated his theory based on their behavior. But, more importantly, by constructing these averages, he was able to quantify the market's movements and analyze the trend.

Students of the market-timing school recognize Charles Dow as the forefather of *trend analysis*. The concepts of his theory are applicable to any kind of business forecasting. They can be used in sales projections, corporate planning, or economic analysis. For these reasons, most successful businessmen carefully monitor the Dow Jones Averages.

THE STOCK MARKET CYCLE AND THE DOW THEORY

Dow observed that during primary market advances or declines the majority of stocks move up and down in unison. In order to quantify and qualify the trend at any point in time, he calculated an average that consisted of 20 industrial stocks— leaders in the most important industry groups. Using this average, Dow formulated his theory on market trends.

According to Dow, a bull market is in progress if successive market advances penetrate previous rally highs and ensuing declines stop short of previous low points. During bear markets, the average breaks down and makes lower lows. Failure of the market to rise above its previous high and to hold above its recent low indicates a *down* trend. Figure 3-3 illustrates the concepts of the Dow theory. Hence our first rule is:

An *uptrend* is a series of higher highs and higher lows, and a *downtrend* is a series of lower lows and lower highs.

Figure 3–3. *Dow Theory Concepts of Trend Analysis*

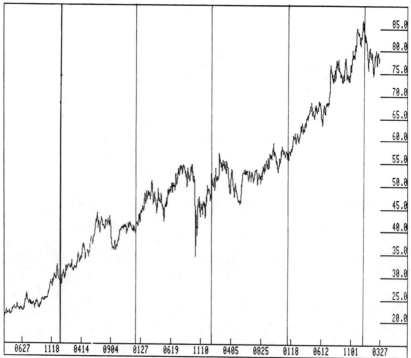

Until 1897, only one stock average was maintained by Dow Jones & Company, Inc., but in that year other averages representing the railroads were devised. The original railroad stock average consisted of 12 stocks. Their prices were added up and divided by 12. Of the original list of Dow's stocks, only General Electric remains as one of the components of the Dow Jones Industrial Average.

Dow compared the industrial average with the railroad average, known today as the Dow Jones Transportation Average. He observed that for a trend to be healthy on the upside, both averages should confirm each other. The trend in the Dow Jones industrial average, representing the state of the productive sector, should be confirmed by the trend in the distribution of output, which is reflected in the Dow Jones Transportation Average. When the two averages stop moving in unison and fail to confirm each other, the underlying trend becomes suspect. In other words, if the Dow industrials score new highs without the Dow Transportation's following suit, then the market trend is reversing. This leads to the second rule:

> The market Averages must confirm each other's movement for the trend to continue on course.

Market timers tend to monitor the Dow Jones Utilities Average as well, for it often leads the broad market action. Because it is sensitive to interest rates, a strong Dow Jones Utilities Average often suggests higher market prices and vice versa.

MARKET MOVEMENTS

Dow cited three main movements taking place in the stock market at any time. William Hamilton described this market action in an editorial published in *The Wall Street Journal* on September 17, 1904.

There are three movements in the market which are in progress at one and the same time. These are, first, the day-to-day movement

resulting mainly from the operation of the traders, which may be called
the tertiary movement; second, the movement usually extending from
20 to 60 days, reflecting the ebb and flow of speculative sentiment
which is called the secondary movement; and, third, the main move-
ment, usually extending for a period of years, caused by the adjust-
ment of prices to underlying values, usually called the primary move-
ment.

As the above statement indicates, Dow categorized the
short-term action of the market as random and of little value.
This, as a matter of fact, concurs with the efficient market
theory widely taught in business schools. The daily market
fluctuations are of little value in forecasting the future course of
the economy or of securities prices. The intermediate-term, or
secondary movement, reflects the sum of investors' sentiment
and is based on published economic statistics and their expectations for the future. According to Dow, the major trend of the
market, or primary movement, cannot be manipulated, as it
represents the intrinsic worth of companies. The long-term
trend has an enviable record for anticipating economic expansion and contraction. It is the major trend that the Department
of Commerce monitors as one of the most reliable leading
indicators of the business cycle. Fascinating, indeed, how
Dow's simple thesis interacts so well with the economic and
fundamental theories. The primary movement is the broad-
based trend, known as bull or bear market, that spans several
years and that varies from one business cycle to another. The
trend should be considered intact until the weight of the evidence suggests a reversal.

Primary bull markets are characterized by a broad advance
in prices caused by a rising demand for stocks. Bull markets are
usually accompanied by continuous improvement in economic
activities. According to the Dow theory, bull market periods
consist of three phases: The first represents reviving confidence
in business conditions and the readjustment of securities prices
to their fair value; the second is the response of stock prices to
earnings improvement; and the third is characterized by over-
speculation, inflated expectations, and rampant, unfounded
hope. This last phase of the bull market is usually accompanied

by rising inflation, expanding economy, improving fundamentals, excessive investor optimism, high-volume activities, and speculative enthusiasm. Typical of the third phase of price advance is a period during which the market is driven by earnings. Such environments tend to be selective, as investors should assess carefully the company and its growth potential during such periods. It is during the third phase of the bull market that only stocks with solid fundamentals advance.

Bull market trends are often interrupted by intermediate-term corrections. During those periods of consolidation, the market digests economic and fundamental developments. Those secondary reactions are deceptive and can last for several months. They represent a pause in the major trend during which the market corrects excesses and reassesses the outlook for corporate earnings and the general economy.

When the bull market matures, prices rise at a much slower rate. Industry group performance becomes mixed, with some remaining strong and others displaying weakness. At such times, the broad market is likely to be locked in a wide trading range lacking the necessary momentum to break out to new highs. A large number of stocks reverse their uptrend and embark on a downtrend of their own, totally ignoring the market action. They skip market rallies and participate with a vengeance in market declines, breaking down to new multiyear lows in the process. Loss of upward momentum, sporadic gains, and the lackluster performance of many industry groups characterize the end of the bull market and the topping process that follows.

Primary bear markets are characterized by a broad based decline in securities prices caused by worsening economic conditions and a pessimistic outlook for investments. As bear market trends proceed, capitulation sets in and stock prices thoroughly discount the worst that is apt to occur. Bear markets have three stages: the first represents the residue of old hopes, based upon which stocks were purchased at inflated prices with the assumption that they would continue to do well; the second reflects the deteriorating business conditions that appear in government economic releases and the cautious stance that investors adopt in the face of the gloomy outlook for corporate profits; the third is characterized by indiscriminate selling of securities, regardless of their value, as investors panic. Fear of loss plagues the final stage of the bear market as securities prices collapse all across the board. Good and bad ceases to matter as emotional reactions replace rational behavior in a panic to exit the market. Expectations at such junctures are usually gloomy, and hope of improvement quickly evaporates.

Bear markets also undergo sharp upward rallies that are treacherous and confusing in nature. Those "bear traps," as they are often called, tend to temporarily revive investors' hopes for the resumption of the bull market; such rallies also squeeze the short positions. Soon enough, however, prices resume their downward slide, shattering any remnants of optimism. During the final phase of a bear market, the economy gradually approaches a cyclical trough. Inflation has already peaked and unemployment is rising. The economic statistics continue to deteriorate, which adds to the state of despair and sense of helplessness among investors.

After the initial stampede, bull markets proceed slowly. Bear markets, on the other hand, are swift and precipitous. They tend to be short but vicious. What a bull market has gained in a few years can be wiped out in a few days. Blue chip and secondary stocks decline in a bear market, no matter how enticing their fundamentals are. A large number of stocks stand to lose 60 percent or more of their value once the market has passed its cyclical peak. Many among those may not rebound in the next bull market and may stay subdued for many years. Some may even fade away slowly and decline to a fraction of the price they once commanded.

In psychological terms, bull and bear markets represent the constant oscillation between greed and fear. In bull markets, investors stay a long while hoping for more profits. They expect tomorrow to continue to be as good as today. When there are major market tops, enthusiasm prevails and speculators are then drawn to Wall Street. The raging bull leaves them with the impression that there is no end in sight to rising, strong prices. The sound economic environment blinds investors to the potential risk that lies ahead, and such blindness can lead to making poor investment decisions. During bear markets, fear drives investors' decisions as wealth dissipates and fundamentals deteriorate. Investors are then shaken by the shadow of gloom, unaware of the great buying opportunities they are presented with. The hefty losses paralyze their judgment and scare them away from seizing golden opportunities.

MARKET MANIPULATION

Can the market be manipulated? According to the Dow theory, the answer is an unequivocal "No" in the long run. Manipulation is possible in the day-to-day operation of the market. These small fluctuations are random and are of little worth to the average investor. They are caused by temporary imbalances. The long-term trend, however, can never be manipulated. A few stocks may experience unexplained movement, but overall, the market is an accurate barometer of the future health of business, and this can hardly be manipulated. William Hamilton, in an editorial in *The Wall Street Journal* published on February 26, 1909, wrote:

Anybody will admit that while manipulation is possible in the day to day market movement, and the short swing is subject to such an influence to a more limited degree, the primary trend must be beyond the manipulation of the combined financial interests of the world.

Because the long-term trend cannot be manipulated, investors should focus on the issue of diversification to overcome the effect of temporary fluctuations on their portfolio. Analyses of the economic, fundamental, and quantitative dynamics can provide an informed assessment of the direction of prices.

THE DOW JONES AVERAGES

The stock market averages are statistical compilations of companies' prices traded on the different exchanges. Their fluctuation represents the overall performance of the securities used in their calculation. The Dow Jones Industrial Average is the most widely followed stock index, often used to judge the direction of the whole market. There are other averages, however, that are of equal, if not superior, importance. By monitoring the behavior of these averages and analyzing their relative positions, the possible future direction of the market, as well as industry groups and stocks, can be assessed. In addition to the Dow Jones Industrial Average, a number of other indexes were created over the years. There are those averages that are broadly-based indexes, such as the Standard & Poor's 500 Stock Index (S&P 500) and The Arnold Bernhard & Co.'s Value-Line index, that reveal the sum of the price performances of a large number of stocks. Monitoring these averages provides a clear picture of the general market direction. Furthermore, there are averages for the secondary and smaller capitalization stocks. Their behavior is very important since their strength or weakness tends to lead large companies around major trend reversals.

Over the years, market timers have developed a number of averages that represent different sectors or industry groups. These indexes consist of stocks sharing the same characteristics and represent the activities of those sectors. Analysis of group averages can indicate their trends and allow the comparison of their performance with the general market position.

The Dow Jones Industrial Averages

This average consists of 30 large companies widely held by both individual and institutional investors. The list has changed over the years. While it is still known as the Dow industrials, it now contains stocks whose main line of business is financial, retail, raw-material sensitive, or service oriented. It is an arithmetic average that is computed hourly by adding up the prices of those 30 stocks and dividing the total by a divisor. Originally, the divisor for the Dow industrials was 30. Over the course of many years, the divisor has been adjusted for stock dividends, splits, and substitutions. At this time, the divisor has a value below one. The importance of the divisor is that the smaller it gets, the more sensitive the average will be to the rise or fall of the Dow components. For example, if the divisor equals one, each dollar gained by any of the 30 stocks will be translated to a point gain in the Dow Jones Industrial Average. If the divisor is .5, it implies that each one point advance in any of the Dow components adds two points to the Dow Jones Average, and so on. The lower the divisor is, the higher the volatility of the Dow Jones Average and the more sensitive it is to gains realized by its own components.

The Dow Jones Transportation Average

This average consists of 20 transportation companies in the trucking, rails, airlines, and air-freight business. It, too, is calculated on an hourly basis, by adding up the prices of those components and dividing by a divisor. This index is the equivalent of the original Dow Jones Railroad Average, on which the principles of confirmation and divergences of the Dow theory were based. The transportation average is sensitive to the business cycle, as it consists of industry groups that are affected by economic expansion and contraction. The majority of the companies whose prices enter into the calculation of the Dow Jones Transportation Average are asset intensive, big capitalization stocks. Airline and railroad stocks are heavily weighted in this index, and its trend is influenced by the trends of both industry groups.

The Dow Jones Utilities Average

Consisting of 15 electric, gas, and telephone utilities, this average is sensitive to trends in interest rates. It is calculated as are the industrial and transportation averages. When interest rates rise, the Dow Jones Utilities Average declines as dividend payouts have to be increased, or as its components lose their investment appeal. In the past, the utilities average led the Dow Jones Industrial Average. Strong performance by utilities stocks may indicate the possibility of decline in interest rates, which is good for stocks. And, vice versa—a weak utilities average may indicate a rise in interest rates, which tends to adversely affect the equity market.

Figure 3-4 illustrates the relationship between the Dow

Figure 3–4. Dow Jones Industrial and Utilities Averages in 1987

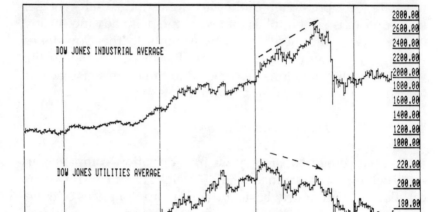

utilities and the Dow industrial before the Crash of 1987. Notice how the utilities weakened ahead of the industrials and gave a warning signal of the October collapse.

The Dow Jones Composite Index

This average is a more accurate index than the Dow Jones Industrial Average. The composite index covers a broader segment of the market—it incorporates the transportation and utilities indexes with the Dow industrials into one single index. It consists of 65 stocks: 30 industrials, 20 transportation, and 15 utilities. In other words, the Dow Jones Composite is the sum of the three main Dow averages. Because of the fact that 35 of its 65 stocks are in the transportation and utilities industries, this index is sensitive to the movements of the stocks in those groups. If the Dow industrials is truly a barometer of the manufacturing and service sectors of the economy, and if the transportation average represents the distribution of goods, then the Dow Jones Composite Index portrays the true state of business on both fronts.

All of these market averages are published daily in the financial section of major newspapers. Investors should monitor such averages' behavior in order to gain insight into the general market trend. The indexes' position relative to each other is important as it may warn of subtle, developing weakness, or may indicate emerging strength. For example, if the Dow industrials rises aggressively to new highs without corresponding strength from the Dow composite, the market's upside potential should be suspected and investors should look carefully for other signs of deterioration. In order for the market trend to continue on course, the averages have to move up or down in sync. When they stop confirming each other's action and go in different directions, a trend reversal may be in the making. The longer the divergences between the averages persist, the more significant the ensuing correction is likely to be. If such a condition materializes, it is advisable to check the economic and fundamental background to verify the outlook for business and earnings. While the Dow Industrials, transportation, and utility averages may not have to confirm each other's new highs on a daily basis, a nonconfirmation that lasts for a few weeks should be taken seriously. A study of the long-term trend of several averages is a must in order to gain perspective on the future market direction. Investors should develop the habit of reviewing charts of the averages that span a number of years in order to observe the market cycle and be aware of its current stage.

THE WORLD OF MARKET AVERAGES

Over the years, many averages have been created to enable investors to analyze the trend of securities prices. Standard & Poor's Corporation developed a series of broad-based averages that not only measure the broad market performance, they also isolate sectors of the market for further, in-depth analysis. Arnold Bernhard & Co.'s Value-Line index consists of over 2000 stocks closely followed by the firm. The Commodity

Research Bureau created several commodities-related indexes for both metals and grains. The Commodity Research Bureau's (CRB) index, is closely followed by economists, portfolio managers, and equity traders. It derives its importance from its relationship to inflation, bonds, and stock price movements. The New York Stock Exchange (NYSE) Composite is an average based on the prices of all stocks listed on the Exchange. It is considered by many professional analysts to be the best barometer of securities trends. In addition, there are averages representing secondary markets and foreign securities. The American Stock Exchange (Amex) and National Association of Securities Dealers Automated Quotation (Nasdaq) averages were constructed to help describe the activities on the American Stock Exchange and the over-the-counter (OTC) markets. The Nikkei Dow Jones, The Financial Times, the Agafi, and the Toronto 300 are examples of securities market averages of Japan, the United Kingdom, France, and Canada.

Not only were broad-based indexes devised; specialized ones also were created. The same principles of indexing are used to calculate industry group averages. These indexes are vital in both the broad and in-depth analysis of industry trends. Several techniques of analysis were specifically designed to compare those group averages to the broad market average. Their performance relative to each other could not have been measured or analyzed without the help of the indexing process.

The larger the number of components used in the calculation of any single average, the better its ability to describe the trend's perspectives. History shows that the Dow industrial's strength at times camouflages subtle weaknesses in the market trend. Representing only 30 large companies, it tends to advance to new highs without the larger number of stocks in the S&P 500 or the NYSE composite. One explanation of this phenomenon, which typically develops around major cyclical peaks, is that since the Dow's components are large, well-established companies with extensive financial resources, they tend to be strong especially at mature stages of a bull market. A broader index, on the other hand, will reveal early signs of deterioration. Many small capitalization stocks, with modest financial strength compared to the Dow's stocks, enter into the calculation of the broad-based market averages. Small- to medium-sized firms usually begin their decline ahead of the large, well-capitalized ones, and this weakness is reflected in the broad-based averages. The Dow is often the last average to decline around major market tops and the first to bottom out when the bear market is about to end. At major market peaks, the Dow's components are much stronger than most stocks used to calculate the S&P 500. Broad-based averages reflect such stocks' weakening position as a trend reversal is taking place. Their weakness reveals the early signs of deterioration as they fail to confirm the strength in the Dow industrials. Figure 3-5 illustrates the relative behavior of the Dow Industrials, the S&P 500, the Value-Line index, and the NYSE Composite. Notice how the averages tend to move up or down together. In late 1983, early 1987, and late 1989, the Value-Line index revealed the weak position of a large number of stocks failing to confirm the strength in the Dow industrials, which continued to reach new highs.

Bear market psychology also has three stages: caution, concern, and finally, capitulation. When investors first become aware of the possibility of a market decline, they still have remnants of hope, although their actions may reflect caution in the face of future uncertainties. But as prices continue to decline, concern begins to surface as fear of losses becomes a serious issue. The last phase of a downtrend often takes the shape of a collapse in securities prices all across the board. The melting down of stocks leads to investor's capitulation and panic selling. This last stage of the bear market tends to witness a precipitous decline in the Dow industrials. Because everybody monitors the Dow, such action reinforces negative investors' psychology and paves the way for a new bull market to climb on the wall of worries. The more broad-based averages, however, may begin to resist the down side selling pressure and refuse to follow the Dow to new lows.

One important broad-based index to monitor during mature bull markets is the Value-Line, which is an excellent barometer of the underlying trend of a large number of securities. Any divergence or nonconfirmation that develops between the

Figure 3–5. *Major Market Averages and the Principle of Nonconfirmation*

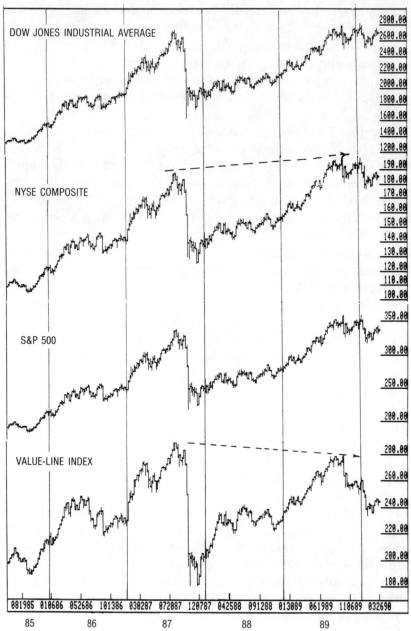

Value-Line and the Dow industrials should be noted with caution—it can be a signal of an impending trend reversal.

Secondary markets are best monitored by the Nasdaq and Amex indexes. A large number of small capitalization stocks enter into their calculation. Their performance relative to the Dow and the S&P 500 can confirm the market's strength in a bull market or reveal the subtle weakness that usually precedes major reversals. During a healthy uptrend, both the blue chip and secondary stocks advance. Weakness tends to develop in the secondary market ahead of important peaks. In bear markets, the decline of secondary stocks confirms the widespread weakness. Finally, around major market bottoms, they tend to resist the decline and often give an early signal of the final lows. Figure 3-6 illustrates the Value-Line, Amex, Nasdaq and Dow Jones Industrial Averages.

Notice how the Value-Line index failed to make new highs in late 1989, which suggests the loss of upward thrust that led to the decline in early 1990. Also observe the weak rebound in both the Amex and Nasdaq indexes since 1987 in comparison with the Dow Jones Industrial Average.

The CRB Index

The Commodity Research Bureau (CRB) index was first published in 1957 and is widely followed by economists, bankers, commercial users of raw materials, portfolio managers, and professional analysts. It is a geometric, unweighted average of 21 commodities figured as a percentage of their future prices in a base year. It is comprised of food and industrial raw materials that are vital to the economy and that could measure inflationary pressures. Experience with the CRB index demonstrates a strong parallel to the Consumer Price index. Moreover, the CRB was found to have a long-term correlation with certain important economic aggregates, such as industrial production, durable goods manufacturing, and capacity utilization. The CRB reflects the future expectations of prices of raw materials, grains, and precious metals. Many experts recognize it as a leading indicator of inflation.

The CRB index can help investors anticipate the likely

Figure 3–6. *Dow Jones, Amex, Nasdaq and Value-Line*

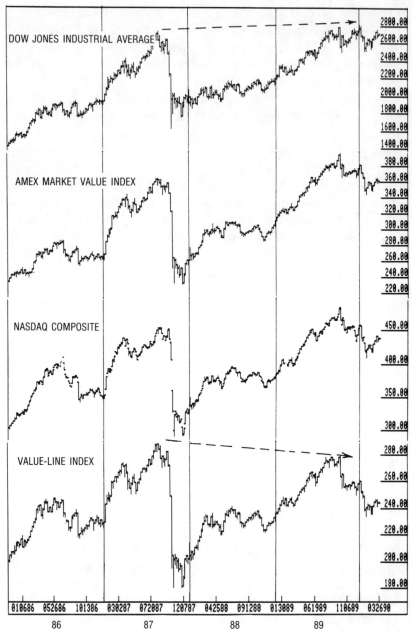

course of the Federal Reserve Board's policy as well as the direction of interest rates and the fixed-income sector. As a matter of fact, the Department of Commerce incorporates commodity prices as one of the widely followed leading economic indicators. The CRB is closely monitored by the Fed as it formulates and manages the monetary policy.

The CRB represents the balance of supply-and-demand forces in the commodities market. Its rise may indicate upward pressure on raw material prices, which will eventually be reflected in the inflation numbers at the consumer end. This can prompt the Fed to tighten its monetary rein and make interest rates advance. The rise of the CRB index foretells the surge in demand for commodities and often anticipates the cyclical expansion or contraction of the economy. When commodity prices advance, business is recovering, and the economy is gaining upward momentum. If the Fed feels that the economy is overheating, it may decide to raise interest rates to cool off excessive demand and to control inflation. And vice versa, a declining CRB index is often interpreted as a reason to expect future Fed easing and downward pressure on interest rates.

Figure 3-7 illustrates the CRB index and some of its components. It is important to note that a rise in the CRB index should be investigated in light of the price behavior of its components. For example, the 1988 drought caused the CRB index to stampede upward. The surge of the CRB index was prompted mainly by the sharp rise of agricultural commodities, such as wheat, corn, and soybeans. At that time, both crude oil and gold prices, considered good barometers of future inflation, were subdued. Should the case have been such that the rise of the CRB index was also accompanied by a firming up of these two commodities, it would then have been a definite indication of a more serious inflation outlook.

Industry Group Indexes

The creation of indexes that help visualize the trend's position has not been limited to the market averages. Companies operating in an industry can be used to calculate a group index that represents the trend of the stocks of the group.

Figure 3–7. The CRB Index and Its Components

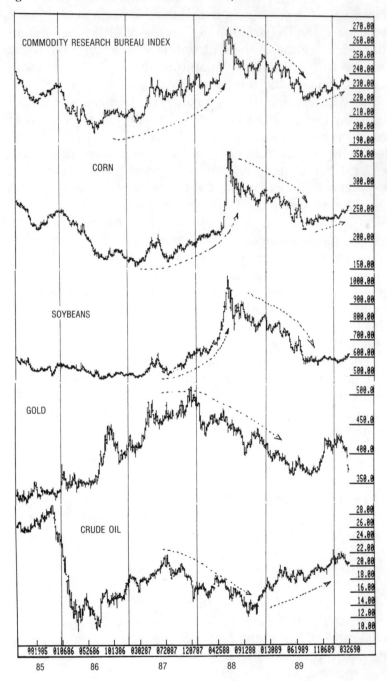

Members of an industry are likely to face similar fundamental factors that affect them all in a similar fashion. The market discounts future sales and earnings growth for the different sectors of the economy, and this is likely to be reflected in the group trend. The industry group indexes are used to compare their performance to the broad market action. Analyzing them can help detect leadership, relative strength or weakness. Such analysis can also serve in studying the health of the prevailing market trend. During bull markets, most industry groups advance along with the major averages. Around important tops, the number of groups participating in market rallies decreases. Investment at such times becomes very selective, with only a few groups advancing. To market timers, the lack of strength in a large number of groups indicates deterioration and the likelihood of a trend reversal. Around major market bottoms, more and more groups resist the downward market pressure. This early sign of strength alerts traders to a potential bull market in the making.

During bull and bear markets, industry groups are constantly rotating in strength and weakness. Investment capital flows in or out of the different groups depending on investors' perceptions of their outlook. The market is composed of a number of industry groups, which in turn consists of a number of stocks. The fluctuation of the broad averages is a representation of the rallies and declines of those groups. In fact, some market timers focus solely on industry group analysis, which tells them a great deal about the market trend. In the long run, market leadership is constantly oscillating between groups as the fundamentals governing their price action keep changing.

In the context of portfolio selection, investors should constantly strive at buying strong groups and avoiding weak ones. Investment returns depend upon the allocation of assets in those industries that command fundamental appeal and that show improving performance relative to the overall market.

Relative Strength

The relative-strength technique of market analysis strives at determining the performance relationship between two quantities. It is used to tell how well any average, industry group, or stock is performing relative to the broad market or to each other. For example, the ratio of the Dow Jones Industrial Average to the NYSE Composite shows how well the prices of the blue chip Dow components are doing relative to all the stocks listed on the New York Stock Exchange. Similarly, the ratio of the drug group index to the NYSE Composite demonstrates how drug companies are performing relative to the rest of the market. The ratio can also be used to study the relative performance of any two industry groups. In the area of stock selection, the same principles can be used to measure the performance of a stock relative to the market averages or its own industry group. In addition, relative strength can be used to compare two stocks within the same group or in two different industry groups. The application of this technique is not limited to domestic securities markets, but can be used to compare commodities to bonds, bonds to stocks, global market averages, and so forth.

Figure 3-8 illustrates the relative strength of the Dow Jones Industrial Average in relationship to the Value-Line index. As the graph demonstrates, there are periods when the Dow has outperformed the more broad-based index and other times when the Value-Line stocks have done better than the Dow's.

Figure 3-9 illustrates the relative strength of the Nikkei Dow Jones of Japan in comparison with the Dow Jones Industrial Average. Notice how the relative strength line helps visualize how well the Japanese market has outperformed the U.S. market in the 1980s.

Figure 3-10 illustrates using the concept of relative strength to show how both bonds and stocks have consistently outperformed gold during the 1980s.

Figure 3-11 illustrates how poorly IBM has done relative to the Dow Jones Industrial average and to the Technology Index since 1984. Also notice how, in January 1990, improving relative strength revealed the early signs of revival in IBM. The same principle could also be used to compare, for example, IBM to another technology stock.

Relative strength is an excellent tool in making investment decisions. Strength of a market, an industry group, or a stock tends to persist for a long time. While most stocks and industry

Figure 3–8. *Relative Strength of the Dow to Value-Line*

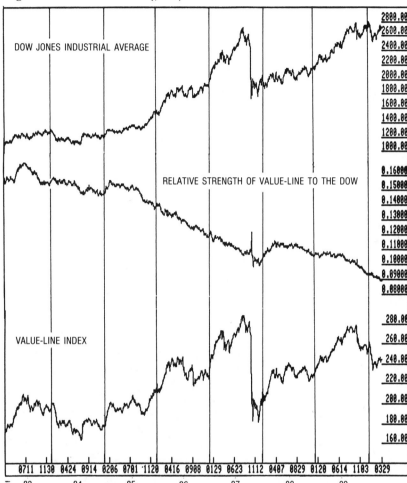

groups rise in a bull market, the speed of the advance varies to a large extent. Investors are better off buying those stocks that lead the way and outperform the market. Those securities can be located by analyzing their performance relative to the broad market. Market leaders are likely to resist correction and advance aggressively on rallies.

Relative strength is particularly helpful in the asset allocation process and diversification among different industry

Figure 3–9. *Relative Strength of Nikkei Dow Jones to Dow industrials*

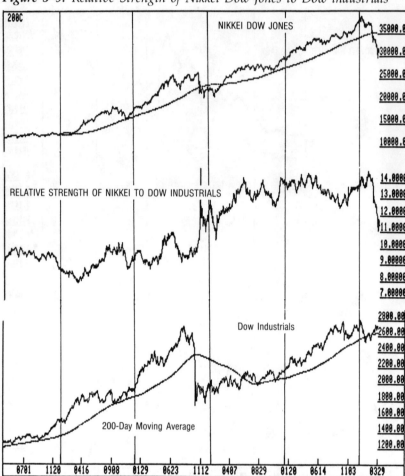

groups. The same principles can be used to compare performance among the different sectors of the market or to study the
relative strength or weakness among the averages on a local or
global scale.

Trendlines. According to the Dow theory, an uptrend is
defined as a series of higher highs and higher lows and vice
versa. When examining the price fluctuation over a period of
time, the eyes are inclined to follow a straight line across the
lows or the highs. This is what trendlines are all about. They

Figure 3–10. *Gold, Treasury Bonds, and the Dow industrials*

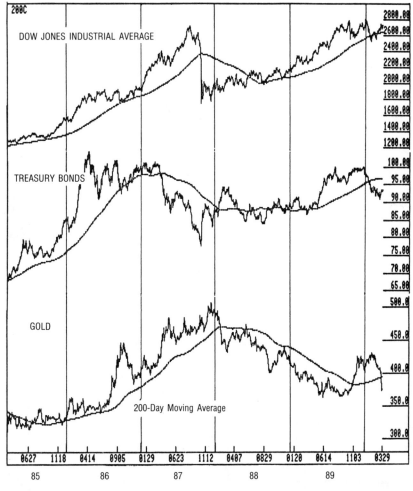

are a natural phenomenon that is an integral part of trend development. There are basically three types of trendlines:

1. Upward trendlines that are obtained by connecting the low points of pullbacks in an advancing trend.
2. Downward trendlines that are obtained by connecting the high points of rallies in a declining trend.
3. Horizontally drawn trendlines that connect the lows and the highs and rallies which form corrections of a trading range, or an indecisive trend.

Figure 3–11. *IBM vs. Dow Industrials and the Technology Index*

The longer the trendline holds during market rallies and declines the more important its violation becomes. If the price pierces through an uprising trendline, the investment position should be reassessed and the possibility of a reversal entertained. If this violation of the trendline comes after a prolonged advance of several months' dimension, the chances are that the new trend will persist for a while and will carry the prices lower. Similarly, when a downward trendline has been intact for several months and a rally pushes the prices above it, one should then look for a bottoming process to develop. But when the downward trendline is violated on the upside, it may not necessarily mean that a trend reversal is imminent. All it may indicate is the exhaustion of price decline and a period of stabilization ahead. Hence, a violation of an upward slanting trendline may indicate an important trend reversal. But a break out through a downward sloping trendline may only mean a period of stabilization has started, without signaling a new major trend.

Trend channels. By drawing a trendline along the tops of rallies and another along the bottoms of corrections, a channel becomes apparent. An up-channel contains the range of price fluctuations in an uptrending market. A channel is helpful in giving a rough estimate of the confinement or borders of the trend in progress. Again, when channels are violated in the direction opposite to the prevailing trend, probabilities will then favor a trend reversal.

If the upper boundary of an up-channel is violated, one should expect an acceleration of the existing trend. The reverse, however, is not true in the case of a downward trending channel. More likely, a bottoming process can be expected to begin rather than an immediate reversal.

Figure 3-12 illustrates two cases of a trend channel. Note that the two channels are in opposite directions, despite their occurrence at the same time in two different stocks. This should emphasize the importance of stock selection, as two stocks could be engaged in completely different trends, ignoring the broad market direction. The importance of micro-trend analysis at the security level could not be overemphasized.

Figure 3–12. *Examples of Up and Down and Neutral-Trend Lines and Channels*

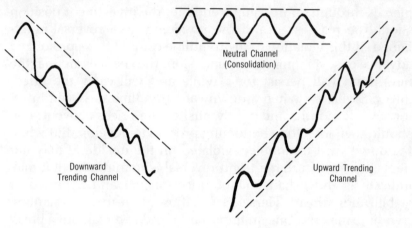

Trendlines are not mystical or infallible. They are helpful in pinpointing the possible direction of the next price movement. A common mistake that amateurs often make is to imagine trendlines for every stock they see. Constructing trendlines is tricky for most beginners. It takes practice and experience for a person to be able to draw them properly. It is easy to see trendlines with hindsight, but it is difficult to anticipate them at an early stage of the trend. They are most useful when they have been violated after a prolonged advance. That is why the importance of the moving average as a trend identifier is emphasized here.

THE MOVING AVERAGE

The moving average method has long been used by professionals in many endeavors to smooth out erratic data fluctuation and project the future. Known as a reliable trend identifier, the moving average minimizes losses and allows its followers to ride most of the advance of a bull swing. Moreover, the moving average system can enhance performance in any kind of market environment. It works well in up and down markets and can be applied in the analysis of the general averages, industry groups, individual stocks, and commodities. Its principles could even be used in detecting loss or gain in earnings, sales, and the economic aggregates' momentum. During periods of high volatility, the moving average can alert investors to potential trend reversal. Although there has been no trading system that comes close to being perfect, the moving average is thought to be adequate and profitable over the long haul. By far, its predictive value is superior to any other method known or used to identify the trend.

Trend followers do not try to forecast the market, rather they capitalize on the prevailing direction of prices and go with the flow. The rationale and reason behind market behavior is of no interest to them; performance is the ultimate goal. In the arena of investing, the key to success is to correctly anticipate the future direction of securities prices. Once the moving average method alerts its practitioner to emerging upward strength, long-term buy positions can be initiated. Similarly, when the moving average warns of the potential for a trend reversal, investors should consider liquidation of current holdings. By adhering to the moving average buy-and-sell signals in trading practice, one is, in fact, letting the market do the talking instead of trying to put a theoretical value on stocks.

Although this method does not allow buying at the absolute low or selling at the top, it provides an alert to important changes that are likely to affect performance. Its predictive value works best in trending markets. But it loses its forecasting value in a trading or neutral market.

For many years, the moving-average technique has been used by statisticians, economists, and corporate planners to smooth out erratic fluctuations of statistical data. The Dow theory practitioners rely on it as a valuable complementary tool in identifying the trend. Moreover, moving averages can also provide a means of detecting trend reversals. Moving averages work well in a trending market. They offer little value during periods of price congestion and indecisive trend direction.

Figure 3-13 illustrates the 50- and 200-day moving averages applied to the case of a stock, an industry group, and a

Figure 3–13. *The 50- and 200-day Moving Average*

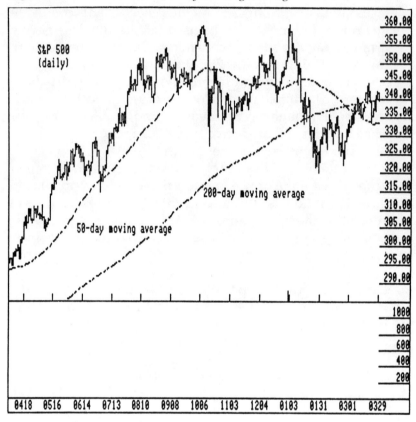

market average. Notice that the point of crossing of the two moving averages confirms the trend in motion. When the 50-day moving average crosses the 200-day moving average from up to down, the trend has reversed into a long-term decline, and a sell signal is initiated. And, vice versa, when the 50-day moving average crosses the 200-day moving average from down to up, a buy signal alert is in force, as the long-term potential is greatly enhanced.

As one of the most viable techniques used by professional market analysts, the 200-day moving average ranks high. Up-trends are characterized by a rising slope of the moving average and downtrends by a descending slope. Following are the rules that should be adhered to when using this system:

1. In an uptrend, investors should initiate and hold long-term positions as long as prices remain above their 200-day moving average. A downside penetration of a rising moving average provides a cautionary signal. After the initial penetration, the failure of the price to rebound above the moving average or flattening out of the moving average should be interpreted as further confirmation of a trend reversal. Notice that the 200-day moving average is insensitive to the sharp fluctuations of price. In addition, after the initial penetration of the moving average, the slope tends to flatten out before the downtrend begins its slide in earnest.

2. In a downtrend, the stock, market average, or industry group is assumed to be in a bear phase as long as the 200-day moving average continues to slope downward. When a price penetration of the moving average to the upside occurs, investors should be alerted to the possibility of a trend reversal from down to up. While a bull swing may not immediately follow, a period of stability and base building can be expected.

The moving average is a generic technique that can be used to analyze the trend of a market, an industry group, a commodity, or a stock. Its principles have long been applied to many real-life statistical analyses. Its use is not restricted to stock market analysis, but also to economic and fundamental data. While it has proven to be of great help in determining trends, it should be applied in conjunction with other methods of analysis and confirmed by economic and fudmamental factors.

CONCLUSION

The Dow theory was the first try at quantifying the market trend. By calculating an average of the price of stocks representing major corporations in the manufacturing sector, Dow was able to study the progression of the market trend. A comparison of the industrials with the transportation averages can reveal diverging performances and signal the onset of a trend reversal. The two averages should confirm each other's action in order for the prevailing trend to continue.

Efforts to refine Dow's work led to the formulation of other averages that represent different sectors of the market. The S&P 500 and the Value-Line indexes describe the trend of the broad market. The Amex and OTC indexes provide a snapshot of the fortunes of secondary stocks. Industry groups have also been ordered to study the rotation of leadership or weakness in the marketplace.

The major or primary trend is the one that investors should focus on. As long as the averages keep scoring higher highs and higher lows, an uptrend is intact and long positions are warranted. Downtrends, according to the theory, are defined as a series of lower highs and lower lows.

Comparison between a number of averages is always preferred, as it demonstrates the relative performance of the different segments of the market. When they all move in unison in either direction, one should expect the prevailing trend to continue on its course. When one or more of the averages fail to confirm the action in the Dow Jones Averages, a possible trend reversal may be expected. The longer those divergences persist, the more severe their implications may be.

Trendlines and moving averages are complementary tools to the Dow theory. They help identify the direction of the trend. Moving averages are ranked among the best analysis methods known to study the underlying trend and to identify points of trend reversals.

The relative-strength concept is also widely used by professional analysts. By plotting the ratio of a stock price to the market or industry average, one can better tell how that stock is faring in comparison with the overall market as well as in its own industry. During market declines, the relative-strength method gives an early clue to future leaders in the market. A stock that resists market decline can be expected to rally strongly once the selling pressure is exhausted (and vice versa).

PART 2

Economic Analysis

☐ 4

The Business Cycle

The farmers say . . . "what does Wall Street know about farming?" Wall Street knows more than all the farmers put together ever knew, with all that the farmers have forgotten. It employs the ablest of the farmers, and its experts are better even than those of our admirable and little appreciated Department of Agriculture, whose publications Wall Street reads even if the farmer neglects them.

William P. Hamilton, 1925

Since Adam Smith wrote his milestone book, *The Wealth of Nations*, the science of economics has taken big strides. Modern finance and accounting theories emerged from economics. The purpose here, however, is to study the interrelationships between the economy and the securities markets. Because financial markets are discounting mechanisms, they tend to lead the economy; they have a good track record at forecasting the expansion and contraction of business activities. Analysis of the economic statistics can help anticipate the end of an economic boom or the onset of a slowdown.

Earnings, dividends, sales, cash flow, and other growth measures pertinent to the financial health of a firm are influenced to varying degrees by economic cycles. Economic expansion sion and an easy Fed policy have a positive impact on the fundamentals governing the prices of securities. The market risk can be controlled better by a thorough understanding of the behavior of the stock prices during the different stages of the economic cycle. By understanding the relationship between the economic indicators and the securities market, the forecast of impending major trend reversals in stocks and bonds can be sharpened. This study begins with a review of key economic indicators and their behavior during past business cycles. Once such indicators' interaction is understood, a better position for assessing their relationship with the equities market can be achieved.

Since 1870, the U.S. economy has experienced 26 recessions. The majority of them have been accompanied by a decline in stock prices. In fact, the market anticipated these cyclical downturns before they were reflected in the economic statistics. Moreover, amid dismal economic predictions, the stock market has staged stampeding advances, announcing the onset of new economic recovery. The fixed-income sector has also responded to periods of rising or declining interest rates accompanying the contraction or expansion phases of the economy. An understanding of the relationship between the economy and the trend in equities and bonds is vital in formulating profitable investment decisions and in taming market risk.

Successive periods of economic expansion and contraction lie at the heart of the free enterprise system. Fluctuations in business activities have been widely used by economists and professional Wall Street analysts to forecast the trend in equities and fixed-income securities. The purpose here is not to indulge in the study of cycles and their basic causes but to understand their impact on stocks and bonds.

THE BUSINESS CYCLE

The business cycle is described as the long-term fluctuations in the aggregate economic activities that occur in a free-enterprise economy. A cycle consists of a primary expansion phase which benefits most business sectors, followed by a broad-based contraction in all economic activities. Cycles are recurrent but not periodic. In the past, their duration varied from one cycle to another. While many business cycles lasted four years, and hence became known as the four-year cycles, they often spanned 10 or even 12 years from start to finish.

In order to understand the cyclical nature of the economy, the forces that influence business and that lead to these periods of recovery and recession must be examined. The nature of the economic policies that bring about these changes must also be determined. These cyclical fluctuations are broad based and have a pronounced impact on the business activities of almost all sectors of the economy.

Inflation and Unemployment

Inflation and unemployment are two important aggregates whose relative trends determine the Fed's policy at different stages of the economic cycle. Rising inflation upsets the balance of purchasing power in the economy. Inflation wipes out wealth and debt and has a devastating effect on people living on fixed incomes. Inflation also makes it difficult for corporations and individuals to formulate and execute long-term plans.

The control of inflation is usually achieved at the expense of rising unemployment. Towards the latter part of a maturing economic cycle, consumer demand increases, as more people are employed and their income is rising. Strains on production capacity mount as supply is unable to expand fast enough to meet the surging demand. Capacity utilization of production resources reaches its upper limits, and inflation begins to rise. The rising inflation prompts the Fed to adopt a restrictive credit policy that eventually brings about a slowdown in demand and an economic recession. During the contraction phase of the economy, the inflation rate slows down and unemployment rises. Once a recession is indicated by the economic statistics, the Fed moves quickly to fight rising unemployment (which is politically unacceptable) and changes its monetary policy to an accommodative one. Consumption begins to expand slowly at first while unemployment declines. Then inflationary pressures begin to mount as the Fed continues to ease the money supply and more people earn income.

This process of expansion and contraction in consumer demand is the basis of the fluctuation of inflation and unemployment during the business cycle. The process plays an important role in determining the monetary policy adopted by the Fed in its effort to manage the economy. To the Fed, inflation is disruptive to all sectors of the economy. Inflation threatens the stability of the monetary system, because it reduces confidence in money. However, inflation can only be controlled at the expense of economic slowdown, recession in business activities, and swelling unemployment.

In order for inflation to slow down, unemployment has to

rise, and vice versa. In the science of economics, this inverse relationship between inflation and unemployment is known as the Philips curve. Figure 4–1 illustrates the correlation between spot prices of raw industrial materials compared with the number of people unemployed. The graph clearly shows the inverse relationship between inflation and unemployment. It is important to note that the peaks of inflation during the past economic cycles coincided with troughs in the unemployment rate. Moreover, peaks in the unemployment rate were not far away from points of reversal in the inflation trend. There is some lead or lag by a few months between these two aggregates. But this real-life example demonstrates an important relationship that is basic to understanding the internal dynamics of the business cycle.

Although inflation and unemployment are key determinants that shape the Fed's policy, they are not the only ones. The Fed also has to consider the trade balance and the dollar's position in the foreign exchange market. It may pay to review here some of the mechanisms used by the Fed to map the nation's economic policies.

The Federal Reserve Board

In 1913, after the banking panic of 1907, the Federal Reserve Board was created to control and manage the economy. The most important role the Fed plays is that of formulating monetary policies that balance inflation and unemployment in a growing economy. The Fed executes desired policies by regulating the liquidity of the banking system. This is made possible by controlling the money supply in the economy and the level of short-term interest rates. To implement its policies, the Fed uses a combination of the following tools:

1. Bank reserve requirements: Banks which are members of the Federal Reserve Board System are required to maintain a percentage of their total deposits as reserve money. That percentage is not lent to the public. When the Fed wants to tighten the monetary policy, it raises the reserve requirements. This action, in turn, lowers banks' liquidity, as the

Figure 4–1. Spot market prices and unemployment

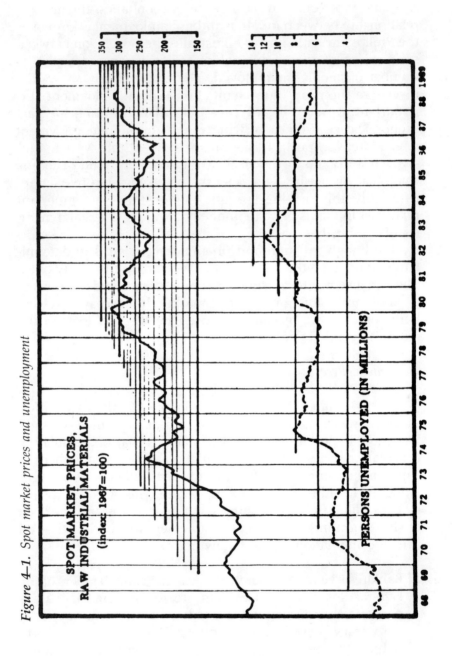

SPOT MARKET PRICES,
RAW INDUSTRIAL MATERIALS
(index: 1967=100)

PERSONS UNEMPLOYED (IN MILLIONS)

available money for lending to both consumers and business decreases. In other words, the supply of credit contracts. This, in turn, translates to reduced consumption and slowed economic growth. The reverse is also true—the Fed can increase banks' liquidity and money available for credit by lowering reserve requirements.

2. Control of the money supply: The Fed buys and sells government securities to member banks. By selling securities, the Fed receives banks' payment by means of Federal Funds checks. This means that the banks withdraw from their reserves at the Fed to pay for these securities. This process leads to lower banks' reserves, and, hence, their ability to extend credit decreases. However, when buying securities, the Fed pays for them in Federal Funds checks, thus injecting money into the banking system. The decision to buy or sell securities is made by the Fed's Federal Open Market Committee (FOMC). The process of purchasing and selling securities leads to expansion and contraction of the money supply.

3. The discount rate: To meet their reserve requirements and increase the amount of money available for credit, member banks borrow from the Fed at the discount window. The Fed is known as the bankers' bank. The discount rate is the interest that the Fed charges member banks on loans, that is the discount rate is the cost of money that banks incur when they borrow from the Fed. This, in turn, establishes a floor under the commercial and personal loan rates that banks charge to their customers. By raising or lowering the discount rate, the Fed tightens or loosens the money supply. This tool has proven to be effective in controlling the amount of money in circulation.

The Fed can also influence liquidity in the stock market. By raising or lowering margin requirements, the Fed can increase or decrease the supply of investment funds that is channeled into equities. Although this option has been available to the Fed, it has seldom been used. The Fed is aware of the domino effect that a stock market plunge can have on the banking system. Since the Great Depression, the Fed has been

cautious when dealing with large market declines. For instance, in the wake of the Crash of 1987, the Fed acted immediately to infuse cash into the banking system in order to
reliquify financial markets. In early 1988 and after the market
stabilized, the Fed proceeded to tighten its monetary policy,
and interest rates rose higher than their pre-crash levels. Having eased the money supply to reestablish confidence and
stabilization in world financial markets, the Fed then proceeded to tighten money to fight rising inflation.

Figure 4–2 illustrates the behavior of interest rates during
and after the Crash of 1987 vis-à-vis stocks and bonds. Notice
that the initial rise of the Federal Funds interest rate caused
nervousness in both the equities and fixed-income markets.
The bond market declined as early as March 1987. At first, the
stock market ignored the rising rates and plummeting bonds,
but it was only a matter of time before the euphoria on Wall
Street come to an end. It did so that autumn, resulting in the
worst selloff in history. Notice that in the wake of the devasta-
tion and fear that plagued the world at the time, the Fed eased
money, and interest rates were allowed to ease. The bond
market immediately rebounded and the equities market stabilized. Although the Federal Funds rate's rose again as early as
the first quarter of 1988, and surpassed the pre-crash highs,
both bonds and stocks were so washed out that contrarian
behavior prevailed until early 1989. The subsequent action of
stocks and bonds was then governed by deteriorating fundamentals, fear of resurging inflation and the decline in corporate
earnings. The stock market trend is closely related to the interest rate direction. That is probably one of the golden rules in
anticipating future equities prices and the likelihood of advance
or decline. The long-term relationship between interest rates
and the equities market will be discussed in depth later.

INFLATION AND INTEREST RATES

The Fed's economic policy is dictated by the relative level
of inflation and unemployment at any given time. A tight
monetary policy and rising interest rates bring about a decline

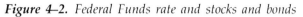

Figure 4–2. Federal Funds rate and stocks and bonds

in inflation, although at the expense of rising unemployment. Figure 4–3 illustrates the relationship between interest rates and inflation.

The graph demonstrates the relationship between inflation and interest rates. Although its use often leads to economic slowdowns, the interest rate is the most effective tool with which to fight inflation. The Federal Funds rate's advance eventually causes inflation to subside. The reason is simple: the rise or fall of interest rates increases or decreases the cost of borrowing. When rates rise, consumption subsides as households defer their purchasing plans. High rates also exercise downward pressure on corporate profit margins and discourage capital spending. The net effect is that rising rates reach a point from which inflation begins to decline, and the general economy contracts. In the past, cyclical interest rate highs have coincided with, and sometimes led, peaks in inflation.

The relationship between interest rates and inflation is very important. The two are positively correlated. When inflation rises, interest rates advance and when inflation declines, interest rates soften. Higher inflation translates into higher interest rates, which adversely affect both the equities and fixed-income sectors. Lower inflation means lower rates, which is bullish for stocks and bonds.

Interest Rates and Industrial Production

Interest rates have an important influence on business activities. Indeed, the cyclical fluctuations of the economy are propelled by long-term interest rate trends. The rise or fall of inflation determines the Fed's policy. Figure 4–4 illustrates the relationship between interest rates and industrial production.

In the past, as the graph demonstrates, the rise of the Federal Funds rate caused a slowdown in economic activities, consumption, inflation, and industrial production. The cyclical highs and lows of the Federal Funds rate tend to lead peaks and troughs in manufacturing activities. The industrial production index (IPI) is one of the four coincident indicators that the Fed monitors. The IPI represents the national output of manufactured goods and is a faithful barometer of the state of the

Figure 4-3. Spot market prices compared with interest rates.

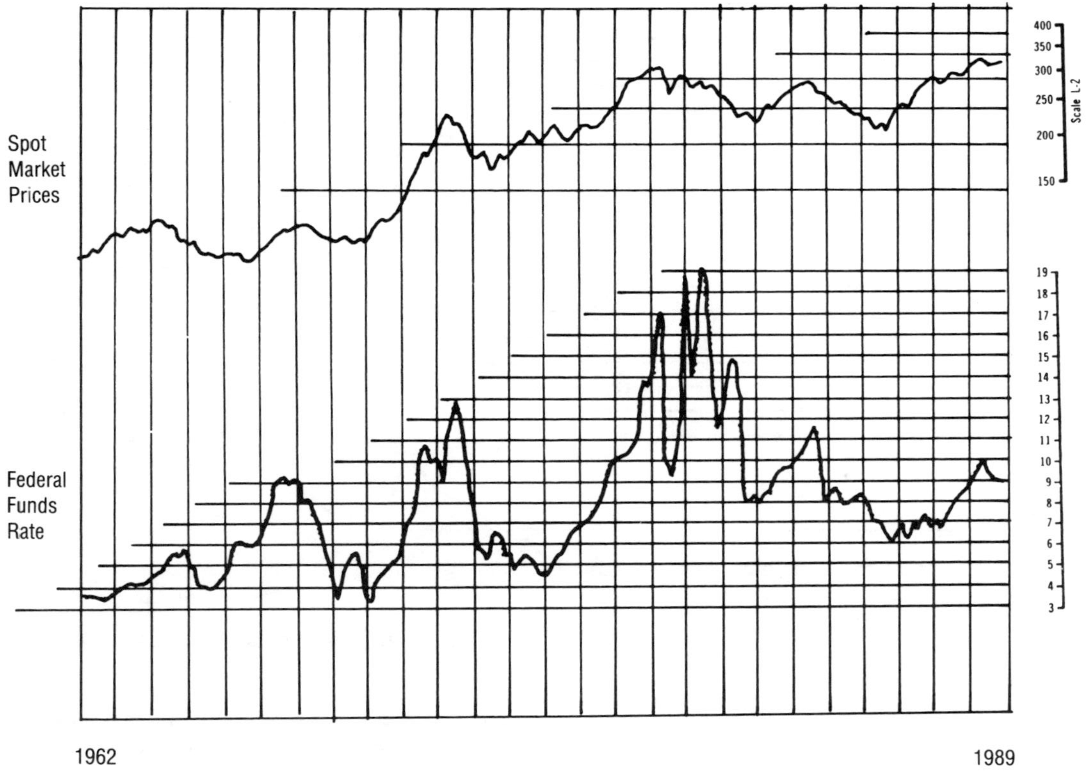

Scale L-2

400 350 300 250 200 150

19 18 17 16 15 14 13 12 11 10 9 8 7 6 5 4 3

Spot Market Prices

Federal Funds Rate

1962

1989

97

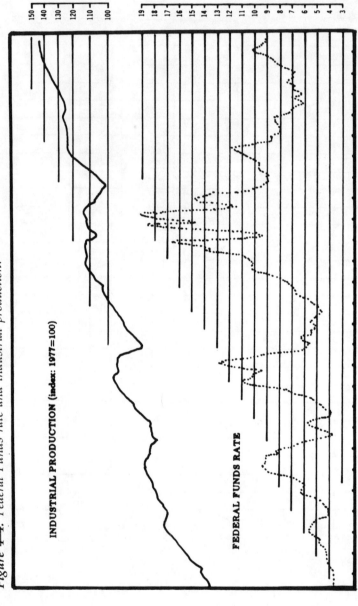

Figure 4-4. Federal Funds rate and industrial production.

economy. A rise in interest rates translates to a higher cost of borrowing, which in turn slows consumption and cools the demand for industrial products. When rates decline, it encourages borrowing, which leads to the expansion of consumer demand and, hence, increased manufacturing. Notice that the rise of interest rates has always led to declining industrial production. The Federal Funds rate trend leads the IPI during both expansion and contraction phases of the business cycle.

Interest Rates and Unemployment

Rising interest rates lead to economic slowdown and higher unemployment, and falling rates are followed by lower unemployment. Figure 4–5 illustrates the inverse correlation between interest rates and unemployment.

In the above figure, the number of months by which rates have led the rise or fall of unemployment varied from one business cycle to another. Also notice that this relationship did not hold in the 1980s. The reason was that the influx of the baby boomers to the job market in the late 1970s and early 1980s caused rising structural unemployment. After this wave of newcomers exhausted itself, there was actually a shortage of skilled labor in many sectors of the economy. The decreasing rate of new entrants to the job market allowed unemployment to continue to drop despite the high real interest rates.

Interest Rates and the Stock Market

The stock market is one of the best leading indicators for forecasting future economic developments—as a barometer, it has correctly anticipated cyclical expansions and contractions before they actually happened by a comfortable margin. The stock market derives its superb predictive value from the interaction of the judgment and knowledge of all of the informed people who take part in the process and from their management of their own interests. This is the invisible hand of the free enterprise system at its best; it is the summary of the collective behavior of those who can effect things while in pursuit of their own interests.

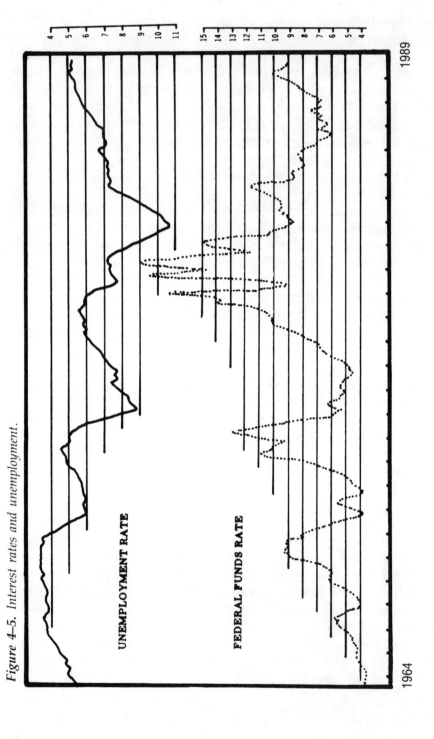

Figure 4–5. Interest rates and unemployment.

UNEMPLOYMENT RATE

FEDERAL FUNDS RATE

1964

1989

In the past, amid booming business, rising industrial production, declining unemployment, and rampant consumer optimism, the stock market has often reversed its bull trend and proceeded on a long-term downward course. A few months later, to the astonishment of investors, the economy suddenly contracted and business conditions worsened. Similarly, in the face of a gloomy outlook, faltering corporate earnings, rising unemployment, plummeting GNP, and overwhelming pessimism, the stock market staged a strong rally and proceeded with a primary uptrend. Shortly afterwards, investors were pleasantly surprised by a broad-based recovery in the nation's economic activities.

Two closely related questions should be addressed at this point: First, how can the stock market anticipate major turning points and assess the outlook for the economy? Second, how do interest rate fluctuations affect stock prices? In order to answer these two questions, an environment in which a tight momentary policy is in place may be considered. At the corporate end, as interest rates rise and consumption slows down, sales decline, inventory accumulates, profits suffer, profit margins shrink, and the prospect for growth appears illusory. As business contracts, the risk of deterioration of the balance sheet and of the internal financial structure of most companies rises. Declining profits force management to resort to debt financing. As interest rates continue to rise, debt service charges increase, thus exercising further pressure on cash flow and other internal resources. In addition, during business downturns market shares may be lost, and technological obsolescence becomes a threat. All of these factors warrant the assessment of risk rather than the search for values in an environment of rising rates.

Contrariwise, when interest rates decline, the economy expands, profits rise, profit margins improve, sales increase, unemployment declines, and economic growth prospects are reinstated. The stock market trends upward as companies' financial conditions improve, expansion in their markets resumes, earnings rise, and their overall intrinsic value appreciates.

The relationship between interest rates and the stock market is illustrated by figure 4–6. It is apparent from the graph

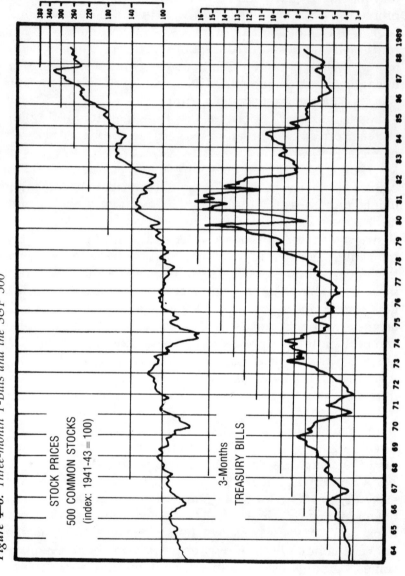

Figure 4–6. Three-month T-Bills and the S&P 500

that the two are negatively correlated. When interest rates move *up* the stock market moves *down* and vice versa. Investors should be fully aware of this relationship, as it is the most important factor that should be considered in assessing long-term trends in the securities market; history indicates that this relationship has held true since the beginning of this century.

The bond market is also sensitive to interest rates. When rates rise, bonds decline, and when rates fall, bonds advance. The relationship between interest rates and the fixed-income sector is well understood, because rate fluctuations have a direct effect on the income derived from bonds. As a general rule, the stock market trend follows the lead of the bond market, which is sensitive to interest rate directions.

On rare occasions the stock market has advanced when interest rates rose; but as rates continued to move up, the market reacted violently. After all has been considered vis-à-vis the impact of interest rates on both stocks and bonds, one sees that, at times, aberrations that lead to substantial rises and falls for no apparent reason do occur. For example, 1962 witnessed a bear market in equities that interrupted the decade's secular bull market. At that time, the general market decline was not accompanied by a corresponding economic slowdown. There was no real explanation for the market weakness from a fundamental or economic standpoint. The internal dynamics prevailed, and investor sentiment drove prices counter to what the business environment should have warranted. This demonstrates that adaptability in investment analysis is of prime importance.

INTEREST RATE TRENDS

Interest rate directions influence the economy, inflation, the equities market, commodities prices, mortgage payments, the job market, corporate capital spending, earnings, sales, profit margins, and so forth. Interest rates are the heart, soul, and life of the free enterprise system. Interest rates are no more or less than the cost of money. When they rise, consumers postpone their buying plans as the prospect of rising unemployment looms threateningly. Job security becomes the major concern determining household-spending patterns. When the economic outlook appears shaky, people tend to curtail their purchase of cars, electronic equipment, furniture, new houses, and many other big-ticket items. Instead, they control their appetite for expanding beyond their means and watch closely for the expected hard times ahead. When interest rates fall, however, the cost of money declines, and consumers become more aggressive in their spending. When the outlook appears sound, they tap their liquid reserves, savings, or credit lines. At the corporate end, as companies begin to feel the retrenchment of consumers' spending, they defer their capital investment commitments and their plans to increase existing production capacity. In the face of rising inventories, companies usually cut their production and lay off workers. When the economy is recovering and consumer demand increases, companies speed up their production and boost their capital investments. They rehire workers to meet new contracts and fulfill orders.

In a free market system, the final outcome is governed by supply and demand. When the economy is in an expansion phase, the demand for business, consumer goods, and mortgage credit is on the rise. Commodities prices and inflation also rise. Short-term rates, especially the Federal Funds and three-month T Bills, respond to inflationary pressures and advance. Sensing the excessive demand and rising inflation, the Fed raises the discount rate, draining liquidity from the system. The upward pressure on interest rates prompts the banks to raise the prime rate. (The interest on short-term loans that banks charge select customers). Mortgage rates then follow suit, which exercises a dampening effect on the housing market. As rates continue to rise, a recession finally takes its toll on all sectors of the economy and inflation begins to subside.

One important indicator that is used to measure the nature of the monetary policy is the spread between the Federal Funds and the discount rate. If the spread is positive, meaning that the Federal Funds rate is higher than the discount rate, the monetary policy in place is restrictive. And contrariwise, if the spread is negative, meaning that the discount rate is higher than the Federal Funds rate, it should imply an accommodative policy to stimulate the economy.

When considering the relative trends of interest rates, the Federal Funds and three-Months Treasury Bills rates lead all other rates. Their rise or fall leads the discount rate, which is then followed by mortgage rates. The prime rate, on the other hand, is a lagging indicator and is the last to advance or decline among all rates. Unfortunately, most investors focus their attention on the prime rate when they should monitor the Federal Funds or Three-months Treasury Bills rate—these are the true leading indicators of the business cycle and of all the other rates. Not only do they represent a good barometer of the future course of monetary policy, they also react faster to inflationary pressures.

The Inverted Yield Curve

When the Fed is set on tightening monetary policy, short-term rates tend to rise faster than long-term ones, producing what is known as an inverted, or negative, yield curve. The importance of such a development is that it has often been followed by an economic recession. In addition, in the past, an inverted yield curve has preceded a period of stock market weakness.

Not all inversions have led to a recession. However, their occurrence should be an alert to potential slowdown and to the possibility of an emerging downtrend in the equities market. In other words, recessions have always been preceded by inverted yield curves, but inverted yield curves are not always followed by recession.

Credit tightening by the Fed causes the inversion of the yield curve as short-term rates rise faster than longer-term ones. Periods of excessive economic growth fuel higher inflation and rising commodities prices. Thus, the inversions tend to coincide with periods of heated economic activities and concern from the Fed about rising inflationary pressures. The advance of short-term rates has a dampening effect on sales and leads to rising inventory. The liquidation process that follows is usually accompanied by cuts in production and rises in unemployment. This ultimately leads to broad-based economic slowdown and a recession in business activities.

When dealing with inverted yield curve periods, it pays to

analyze the causes of the inversion and the long-term outlook for inflation. Temporary or cyclical cost-of-living rises are a natural phenomenon in a capitalist economy. They are the reason for the fluctuation of the aggregates while current policies attempt to stabilize future growth prospects without causing too much inflation. Such cyclical inflationary pressures are often accompanied by a higher rate of advance of short-term rates than with long-term ones. Almost always, the yield on one-year Treasury notes advances faster and higher than do Treasury notes due in ten years. However, if inflation is in a secular or long-term advance due to structural factors, such as demographics, wars, or a cartel's controlling the price of a vital commodity like oil, then long- and short-term notes may rise in unison. But, even under such circumstances, one should expect the short-term maturity rates to surpass the longer-term ones.

ANATOMY OF THE BUSINESS CYCLE

In order to gain perspective on economic dynamics, the impact of interest rates on the different sectors of the economy during the span of a full business cycle should be examined.

In economics, inflation has been defined as too much money chasing too few goods. Periods of rising inflation trigger a restrictive monetary policy and a rise in interest rates. This, in turn, leads to a reduction in the money supply, which causes unemployment and economic slowdown. During an economic slowdown, auto sales and housing starts decline. These two vital sectors, in particular, are sensitive to consumer spending and interest rates.

Furthermore, the slowdown in consumption leads to a cycle of inventory accumulation in the manufacturing sector. The corporate balance sheet becomes highly illiquid as the cost of servicing debt keeps rising and demand for goods falters. Companies are then pressed to cut down on their capital spending for plants and equipment. As sales continue to slacken under the impact of rising rates, and production exceeds demand for goods, hiring freezes and layoffs become widespread. Help-wanted advertising falls, reflecting the tight job market. Inflation slows down and begins to subside. The stock market is now in a free fall and a bear market is in progress on Wall Street. This stage of the business cycle is characterized by credit risk and witnesses declines in corporate earnings as profit margins shrink. Also typical is a decline in real GNP, industrial production, and capacity utilization.

Simultaneously, housing activities decline precipitously, unemployment rises, and consumer sentiment becomes pessimistic. Companies trim their production and are pressed to liquidate their rising inventory. The process of inventory liquidation is characterized by massive markdowns and reduction in production schedules, which also implies more layoffs. Unemployment numbers, being a lagging indicator, worsen, and the issue of job security drives consumers to cut back further.

In order to formulate policy, the Fed monitors the leading, lagging, and coincident indicators. These aggregates report on the state of the different sectors in the economy and measure the level of business activities. The economic indicators will be studied in the next chapter.

At this juncture of the business cycle, the leading indicators turn downward. The Fed's priority shifts from a restrictive monetary policy to a more accommodative one. The prime goal is to stimulate the sagging economy rather than to fight inflation. The rising unemployment and the slowing down of credit are the new enemies that the Fed policy targets. An eased monetary policy implies allowing interest rates to fall. The Federal Funds rate begins to decline, accompanied by a cut in the discount rate. An expansion in the money supply is in order. The stock market stages a strong rally characterized by broadly-based advances in prices. The leading indicators reverse their trend from up to down. Although industrial production may continue to fall and unemployment continue to rise, it is only a matter of time before these trends reverse.

Moreover, in the early stages of the Fed's easing process, the GNP may still be declining and sales may remain sluggish. Typically, consumer sentiment is in the doldrums and prophecies of a depression, or at least a severe recession, make the headlines in major newspapers. The economic forecast is gloomy, and corporate earnings are revised downward. Investors are uncomfortable, to say the least, and their focus is on risk rather than on potential reward.

Then, in the face of all these uncertainties, the stock market and housing starts rebound sharply. The leading indicators reverse their downward trend, announcing the beginning of a new phase of economic recovery. Despite these positive developments in an environment of declining interest rates, investors' psychology remains skeptical for a while as the lagging economic statistics project further softening of business.

As time goes by, the green light slowly appears as inflation continues to stabilize. Many investors, feel that it is again safe to invest in the stock market, and real demand for stocks expands. The economic recovery is at full speed, and consumption is accelerating upward. The price of raw materials stops declining and reverses its trend. Inflation is about to soar and the whole cycle is about to begin all over again.

Interest Rates and the Housing Market

The impact of interest rate trends on all sectors of the economy cannot be underestimated. A particularly sensitive area is the housing market, which has an inverse relationship with interest rate trends. When the Fed tightens and rates rise, the building industry suffers and when the Fed is easing and rates decline, the housing market revives. Cyclical downturns are led by shrinking demand for durable goods—mainly, housing and autos. Because these two sectors influence the activities in almost all other industries, their impact intensifies the downward pressure of recessionary forces.

Figure 4–7 illustrates the cyclical behavior of newly authorized building permits versus the three-month Treasury Bills rate. The graph demonstrates clearly the negative correlation between these two economic aggregates. Notice that peaks in building activities materialized shortly after a cyclical low in rates was reached. As soon as rates reversed their long-term trend, the housing market began its slowdown. Then, as rates gained upward momentum, the fall in the real estate market accelerated. In addition, cyclical peaks in interest rates led the housing market troughs by a few months. Moreover, the housing market blossomed most after rates precipitated downward, usually as recessions were in force and the Fed was easing fast to prompt an economic recovery.

Figure 4-7. Housing permits compared with T-Bonds.

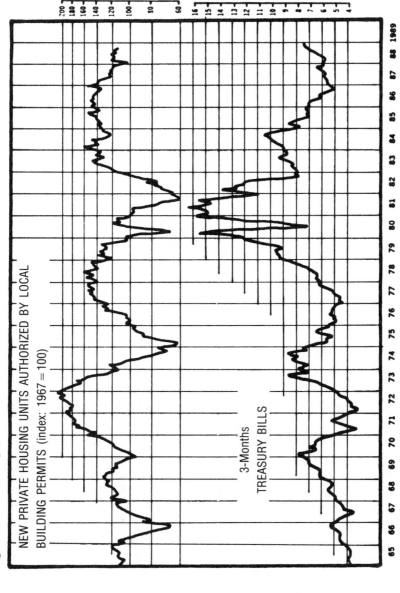

109

Inflation and the Capacity Utilization Rate

In order to understand the behavior of inflation during the business cycle, the relationship between spot market prices of raw materials as compared with capacity utilization must be examined.

Figure 4–8 illustrates the cyclical correlation between these two economic aggregates. Capacity utilization tends to reach its limits ahead of spot market prices. The congestion stage near cyclical saturation levels tends to occur shortly before the acceleration of inflationary forces. During economic expansions, when supply fails to satisfy rising demand, spot market prices of raw materials accelerate upward. This, in turn, forces the Fed to tighten money sharply and pushes interest rates up. Similarly, capacity utilization reaches its cyclical trough before spot market prices. When the slowdown is at its full force, near recession troughs, supply far exceeds demand and inflation is subdued. Only when interest rates begin to head downward and the Fed eases up does inflation regain upward momentum. In the past, when capacity utilization reached 85 percent to 90 percent capacity, a cyclical peak in economic activities was not far behind. Similarly, when it declined to 70 percent or below, the Fed eased, interest rates declined, and a cyclical trough was within sight.

Unemployment and Help-wanted Advertising

The Fed is constantly implementing policies to balance both inflation and unemployment. The Department of Commerce reports monthly on help-wanted advertising. This indicator is vital in analyzing the outlook for the job market. Figure 4–9 illustrates the number of persons unemployed compared with help-wanted advertising in newspapers. These two aggregates are inversely related: During phases of economic expansion, help-wanted advertising rises. When the economy stops advancing, it implies that the outlook for the job market is growing cloudy. The graph also demonstrates that cyclical higher in unemployment have been accompanied by early signs of strength in the job market. This is usually reflected by a rise in help-wanted advertising.

Figure 4–8. *Capacity utilization compared with spot market prices.*

INFLATIONARY PRESSURES

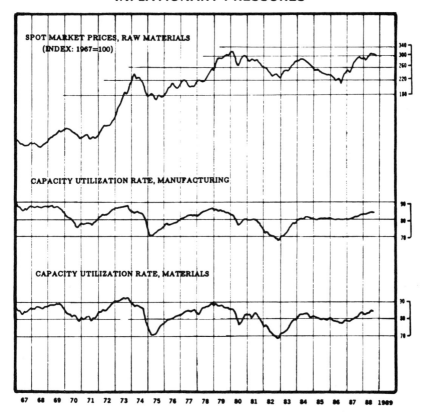

Interest Rates and the GNP

The Gross National Product is as sensitive to interest rate fluctuations as all the other economic aggregates. The Nominal GNP is measured without any adjustment to inflation. Real GNP, on the other hand, measures the total output after accounting for inflation. In this study, the Nominal GNP behavior is compared to interest rates to analyze their relationships. Figure 4–10 illustrates the Nominal GNP vis-à-vis the Federal Funds rate. During previous business cycles, the rate of growth of the nominal GNP materialized in the face of rising rates. The peak in rates occurred after the GNP started to slow down, as indicated by the arrows. The low points of GNP growth were

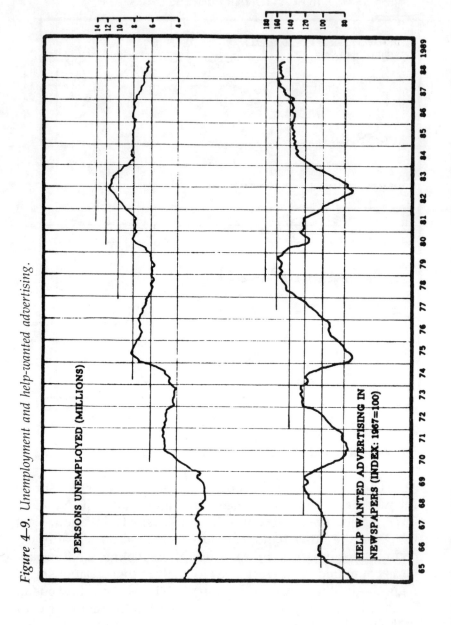

Figure 4–9. Unemployment and help-wanted advertising.

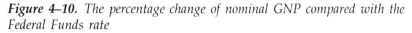

Figure 4–10. *The percentage change of nominal GNP compared with the Federal Funds rate*

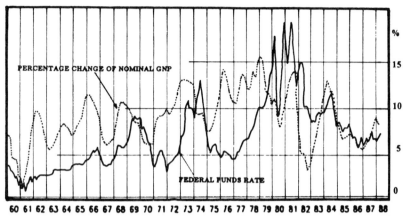

reached after interest rates precipitated in a long-term downtrend. Also notice that percentage changes of the Nominal GNP peaked around 10 percent to 12 percent, with only two exceptionally strong years between 1976–78. During those years, inflation was rampant and real interest rates were low, which may have helped prolong economic expansion. Cyclical peaks in interest rates were reached only after economic statistics indicated that the Nominal GNP growth was rising at a slower rate displaying loss of upward momentum in economic activities.

Inflation and the Stock Market

The trend of inflation is a key economic aggregate. Not only does it affect all sectors of the economy, it also shapes the monetary policy of the Fed, determines the direction of interest rates, and influences the equities and fixed-income securities prices. Figure 4–11 illustrates the relationship between the S&P 500 and spot market prices. The two indicators are inversely correlated. Rising inflationary pressures adversely affect the stock market and lead to major cyclical peaks in securities prices. Over the years, the relationship has been irregular. Soaring commodities prices have propelled severe bear markets. In the 1970s, the hefty rise in inflation prompted a stagnant market that fluctuated in a broad trading range. The boundary of this range contained the cyclical fluctuations. In the 1980s, the high real interest rates stopped inflation in its tracks and interrupted the unrelenting rise of the previous decade. Meanwhile, equities prices sold close to their book value at historically low price/earnings (P/E) ratios. The reasonable valuation and the subdued outlook for inflation triggered one of the strongest uptrends in history. Notice that spot market prices peaked ahead of stock market prices. Moreover, they made their cyclical lows and started heading up before the S&P 500 finally topped.

Unemployment and the Stock Market

The stock market is a leading indicator whereas unemployment is a lagging indicator. The two are inversely correlated such that bull markets have been accompanied by expanding economic activities and declining unemployment. Contrariwise, bear markets have progressed in environments characterized by slowing business conditions and rising unemployment.

Figure 4–12 illustrates the relationship between the two indicators. The point that needs stressing is that bear markets start when unemployment numbers are low. Because most investors base their judgment on recently published economic reports, the favorable outlook for jobs often camouflages the subtle weakness developing in the equities markets. Stock market peaks are seldom noticed amid environments dominated by positive economic news and declining unemployment. Moreover, the graph makes clear that stock market troughs materialize while unemployment is still rising. This treacherous relationship also prevents investors from capitalizing on the great opportunities that develop at the end of a cyclical downturn.

FOCUS ON ECONOMIC ANALYSIS

A comprehensive economic analysis must examine the interaction of consumer and capital spending, the outlook for corporate profits, the activities in the durable goods sectors,

Figure 4–11. The S&P 500 and spot market prices.

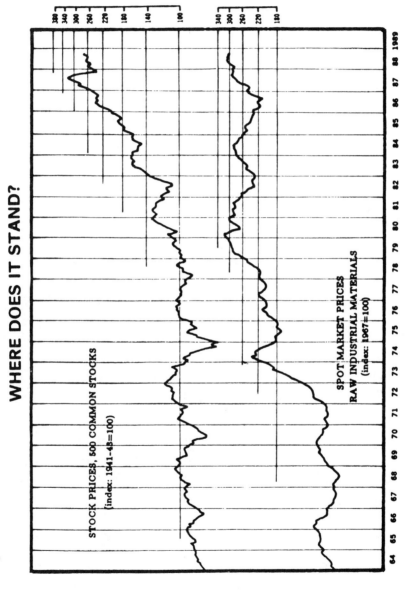

WHERE DOES IT STAND?

STOCK PRICES, 500 COMMON STOCKS
(index: 1941-43=100)

SPOT MARKET PRICES
RAW INDUSTRIAL MATERIALS
(index: 1967=100)

Figure 4–12. Unemployment and the S&P 500.

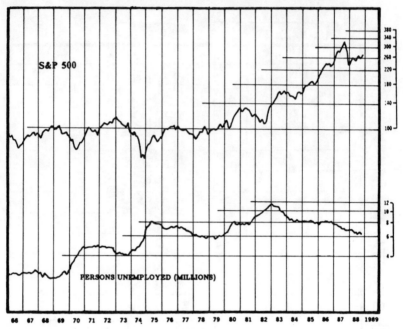

international trade, the dollar, industrial activities, employment, inflation, leverage, and the monetary and fiscal policy in place at any given time. All these factors are interrelated like a honeycomb, such that a change in any of them reverberates throughout the economy. So far, inflation, unemployment, and the monetary policy have been focused on and their behavior during the business cycle has been examined.

The rate of increase in inflation, however, is determined by the intensity of consumer demand and corporate capital spending. Meanwhile, the durable goods sectors, especially the housing and auto markets, are highly sensitive to interest rate trends and the current monetary policy, as these foster or dampen the demand for credit. International activities are highly dependent on the global trends of interest rates and foreign exchange perspectives. Leverage is another factor that controls the flow of spending in the economy at both the consumer and corporate levels. Any rise or fall in any of these economic aggregates swiftly affects others, with major implications that are eventually discounted by financial markets. In their actions and reactions, these aggregates produce the economic catalysts that shape primary bull or bear markets in both the equities and fixed-income markets.

The Consumer

The consumer is an important ingredient in economic analysis. Consumer spending is the locomotive behind business activities. Much depends upon the employment outlook, the savings rate, and household debt levels. Over the lifespan of the cycle, consumer spending habits are measured using several economic aggregates that are closely monitored by the Fed.

Figure 4–13 illustrates the year-to-year change in consumer spending. In the past, cyclical peaks occurred when the growth of real personal consumption expenditures hovered around the 6-percent level. The rate of change of this indicator lagged peaks and troughs in the stock market. Consumer spending is more of a coincident indicator of actual economic activities. Not surprisingly, consumption tends to decline during recessions and expand during economic recoveries.

Consumer sentiment is measured by the consumer confidence index. Two series are used to determine the state of consumer optimism or pessimism: the Conference Board Consumer Sentiment Index (CBCSI) and the University of Michigan series. These indexes differ slightly, but they are both thought to be good representations of consumers' optimism/pessimism level. The difference between the two indexes is in the process of gathering statistics and the number of households included. Over the full span of the business cycle, consumer confidence statistics have shown a tendency to coincide with economic activities. When the economy appears to be weakening and the prospects in the job market look uncertain, consumers tend to postpone their purchasing commitments. Big-ticket item vendors feel the impact of this increasingly conservative spending attitude. Despite the rebates that auto manufacturers offer in the latter stages of the business cycle,

Figure 4–13. Consumer spending during the business cycle.

Real Personal Consumption Expenditures

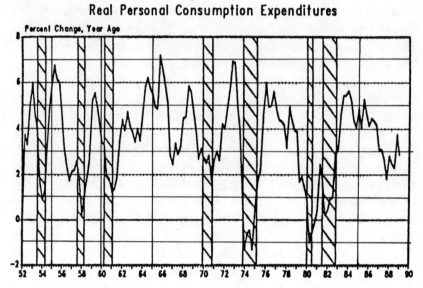

Percent Change, Year Ago

sales sag. Housing starts also tend to suffer during periods of rising interest rates and tight money. The debt services on these big-ticket items prohibit a large cross-section of households from being able to service these debts. Consumer curtailment of spending on these capital goods items has tended to have a pronounced effect on sales and consumption of a broad range of products and services.

Figure 4–14 illustrates the behavior of consumer sentiment during the business cycle. Optimism is high when the outlook for economic growth is encouraging, and vice versa. Notice on the graph that sentiment, a lagging indicator, hits its cyclical trough a little after the economic recovery has actually started. The sharp rebound in consumer sentiment characterizes the end of the business cycle and lags the trough in the stock market. The importance of this indicator is that it affects consumer spending. When people are optimistic about the future, they spend more and save less, which fuels economic expansion.

When a recession is about to begin, the job market becomes tight. Help-wanted advertising declines and the unemployment rate starts rising. In addition, consumer confidence deteriorates, which affects sales; also, the ability to service debt leads to increased cautiousness compared with periods of economic expansion. The slowdown in personal income also adds to a feeling of consumer vulnerability and prompts consumers to defer their buying plans to the future.

During phases of economic expansion, consumers tend to save less and consume more. The savings rate rises during economic slowdowns and continues to run high well after the new phase of expansion is on stream. In the 1980s, the savings rate plummeted to extreme levels, lower than during previous cycles of economic boom. This can be explained as being a residual effect, an aftermath, of the rampant inflation of the 1970s, which left behind a shaken faith in the value of savings. Having seen how savings could erode quickly because of runaway inflation, the attitude of the consumers shifted from saving to consuming. The decline in the savings rate may also be explained by demographics and the impact of the baby boomers on the economy. Youthful household finance patterns are characterized by high consumption, low savings, and a willingness to take above-average risks. With the stock market enjoying one of the greatest bull markets of all times and real estate appreciating at unprecedented levels, consumers tapped

Figure 4–14. The consumer confidence index.

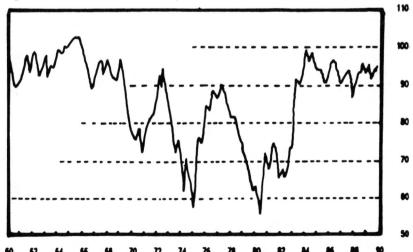

into their savings to finance ambitious consumption and investment plans. In general, the real slowdown in consumer spending accompanies the loss of income, and this happens when unemployment keeps rising.

The result of consumer spending, sentiment, savings rate, and the outlook for the job market affect sales of durable goods, housing, and automobile manufacturing. Interest rates rise when periods of tight money depress demand for production in these two vital sectors of the economy.

Capital Spending

At the corporate end, investment spending on nonresidential fixed activities lags the initial expansion phase of the economy and accelerates upward as the cycle matures. In the past, the peak of this indicator coincided with the peak of the business cycle, and bottomed after the next expansion phase was well on its way. The reason for this is that corporate planning to expand existing manufacturing capacity is prompted by rising consumer demand. Expenditures on machinery, information, and other industrial equipment soars as the economic cycle matures. The congestion in production facilities and backlog of orders prompt management to spend on new facilities to satisfy the expected rise in consumption. Inflation accelerates during this final stage of the cycle, which compels the Fed to tighten money—then rates rise, demand subsides, and inventory rises. Figure 4–15 illustrates capital spending on nonresidential fixed investments in billions of dollars. Although this economic aggregate continues to expand during every new business cycle, the fluctuations portray the expansion and contraction that characterize the different stages of business activities.

CONCLUSION

In the foregoing discussion, we introduced the most important characteristics of the business cycle. The Fed is in charge of managing the economy to balance the level of inflation and unemployment. The two economic aggregates are inversely correlated. When inflation rises, unemployment declines and vice versa. On rare occasion, a period known as "stagflation" resulted during which both inflation and unemployment advanced simultaneously.

Through its open market operations and controlling the level of interest rates in the economy, the Fed is able to slow down or stimulate economic activities. When analyzing economic trends, investors should study consumption, capital spending, and the impact of the monetary policy adopted by the Fed. Phases of economic expansion are followed by periods of tight money and a broad based slowdown in business activities. The stock market has always been able to discount future events and anticipate prosperity and recession. By forecasting the direction of the economy, the market was able to assess the impact of the outlook on corporate earnings, sales, and the general financial conditions of companies in the different industry groups.

By digesting the factors that influence the business cycle, investors could tame the market risk and minimize their portfolios' exposure to losses during downtrends. Applying the proper investment strategy to fit with economic forecasts could enhance final results.

Figure 4–15. Capital spending on nonresidential fixed investments.

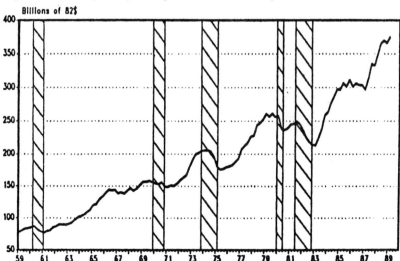

❑ 5

The Economic Indicators

If a speculation keeps you awake at night, sell down to the sleeping point.

Dickson G. Watts

Economic recoveries and recessions have a direct impact on corporate earnings, sales, profit margins, and the overall financial health of all companies. In order to gain perspective, past economic indicators should be monitored so that their behavior can be interpreted in light of their history near cyclical peaks and troughs. Such junctures have common characteristics, which indicate the exhaustion of the long-term business trend.

The economic indicators are vital barometers of forthcoming developments that can affect the well-being of companies in all industries. The fundamental forces governing earnings are influenced by the state of business. Without proper analysis, the process of forecasting the future of key financial ratios becomes an exercise in futility. Many bright industry analysts fail to consider the negative implications of a recession on corporate earnings. The alternative they often choose to follow is that of revising their projections downward, when it is too late for investors and portfolio managers to react. If they had made their estimates after conservative assessment of the business cycle, they could probably have anticipated the news instead of reporting it.

During business cycles, investments tend to lead production and employment. Early commitments, such as new housing permits and durable goods orders, lead industrial production and final sales. Capital spending decisions are based on anticipated future demand in light of existing industrial capacity. Some of these aggregates reflect increasing consumption before they actually translate into final sales. These aggregates can give early warnings of deteriorating economic conditions and lead the slowdown or recovery of the economy. Other indicators, especially those related to employment, may lag the business cycle and can only serve in formulating long-term policies. Because of the leading and lagging nature of the economic indicators, three indexes were constructed to incorporate those series that share similar cyclical characteristics. What are known today as the leading, coincident, and lagging indicators provide the Fed with vital timing elements with which to manage the economy and implement appropriate policies during the different stages of the business cycle. These indicators are discussed in full in the following pages.

THE LEADING INDICATORS

In order to monitor the economy, an index of eleven leading indicators was constructed. The 11 leading indicators are (1) the average weekly hours of production, (2) average weekly initial claims for state unemployment insurance, (3) manufacturers' new orders for consumer goods and materials, (4) vendor performance, (5) contracts and orders for factories and equipment, (6) new private housing permits, (7) the monthly change in manufacturing and trade inventories, (8) change in sensitive materials prices, (9) stock prices and the S&P 500, (10) money supply M2, and (11) the index of consumer expectations. Over the years, the trend of the index comprising these indicators has given reliable signals ahead of major cyclical peaks and troughs. The eleven leading indicators were chosen to indicate production activities, inflation, monetary policy, consumer sentiment, and orders for plants and equipment. The index incorporates the following economic indicators:

Average Weekly Hours of Production in Manufacturing

This monthly indicator is compiled by the DOL's Bureau of Labor Statistics. It is based on payroll reports from a large sample of companies and is published in the Department of Labor Statistic's "Employment and Earnings" report. This index represents the average hourly pay per week, and includes the number of hours worked as well as vacations, holidays, sick days, and all other paid leave.

During phases of economic expansion, this indicator rises, confirming the increase in industrial production. When the average number of hours worked decline it is usually forecasting a slowdown in manufacturing activity. The lead period at major economic peaks is longer than at cyclical troughs.

When this economic indicator loses its upside momentum, it may signal the onset of a recession. From a strategic standpoint, investors should then reduce their securities holdings, raise cash, and become more selective, for a defensive investment environment is likely to develop. At such junctures, the equities market is likely to be topping a process characterized by narrow advances by a few industry groups that have a compelling fundamental appeal. The majority of stocks, however, either decline or are unable to gather enough strength to score new highs. Although this indicator can give early warnings of market peaks, it should not be used alone in judging where the economy is going. Its forecasting value does not match other, more powerful, leading indicators. But it can be helpful in timing major trend reversals in the economy, or the proximity of the end of a primary economic expansion.

Figure 5–1 illustrates the average weekly hours of production compared with the S&P 500. Its predictive value is limited to the long-term potential of the market trend. When analyzed in conjunction with other aggregates, this series can indicate the exhaustion of upward momentum. This average's decline from peak points tends to be gradual, but its advance is usually sharp during cyclical recoveries. Seldom has a bear market started when this indicator was trending upward.

Average Weekly Initial Claims for State Unemployment Insurance

This indicator is compiled by the DOL's Employment and Training Administration and is published in the "Unemployment Insurance Claims" report. It indicates the number of

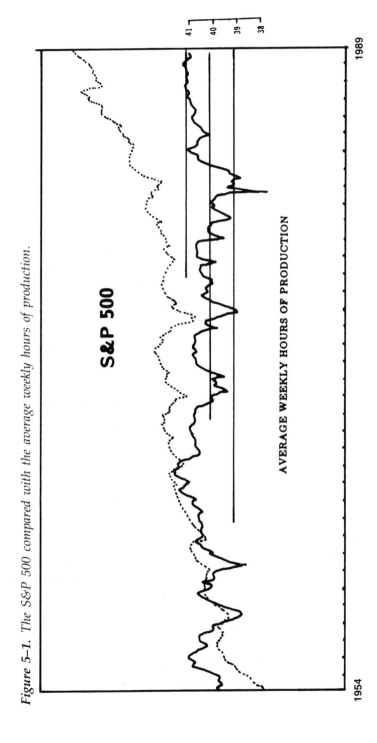

Figure 5–1. The S&P 500 compared with the average weekly hours of production.

127

claims made each week for unemployment insurance. This indicator is a good barometer of the employment outlook. At major turning points, this indicator tends to rise ahead of the economic slowdown. Its accuracy is not as good as other leading indicators, but it does give early signs of an impending slowdown or the beginning of a recovery.

Figure 5–2 illustrates the behavior of this indicator during the different stages of the business cycle. The scale used is inverted such that its decline indicates rising claims for unemployment insurance. Notice how this indicator kept scoring lows during cyclical downturns in the 1970s. The cause of this rise in claims was due to demographic factors. The baby boomers' entrance into the job market far exceeded the rate of job creation, which led to a tight employment market and an abundance of labor. In order to forecast the outlook for the job market, investors are better off monitoring this leading indicator rather than the monthly unemployment statistics, which are a lagging indicator.

Manufacturers' New Orders for Consumer Goods and Raw Materials Industries

This indicator is compiled by the Census Bureau from reports on sales and unfilled orders gathered from a large number of firms. This indicator measures new orders for consumer goods and materials. It includes all new orders during a given month, less cancellations of previous orders. The ordering of goods leads to their physical production. Any weakness in this indicator represents a softening of future demand. Figure 5–3 illustrates the manufacturers' new orders compared with the S&P 500. This indicator may not help time the exact peak of the business cycle or the stock market, because it tends to remain strong into the early stages of a recession. At cyclical troughs, too, new orders begin to rebound at the end of the recession after other indicators have already signaled the onset of a new phase of economic expansion. This indicator's true value is in its ability to confirm the other indicators at major turning points. In the past, a rebound in new orders at the end of a recession was triggered by rising consumer demand.

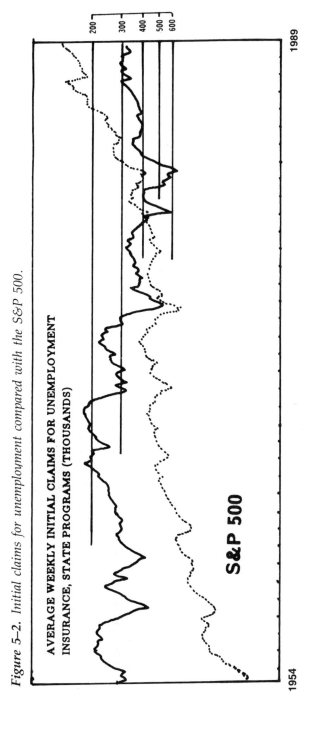

Figure 5–2. Initial claims for unemployment compared with the S&P 500.

129

Figure 5–3. Manufacturer's new orders compared with the S&P 500.

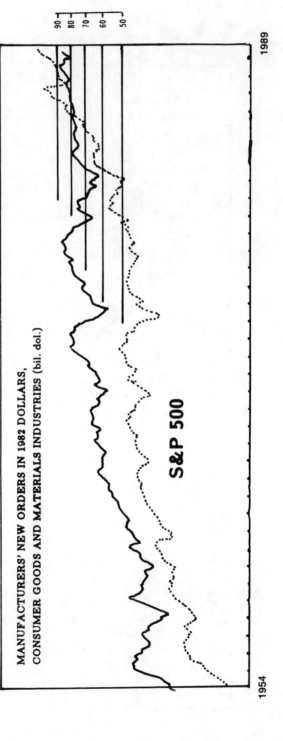

MANUFACTURERS' NEW ORDERS IN 1982 DOLLARS,
CONSUMER GOODS AND MATERIALS INDUSTRIES (bil. dol.)

S&P 500

1954

1989

90
80
70
60
50

Vendor Performance

The vendor performance indicator measures the percentage of companies receiving slower deliveries. It is a diffusion index, indicating the breadth of consumer demand and the pace of economic activities. The expansion phase of the economic cycle is usually accompanied by increasing business activities and an increase in orders and backlogs. This results in slower delivery of goods and orders by suppliers. Contrariwise, when the economy is contracting vendors are able to deliver orders more promptly as demand is sagging. Toward the end of the cycle, this indicator rises as orders are flowing in faster than vendors can deliver them. When this indicator starts declining, a sluggish business environment is to be expected.

Figure 5–4 illustrates the historic behavior of vendor performance during the economic cycle. The graph demonstrates that peak economic activity occurred when the slower deliveries diffusion index hovered around the 75-percent level. Troughs in the business cycle were reached when this indicator declined close to 25 percent. This diffusion index cannot be used to forecast the stock market trend. In 1973, the index continued to advance when the stock market was already in a major downtrend. During the 1984–86 period, the index failed to reflect the great upside momentum that swept the equities market.

Contracts and Orders for Plant and Equipment

This indicator measures the value of new contracts awarded to building, public works, utilities contractors, and new nondefense capital goods orders received by manufacturers. An increase in orders for factories and equipment reflects confidence in the future. A rising new-orders trend can have a positive impact on many other sectors of the economy.

Figure 5–5 illustrates the behavior of this economic aggregate during the stages of the business cycle. Such new contracts tend to accelerate upward as the expanding economy matures. In the past, this indicator continued to decline for a

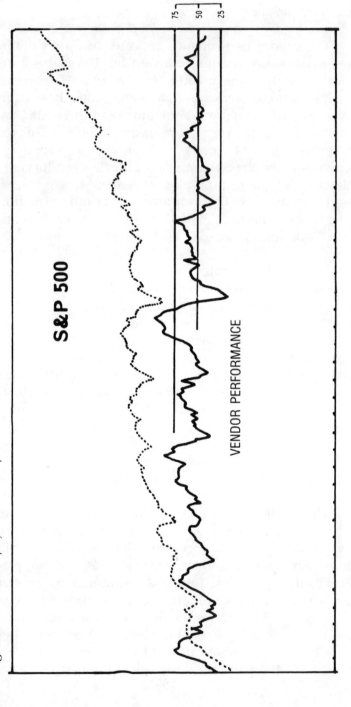

Figure 5–4. Vendor performance compared with the S&P 500.

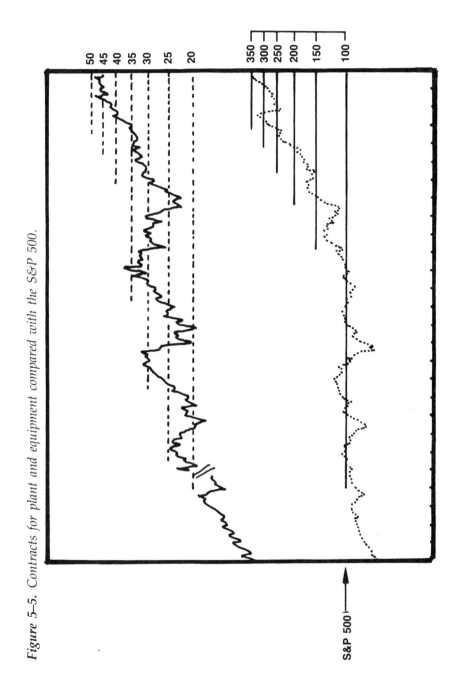

Figure 5–5. Contracts for plant and equipment compared with the S&P 500.

133

few months after the cyclical trough had been reached, as in the 1973–75 and 1982–83 periods. Contracts and orders for plant and equipment can be canceled as business conditions deteriorate. The decision for buying new plant and equipment is made by a corporation in order to expand its production capacity. This indicator may continue to rise during the early stages of a showdown. Its leading nature, however, comes from the fact that as consumption declines and inventories mount, corporations cancel out a portion of their planned investments in new plants and equipment. In addition, the new contracts indicator is early at sensing the end of an economic recession and the beginning of a new cycle of business recovery. This indicator has no value in predicting the trend in the equities or fixed-income markets. Its usefulness is limited to confirmation of the progression of business contraction or expansion.

New Private Housing Permits

The housing sector is vital to many sectors of the economy. Housing slowdowns lead to contraction in several industries, as sales of many industrial goods and services contract accordingly. Thus, building permits are an excellent leading indicator for both the housing market and the equities trend. The number of houses under construction is revealed by the permits authorized. Several months may elapse between the issuance of a permit and the actual completion of a house. A rise in building permits today should lead to increased expansion in the housing sector in the future. A decline in the number of newly authorized permits, however, signals a cautious mood and slackening housing demand. Such conditions usually precede softness in the housing market and in the whole economy.

A slowdown in the housing market leads to a broad-based economic contraction and a recession. This important leading indicator is by far the most accurate of them all in forecasting the onset of a business slowdown.

Figure 5–7 illustrates the historic behavior of new housing permits compared with the S&P 500. Of all the leading indica-

Figure 5–6. *New housing permits and the S&P 500.*

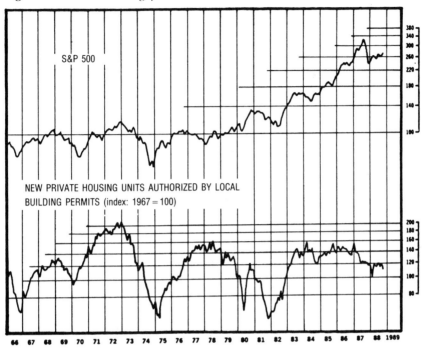

S&P 500

NEW PRIVATE HOUSING UNITS AUTHORIZED BY LOCAL
BUILDING PERMITS (index: 1967 = 100)

tors, the value of this economic aggregate cannot be matched. It leads the economy and the stock market at both peaks and troughs. It reversed its trend with the stock market top in 1972, and led the 1981–82 recession. Despite the phenomenal rise in both the stock market and housing prices in 1987, the housing permits displayed consistent deterioration. This flashed a warning signal well ahead of the Crash of 1987. Around cyclical troughs, this indicator rebounded in 1970 and late 1981 before the final bottom was reached in securities prices. A revival in this indicator bodes well for the stock market, and its weakness is a cautionary signal. This is one indicator that investors need to monitor closely, as it has an excellent forecasting record.

Monthly Changes in Manufacturing and Trade Inventories

This index measures the monthly change in manufacturing and trade inventories on hand and on order, adjusted for

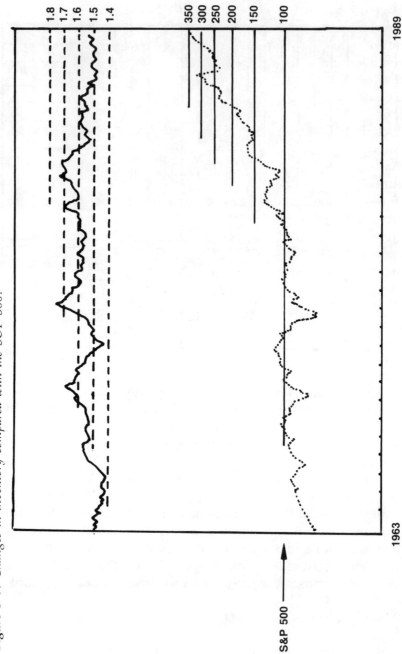

Figure 5–7. Changes in inventory compared with the S&P 500.

136

inflation. When the economy is expanding, manufacturers allow business inventories to rise, as they expect continuous future demand. When the economy shows early signs of sluggishness, inventory liquidation starts and further inventory control measures are strictly adhered to. Notice that inventory accumulation towards the latter stages of the business cycle results in increased storage costs and interest expense for producers. The process of inventory liquidation is often accompanied by reductions in work force. The rise in unemployment that follows adds to consumers' pessimism about the future outlook and often precipitates the economic decline. The 1974–75 recession, in particular, was characterized by a huge inventory accumulation. Since that time, with the help of computers, more control of inventories has been achieved. Business managers prefer to lower their ratios of inventory to sales to avoid the extra expenses and the subsequent painful liquidation process that follows.

Figure 5–7 illustrates the change in inventory levels during previous business cycles. This indicator offers little help in anticipating major stock market turning points. Its value is limited to confirming the exhaustion of business expansion and contraction phases.

Changes in Sensitive Materials Prices

Rising demand for goods and services in an expanding economy exercises upward pressure on commodity prices. A decline in business activity has the opposite impact on prices. Rising prices of sensitive materials often lead to a rise in interest rates. The Fed is constantly fine tuning its policies in order to control inflation while allowing business growth to stay on course. As inflation gains upward momentum, the FED adopts a tight monetary policy and allows interest rates to rise. Such a policy tends to cool off consumers' demand, as it raises the cost of borrowing for both producers and consumers. After inflation is brought under control, the Fed becomes more accommodative and allows interest rates to decline. Such a policy reignites consumption and prompts a new recovery cycle of the economy to start. Raw materials prices are sensitive to the inventory cycle. In a heating economy, inventory accumulation is usually accompanied by rising commodity prices as capacity utilization reaches its limits. Moreover, inventory liquidation takes place as demand for goods and services softens, which implies a general decline in inflation and commodity prices.

Stock Prices and the S&P 500

Stock prices lead the business cycle long before any strength or weakness appears in the economic aggregates. The equities markets are well known for their ability to digest and discount the impact of prevailing economic policies on earnings, sales, dividends, and profit margins. The stock market is by far the best of all the bellwether indicators of future economic conditions. It often slides into a downtrend at the onset of a slowdown in business and stages a strong advance in anticipation of the recovery that follows. While this ability of the stock market to lead the economy has become a controversial issue, it is fair to say that although it is not 100 percent accurate, its powers of prediction should never be underestimated.

Figure 5–9 illustrates the behavior of corporate earnings vis-à-vis the S&P 500. The trend of the equities market leads corporate profits near cyclical peaks and troughs. Notice that in terms of 1982 dollars, profits were unable to regain momentum during the economic recovery. Profits failed to surpass levels reached in the late 1970s. As the graph demonstrates, the great bull market of the 1980s can hardly be explained by corporate profit performance. Profits barely matched their peak scored in 1979.

Money Supply M2

Every week, the Fed publishes the money supply figures. An expanding money supply may suggest that the Fed is easing its monetary policy to stimulate business. When this starts to happen, in the wake of a recession, it can have a positive impact on stocks and bonds. As the economy continues to recover, a rising money supply can have a mixed influence on the performance of industry groups. It can also ad-

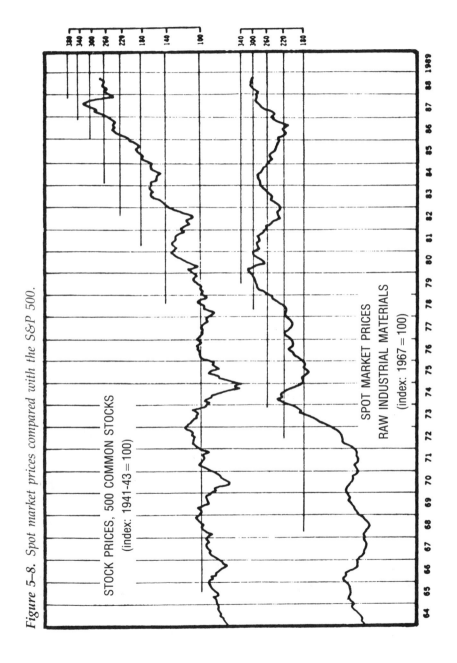

Figure 5–8. Spot market prices compared with the S&P 500.

STOCK PRICES, 500 COMMON STOCKS
(index: 1941-43 = 100)

SPOT MARKET PRICES
RAW INDUSTRIAL MATERIALS
(index: 1967 = 100)

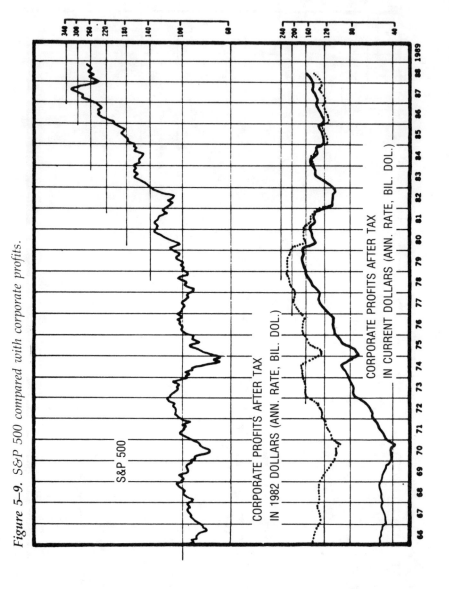

Figure 5–9. S&P 500 compared with corporate profits.

140

versely affect the fixed-income sector as inflation keeps rising
and interest rates have to be raised to fight it. In general, a
growing money supply bodes well for the future of the economy. A declining money supply, however, can signal a stringent economic policy in the making. A declining money supply
can also imply that the Fed is fighting inflation. In a broad
sense, this means that interest rates are rising to fight resurging
inflation. Late in a maturing business cycle, the initial decline
of the money supply is accompanied by weakness in the bond
market; but as the money supply continues to shrink, the bond
market strengthens and the stock market enters a bottoming
process.

Figure 5–10 illustrates the Money Supply M2 in billions of
dollars compared with the S&P 500 since 1962. This indicator
has little value in forecasting the equities market trend, since it
has coincided with and sometimes lagged the cyclical peaks
and troughs. When M2 is rising, in general, further gain in

Figure 5–10. *The money supply M2 compared with the S&P 500.*

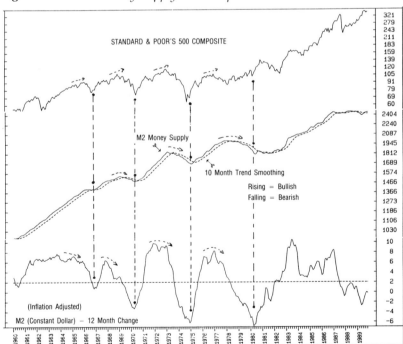

equity prices may be anticipated. The reverse is also true since declining money supply portrays a retrenchment in liquidity typical of a tight monetary policy. The 12-month rate of change of M2 has an excellent track record at predicting major turning points in the market. Since the early 1980s, however, the money supply indicators have had poor predictive value in timing the trend in the stock market.

Index of Consumer Expectations

Psychology is a key factor in determining the level of consumption in the economy. Confidence in the future leads to increased spending and consumption, but pessimism makes consumers more cautious and compels them to postpone their buying plans. Recognizing the impact of consumer psychology on business, the Fed carefully monitors this indicator. The Department of Commerce has added this indicator to the list of leading indicators in order to measure people's confidence in the business outlook. Figure 5–11 illustrates the behavior of consumer sentiment during past business cycles. In the 1960s, optimism prevailed. The inflationary 1970s severely affected consumer sentiment; there was little faith and conviction in the economic outlook. In the 1980s there was a renewed vote of confidence; inflation subsided and unemployment declined to multiyear lows.

A REVIEW OF THE LEADING INDICATORS

The study of the leading indicators can help control the market risk and enable anticipation of long-term business trends. The indicators may not be of much help in predicting the short- or intermediate-term market fluctuations, but they are effective at forecasting major cyclical turns. As Professor John Samuelson once said, the leading indicators did forecast nine of the past six recessions. The 11 leading indicators have peaked ahead of the economy by a comfortable margin, although at major cyclical lows, these indicators have turned ahead of the economy by only a relatively short interval (one to two quarters).

Figure 5–11. Index of consumers' expectations compared with the S&P 500.

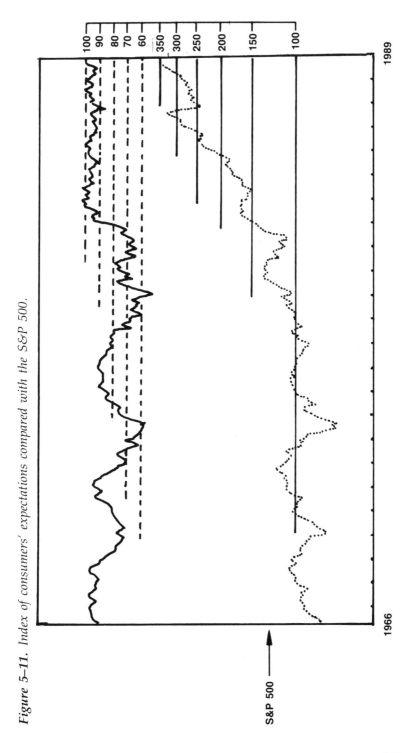

S&P 500 ──────▶

1966   1989

143

The most valuable among these indicators are the number of new private housing permits, money supply, stock prices, the change in sensitive raw materials prices, and the index of consumers' expectations. Housing permits tend to slow down ahead of all other indicators, including the stock market. They are particularly sensitive to interest rates trends and proved to be a good barometer of the Fed's policy. Money supply figures are the driving locomotive of the economy. When they expand, business booms, and when they contract the economy recedes. The stock market reflects the opinion of knowledgeable business professionals about the likely outlook of the economy. While it is influenced to a large extent by investors' psychology, it still tends to adjust to anticipated future events. Its track record is enviable indeed in foretelling the future course of business. As to the changing raw material prices, they reveal a great deal about the future outlook for inflation. Once a trend has been established, one can safely say that it is only a matter of time before the Fed adopts an economic policy to reverse it. If inflation is on the rise, the FED is likely to tighten. If it is declining and unemployment is rising, the FED would be expected to ease.

Figure 5–12 illustrates the relationship between the indexes of the eleven leading indicators and industrial production. The lead around major cyclical peaks and troughs can be clearly identified. The lead and lag time varied between 4 to 9 months from one cycle to another.

Consumers' expectations play an important role in stimulating demand for goods and services. Confidence in the economic outlook stimulates consumption. However, consumers' retrenchment leads to sluggish sales and accumulation of inventory. Accordingly, consumers' expenditures affect the final sales, capital spending, profitability, earnings, and growth potential of companies in most sectors.

The 11 leading indicators derive their forecasting value from the fact that they measure decisions that are made by business executives before the production process begins. The leading indicators measure the pace of industrial production, the rate of change of raw material prices, the level of corporate capital spending, and the consumers' confidence level. For

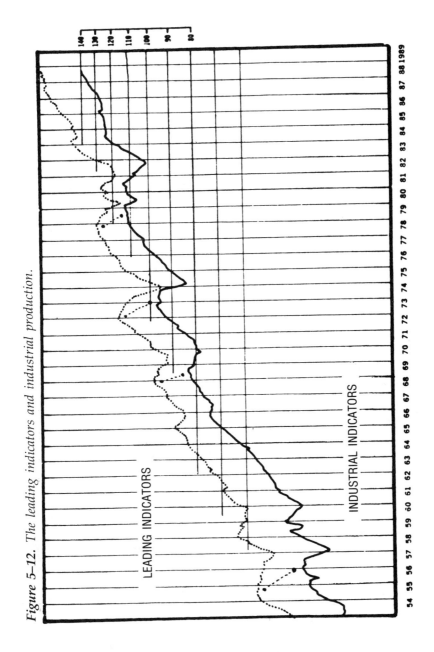

Figure 5–12. The leading indicators and industrial production.

LEADING INDICATORS

INDUSTRIAL INDICATORS

example, the number of new private housing permits applied for prefigures the amount of activity in the construction industry. When the number of applications for new permits recedes, it tends to reflect a softening demand that builders can detect in the marketplace. Similarly, the number of manufacturers' new orders for plants and equipment is tied indirectly to sales growth targets. Such decisions are usually made before the final production of goods. The average weekly hours of production, the initial claims for unemployment, vendor performance, and the index of consumer expectations all could give helpful signals ahead of any slowdowns in production or consumption of goods.

The leading indicators have an excellent record of anticipating expansion or warning of an impending slowdown. Most of the 11 leading indicators are sensitive to the Fed policy and the long-term trend of interest rates. When all is said, the state of the leading indicators is vital in analyzing the business cycle and forecasting major turning points in the economy. Once a projection of the future course of the economy has been postulated, the investment choices could then be selected in light of the potential risk.

THE COMPOSITE INDEX: THE FOUR COINCIDENT INDICATORS

The index of the four coincident indicators reflects the state of business at the time they are reported by the Department of Commerce.

The four coincident economic indicators are (1) employees on nonagricultural payrolls, (2) personal income less transfer payments, (3) state of industrial production, and (4) manufacturing and trade sales. Their importance derives from the fact that they confirm the recovery or the slowdown of economic activities as they are happening. They move directly with the business cycle and show what is happening in the real world. Economic peaks and troughs are determined at the point from which they reverse their long-term direction. When the coincident indicators start rising, they usually continue uninterrupted on their course. They carry within their initial move from major cyclical lows a decisive upward momentum that represents the expansion in all sectors of the economy. The coincident indicators are closely monitored by the Fed in order to get a sense of where the economy is heading. They help the Fed adjust its monetary policy to control inflation and the economy at large. But, as far as the stock market is concerned, the forecasting value of the coincident indicators is of little value, since their fluctuations coincide with the business cycle, while the stock market leads it. The coincident indicators can best be used to study the peculiarities of the business cycle and to verify the predictability of the economic indicators. The coincident indicators can also be used to identify secular growth periods that last for many years. These indicators are fully described below.

Employees on Nonagricultural Payrolls

The total number of persons employed in the non-agricultural sector is monitored as a coincident indicator. When the economy is expanding, this indicator tends to rise, and vice versa. From among all the leading, lagging, and coincident indicators, the number of employees on nonagricultural pay-rolls provides the least help in forecasting either future economic conditions or the direction of stock market prices. However, this index can provide some valuable information about changes in demographic trends which, in turn, can be used to verify the extent to which an economic recovery has been able to create new jobs.

Personal Income Less Transfer Payments

Increases or decreases in personal income are directly dependent upon the employment environment. Personal income measures the amount of compensation received by households and the rise or decline in the wages earned at any given time. Personal income is a useful measure in confirming the trend in consumer demand. Moreover, when analyzed in light of the savings rate per household as well as consumers' expectations,

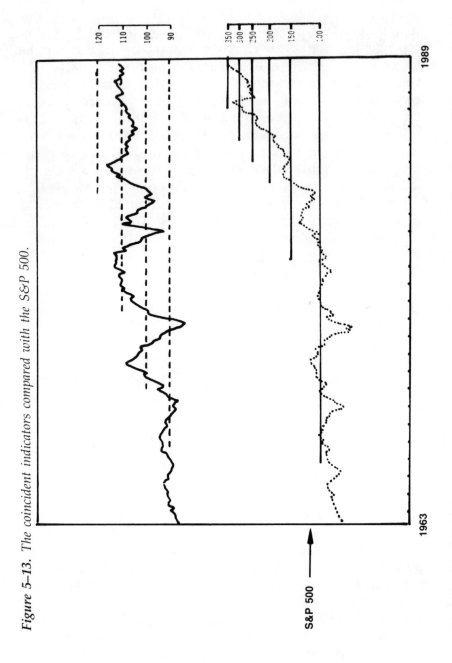

Figure 5-13. The coincident indicators compared with the S&P 500.

148

it helps estimate the cushion in case of a severe economic decline. Incomes tend to rise in sync with the economy but flatten out as a business slowdown is about to ensue. As personal income rises, it implies that households could have more disposable income to spend on their consumption needs. Moreover, an increase in personal income enables consumers to pay their debt and reliquify their balance sheet. During phases of economic contraction when consumer expectations are low, any gain in personal income is channeled toward increasing savings and reducing debt. Since the consumption expenditures per household play an important role in triggering the slowdown or expansion of the economy, the personal income indicator is an important component in analyzing the future course of business and the potential vulnerability of the economy to any retrenchment.

Rate of Industrial Production

The industrial production index is published monthly by the Fed. This index measures the output of the nation. As long as it is rising, one can assume that the upward trend is still intact. When production stops advancing, it signals the onset of a sluggish business environment. Its decline marks the peak in economic activities for the business cycle. Normally during phases of contraction, industrial production declines in response to interest rate rises and the general lack of consumer demand. This indicator is very useful in relation to the behavior of all the economic indicators.

Manufacturing and Trade Sales

The manufacturing and trade sales index measures the dollar amount of manufacturing and wholesale and trade businesses. This volume moves up in an expanding economy and down when business contracts. As with most other economic indicators, the trend of this indicator mirrors the real condition of the economy. A bear market has never started when the coincident indicators were rising and interest rates declining. Typically, when a new recovery in business activity begins, the

Figure 5–14. Industrial production compared with the S&P 500.

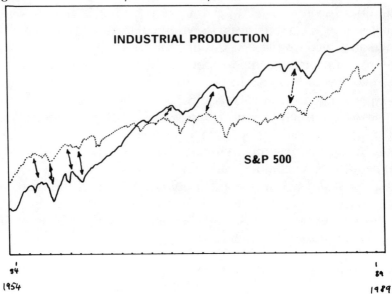

Fed is easing and interest rates should be declining. When this condition prevails and the coincident indicators advance, the stock market is likely to anticipate a broad based rebound in economic activities and stage a primary uptrend. And vice versa, when interest rates are rising and the Fed is tightening, the economy is likely to slow down. The stock market is mostly vulnerable when interest rates are advancing and the coincident indicators declining.

THE LAGGING INDICATORS

The Department of Commerce also reports on an index of lagging indicators (for a comparison of the lagging indicators and the S&P 500 see Figure 5–15) that represents 7 different types of economic series. These indicators usually continue to decline after the trough of the business cycle is reached and the next business recovery has begun. They have no value in predicting stock prices or other economic statistics. The best use of the lagging indicators is to spot emerging trends of a structural nature. When the lagging indicators start to rise, they confirm that the recovery has been in progress and is now well on target. Once this happens, it is normal to expect the rebound to proceed on course for a while before the next contraction phase begins. The composite index of the seven lagging indicators consists of: (1) The average duration of unemployment, (2) The ratio of manufacturing and trade inventories to sales, (3) The change in the index of labor cost per unit of output, (4) The average prime rate charged by banks, (5) Commercial and industrial loans outstanding, (6) The ratio of consumer installment credit outstanding, and (7) The change in the consumer price index for services. These lagging indicators are examined here.

Average Duration of Unemployment

This indicator measures the average number of weeks that an unemployed person has been out of work. It is an indicator of long-term unemployment, or structural unemployment. When this indicator reaches new highs relative to previous cycles, it may reflect on the inability of the economy to create enough new jobs to accommodate the influx of new entrants to the labor market. When this index reaches abnormally low levels, it may signal shortages in the labor market. During the 1970s, this indicator reached extreme highs when it reflected the invasion of the baby boomers into the job market as well as the large number of new female employees. In the 1980s, the proliferation of the service sector has allowed the economy to create new jobs to accommodate that influx. Moreover, as the economy recovered from the 1982 recession, the decline of this indicator has signaled the shortage of labor that is expected to result from the baby bust—the low birth rate of the 1960s.

Ratio of Manufacturing and Trade Inventories to Sales

This ratio represents the state of consumption and sales of manufactured goods during the business cycle. When the economy expands, this ratio rises. The reverse is true when shortages in the face of rising demand materialize because manufacturers have not yet planned sufficient production to

Figure 5–15. The index of lagging indicators compared to the S&P 500.

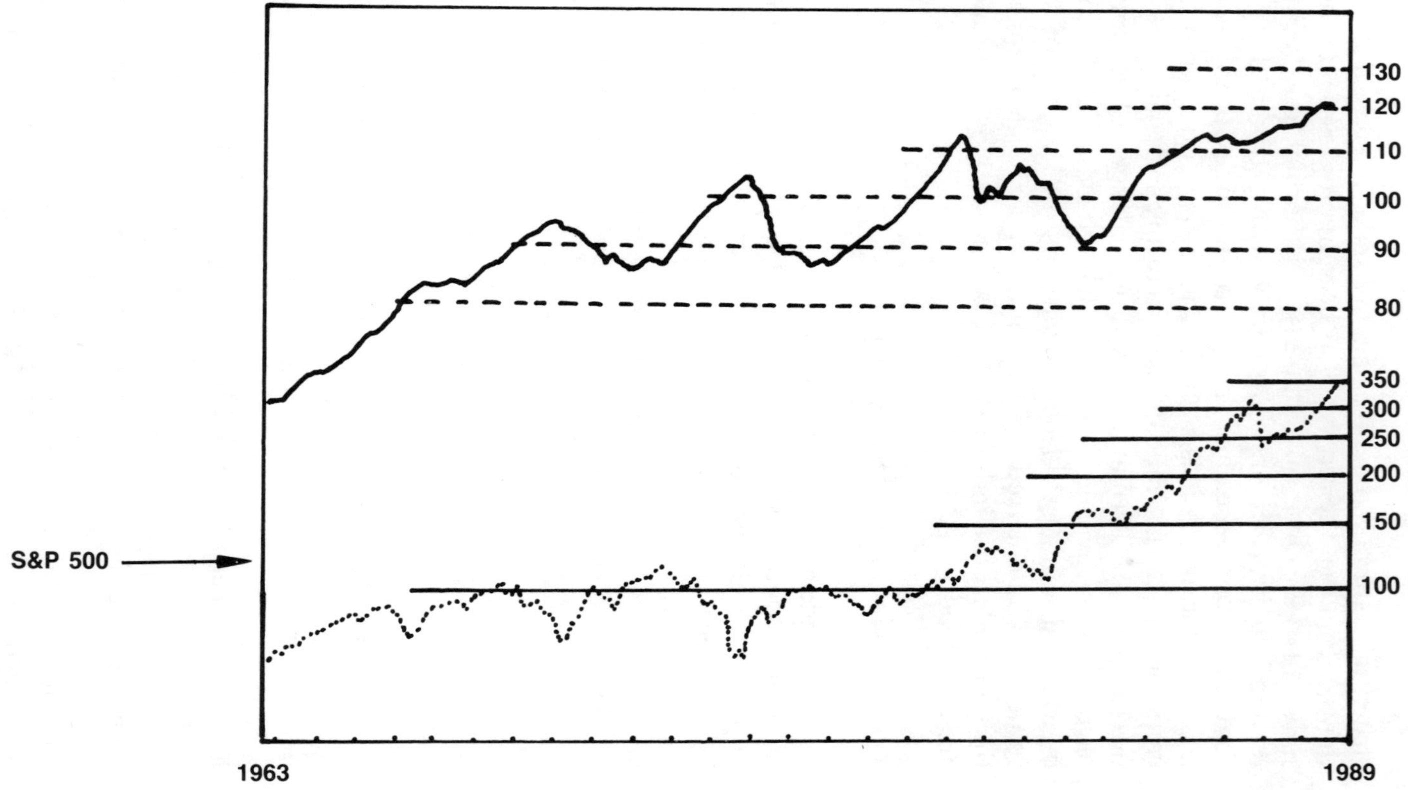

152

match rising sales levels. Sometimes this indicator is used to detect imbalances that often set in during business cycles that have been characterized by excessive optimism.

Change in Index of Labor Costs per Unit of Output

Labor costs increase as the economy expands and decrease as the economy contracts. Such costs lag peaks and troughs as they only move up after pressure due to shortages or excesses has been allowed to build in the job market. Moreover, the change in labor costs can be an indication of productivity levels and inflationary pressures. When labor costs increase fast, inflation is rising and productivity is declining, and vice versa. The change in labor costs also influences profit margins. In labor-intensive industries, a big rise in labor costs tends to exercise downward pressure on profitability and margins.

Average Prime Rate Charged by Banks

The prime rate is the short-term interest on loans that banks charge their best customers. Although it is a lagging indicator, it may have a psychological impact on borrowing and credit. In addition, because most investors closely monitor the prime rate, their expectations about the outlook of the economy may be influenced by its rise or decline. This index, in the past, tended to affect stock prices and the overall consumption level in the economy.

Commercial and Industrial Loans Outstanding

Corporate borrowing is an important indicator of leverage on the balance sheet. Although it is a lagging indicator, its significance is of long-term effect on the financial health of companies. When analyzed in light of the ratio of long-term debt to total capital it may be of better use to judge the extent of exposure to creditors. Moreover, when combined with other debt-related measures, such as debt service as a percentage of total cash flow, it may show the real financial vulnerability of the corporation to future business downturns.

Consumer Installment Credit Outstanding to Personal Income

As the business cycle matures, income declines faster than debt. When the economy falls into a recession, this indicator tends to initially rise due to declining income. As consumers slow their demand for credit in the face of an uncertain economic outlook, this indicator begins to falter. When the debt to personal income ratio is high and the savings rate is low, it can mean an above-average decline in consumption lies ahead. It usually suggests a sluggish retail figure for the time necessary to bring savings to higher levels and credits to lower ones.

Change in Consumer Price Index for Services

When there is a broad-based increase in prices at the raw material end, it tends to filter out to consumers, slowly lagging the economy. The price increase in services continues well after the slowdown is on its way. Prices typically continue to rise into the recession and decline when consumption begins to subside and inventory is rising. The decline in the service prices may reflect the sales campaigns that retailers resort to in their effort to liquidate inventories and the cut in service prices of other institutions in their effort to boost sales volume.

MEANING OF THE ECONOMIC INDICATORS

The leading, coincident and lagging indicators (See Figure 5–16) are important economic aggregates that should be carefully monitored. As they fluctuate during the business cycle, they could alert investors to potential future economic trends. A thorough analysis of the economic indicators could help anticipate major trend reversals. It could also confirm an expansion or a contraction phase in progress. The stock market reacts to economic development. The market risk, which cannot be diversified, is born out of those long-term swings in the economy, which in turn affect earnings and sales growth.

Hence, when the economic indicators are pinpointing to a period of business recovery ahead, the stock market is likely to

Figure 5–16. The leading, coincident, and lagging indicators.

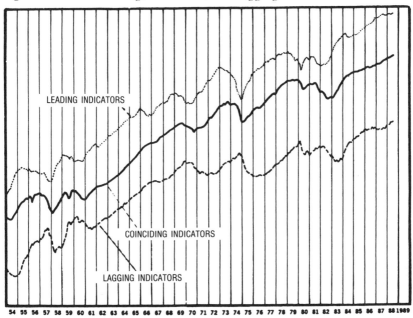

be favorable. When the indicators begin to display weakness, the securities portion of the portfolio should be reduced as the stock market would have to become more vulnerable to negative surprises. The leading, coincident, and lagging indicators are only helpful for the long-term buy-and-hold investors. Their behavior is repetitive in nature and historical comparison to their prior juncture could be enlightening. But because of their long-term forecasting nature, they offer no help in sector analysis, asset allocation, or stock selection. All the economic indicators could offer is an alert signal to the potential future course of the economy.

The economic indicators could be a way to deal with the systematic risk. By digesting their behavior at the different stages of the business cycle, investors may be able to better anticipate future economic trends. This, in turn, may help control the market risk and structure a portfolio according to forecast. The market risk may not be completely eliminated, yet it may be reduced or tamed by proper economic analysis of the indicators. The leading indicators, in particular, offer the greatest help in anticipating major turning points in the economy. The coincident and lagging indicators serve a confirming function of the possible emerging trends and could also alert investors to secular movements in the aggregates.

CALENDAR OF BUSINESS INDICATORS

The following is the approximate timing of the announcement of economic statistics. This schedule may change from month to month. Assuming that a month has five weeks, the following order of announcement of statistics is to be expected:

First week:
- ☐ Purchasing Managers Index
- ☐ Construction Spending
- ☐ Factory Orders
- ☐ Domestic New Car Sales
- ☐ Chain Stores Sales
- ☐ Civilian Unemployment Rate
- ☐ Payroll Employment
- ☐ Average Hourly Earnings

Second week:
- ☐ Consumer Installment Credit
- ☐ Wholesale Inventory
- ☐ Housing Completions
- ☐ 10-Day Car Sales
- ☐ Producer Price Index
- ☐ Retail Sales
- ☐ Industrial Production Index
- ☐ Capacity Utilization

Third week:
- ☐ Business Inventory
- ☐ Merchandise Trade
- ☐ Consumer Price Index
- ☐ Housing Starts

Fourth week:
- ☐ U.S. Treasury Balance
- ☐ Durable Goods Orders
- ☐ Employment Cost Index
- ☐ 10-Day Car Sales
- ☐ GNP

           ☐ Import Price Index
           ☐ Personal Income
           ☐ Personal Consumption Expenditures

Fifth week: ☐ Agricultural Prices

SUMMARY

The Commerce Department publishes a wealth of economic statistics that could be used to interpret the prevailing business condition and forecast the likely future direction of the economy. The cyclical nature of the aggregates adds an important measure of predictability to their probable progression. They tend to display common characteristics around major economic peaks and troughs.

The foregoing discussion of the leading, lagging, and coincident indicators explains a great deal of the behavior of the economy at the different stages of the business cycle. A careful study of their historic behavior could help anticipate the risks and rewards that have to be considered in the investment process.

The trend of interest rates influences the activity of all the economic aggregates and the stock market. Furthermore, the behavior of security prices is correlated to the business cycle and the economic indicators. An assessment of where the aggregates stand is a first step towards realizing the stage the business cycle is at and hence implementing the necessary strategy to the investment portfolio structuring process.

PART 3

Fundamental Analysis

❑6

The Fundamental Catalyst

*Each kind of person needs a different kind of stock:
Risk situations for the bachelor with more than
enough to live on; growth situations for the young
family building an estate; chance-taking
commitments for the older couple whose children
have left the nest; and safety for the person whose
earnings days are over.*

Burton Crane

The fundamental school of securities analysis is by far the most widely used by the majority of Wall Street professionals. Fundamental analysis strives at determining the intrinsic value of a company and evaluating its future earnings power and growth potential. These constitute the company's firm foundation. The fundamental approach goes a step further—it suggests that if a stock is selling at a price deemed undervalued based on its intrinsic worth, the stock should be bought. Furthermore, this stock should be held until full valuation is achieved. That is why fundamental analysis is best suited for passive portfolio management and serves long-term investment objectives well. Fundamentalism lacks the timing aspects that economic and market-timing analyses add to the investment process. Instead, fundamentalism concerns itself with the *what* to buy question without weighing the opportunity cost of having to wait for the market price to adjust fully to its true value.

Theoretically, the objective of the fundamental approach is to determine the trend of the underlying value of a security, around which the price may fluctuate. The challenge comes in when the business cycle fluctuations are added to the equation. Moreover, the fundamental method ignores the psychological factors that influence investment decisions. It is well known that the value of any investment is a function of the perceived worth that investors attach to it. At times, a reasonably valued stock may rise if investors perceive it to be relatively cheap. Moreover, a stock may sell far below its fundamental value for an extended period of time without appreciable advance. After all, who can tell the market what a stock should sell at?

Fundamental analysis is at the heart of the theory of rational expectations but hardly offers any strategies with which to cope with periods dominated by crowd behavior. At times of great emotional despair or of unbounded optimism, securities prices can melt down to bargain levels or be driven to euphoric heights. Panics can bring the price of the mightiest of stocks to a fraction of what their underlying fundamentals may suggest. After a bull market has been in progress for a while, great expectations may push a stock price to levels that are above its true value. These times of excesses usually happen at the culmination of a bull or a bear market, when greed and fear replace reason. The fundamental school leaves a lot to be desired during such critical junctures—it fails to deal with zealous expectations.

HISTORICAL DEVELOPMENTS

Benjamin Graham, the father of the modern school of fundamental analysis, was born in England in 1894. In 1934, with David Dodd, he wrote *Security Analysis*, the book that became the bible for proponents of this philosophy. His approach to investment analysis advocated the value-based selection of securities that meet solid earnings and growth criteria. He believed that the intrinsic value of a corporation is sooner or later going to be recognized by the market. His method of market analysis gained popularity after the Crash of 1929, as the investment community searched for super-conservative strategies following the sour experience of the Great Depression.

Prior to the landmark work of Graham and Dodd, the firm foundation concepts as known today were in search of an identity. Near the turn of the century, the book value or asset valuation was the most critical factor in formulating investment decisions. Balance sheets were carefully assessed to estimate the intrinsic worth of a company. After World War I, the theory was abandoned in the wake of the runaway inflation that followed. The viability of the book-value theory could no longer be accepted. Back then, investment banking activities were technically absent, and mergers and acquisitions were barely known. The inflation era challenged the tenets of this theory, because investors were unable to estimate what the real value of the underlying assets was.

The Price/Earnings Ratio

In the mid-1920s, Benjamin Graham emphasized the importance of the present and future earnings power of the firm. Since those days, the financial community has adopted this method as the main determinant of a company's fundamental soundness. Proponents of this philosophy rely heavily on forecasting future potential profits and earnings per share. The market price of a security is then divided by the earnings per share. The outcome became known as the Price/Earning (P/E) ratio. Comparison of P/E values of the overall market relative to its historical perspectives is then performed. A low P/E ratio implies that the market is deemed cheap and aggressive accumulation is warranted.

A company's P/E ratio is also compared to the market's as well as to its own industry group's to verify investment appeal. Graham formulated what he called "the central value" of a stock by capitalizing the average annual earnings by a factor equal to twice the interest paid on the highest grade corporate bonds. Several modifications followed to allow for cyclical expansion and contraction.

Time and again, all these theories, though conservative, have not factored in investors' perceptions of value. Subjective opinion of what a stock should sell at is, at times, completely different from today's sophisticated accounting estimates. It is because of this psychological perception of value that investors are willing to pay different P/E multiples for different stocks. Growth companies, for example, hold promise of accelerating profits and, hence, command a higher ratio than those in a maturing industry.

FUNDAMENTALS: THE TREND CATALYST

Fundamental analysis is an effective way to study a firm's financial position. Although it lacks the timing element, it stands at the core of the trend analysis theory. Understanding the financial underpinnings of a company helps investors evaluate the comparative worth of a stock. Fundamental analysis is considered the most important catalyst propelling prices on since Wall Street, since fundamentals determine the long-term trend of stocks.

Demand for a security is triggered by investors' perceptions that it is selling far below its intrinsic value. When expectations of robust future earnings prevail, genuine buying interest pushes the price upward. However, if the company's fundamentals deteriorate, investors sell the security to protect themselves from staggering losses. In such cases, the oversupply of the stock depresses its price and propels a downtrend.

FINANCIAL STATEMENTS ANALYSIS

Thorough fundamental analysis begins with a review of the financial statements released by the corporation to its shareholders. The most important sources of information about a company are the balance sheet and the income statement.

The following pages present a comprehensive review of the tenets of fundamental analysis. It is not meant to be the most detailed study of financial reports and does not delve into the sophisticated interpretation of fundamental data. Certified public accountants are in a better position to assess the overall financial position of a firm. What is wanted is to pave the way for the final integration of the fundamental catalyst with the economic and market-timing techniques into a multidisciplinary approach that can enable better investment decisions.

THE BALANCE SHEET

The balance sheet is a summary of the firm's financial position at a given time. It is like a snapshot of the company's fundamentals on a specified date. The market is constantly changing and so are the company's sales figures, inventory levels, cash components, and the like. The balance sheet consists of two sides: the assets side and liabilities and the stockholders' equity side. The assets side of the balance sheet is a representation of the liquid and illiquid assets of the corporation. Cash, cash equivalent, raw materials, work in process, finished inventory, land, property, equipment, and any prepayment of future obligations are among the tangible assets of a firm. The liability and stockholders' equity side of the ledger are the sum of all short and long-term liabilities and shareholders' equity in the corporation. The two sides of the balance sheet should be equal. The difference between the total assets and total liabilities represents the shareholders' equity or stake in the company after all obligations are paid off.

ASSETS

In evaluating the asset side of the balance sheet, the proportions of these categories relative to each other and relative to the total assets should always be looked at. Asset growth is an important factor to consider, providing that there is not a substantial and disproportionate increase in inventories or receivables. The cash level is more significant during periods of economic slowdown because it provides the company with alternative low-cost financing and enables the company to exploit market opportunities by using internal financing.

Current Assets

There are several types of current assets. Among them are cash and marketable securities, accounts receivable, inventories, and prepaid expenses. The following is an examination of their characteristics.

Cash and marketable securities: This balance sheet item is a good indicator of liquidity. The cash on hand and temporary investments of excess cash in highly liquid short-term government securities are of special importance. They can be used to exploit market opportunities as they arise.

Liquidity also helps a company meet any short-term obligations and gives management freedom of action. When cash and its equivalent are low, it can mean that the company may have difficulty paying current debts. This can lead to forced liquidation of assets, even long-term investments. Too much cash, however, can indicate the inability of management to plan, diversify, and expand its portfolio of businesses into other growth horizons. High cash levels can also make a company a target for a takeover attempt.

Accounts receivable: This category represents the amount of money that has not yet been collected from customers for delivered goods. Too much in receivables may indicate the inability of the company to collect what is owed to it. Customers are usually given the option to pay for the merchandise within 30, 60 or 90 days. Some customers fail to pay what they owe. When this occurs, the firm writes off those receivables as bad debt that it cannot collect. When the amount of uncollected receivables runs high, the firm runs the risk of losing great sums of capital which may eventually lead to total bankruptcy.

Inventories: These may be raw materials that will be used in the production process, finished or semi-finished products that are in the manufacturing stage, or finished goods that have not yet been sold but are ready to be shipped to customers. During slowdowns, inventories accumulate as sales sag. This prompts management to slow down on the production schedule and cut its work force until inventories are liquidated. Too much inventory means that too many production resources are left idle. Inventory accumulation can lead to significant losses, especially in high-tech industries. The declining demand during a recession makes it hard for those companies to recover their research and development expenses. By the time the economy is expanding, obsolescence may have done away with the usefulness of the product. The inability of a company to estimate the demand for its products during recessions can lead to severe financial deterioration. Moreover, during phases of economic contraction, a company stands to lose market share. The level of inventory determines the extent of the financial damage the firm may suffer.

Prepaid expenses: These are payments made on some of the company's obligations before they are due, such as rent, insurance premiums, advertising costs, and so forth. The smaller this figure on the balance sheet, the more cash on hand there will be, which brings back the issue of liquidity.

Total current assets: These are the sum of all the above items. They are what generate revenues, sales, and profits, which will be used to determine the value of the stock in the open market. Remember that inventories, when sold, become receivables, and receivables, when collected, become cash—and the production cycle continues.

Fixed assets: The fixed assets are the capital investments that the firm acquires to run the business. They include property, plants and equipment, land, trucks, automobiles, furniture and any other asset needed in the production and selling process. These assets are carried at cost, and accounting methods fail to represent their real market value. Note that this balance sheet category is of great importance in measuring the book value of the company. During the 1980s, many companies had assigned to their real estate holding a value far blow the market value. This triggered the big wave of takeovers and leveraged buyouts. The asset strippers bought the company and then sold its real estate holdings, which often allowed their buyers to recover the price they paid, in the open market. Afterwards the acquirer was left with a going concern at next to nothing in cost and had the chance of keeping the business or putting it back on the market as a new issue. Given the great boom in the housing market in the 1980s, corporate real estate was reported at far lower value than its real market price.

Accumulated depreciation and depletion: The net fixed asset is calculated by deducting the amount of accumulated depreciation from the original cost of the property, plant, and equipment. The term "depletion" is usually used for oil companies and mining stocks, because their precious unused reserves deplete rather than depreciate.

Good will: This is the value assigned to the name of the corporation, its reputation, its type of industry, the patents it holds, and many other factors.

Total assets: Total assets are the sum of the above-mentioned factors. When the total assets are divided by the number of employees, the assets per employee ratio figure is obtained. This number can be compared on a year-to-year basis to verify the growth of assets per number of employees. A more comprehensive analysis of fundamental trends will be possible once financial ratios are explained.

LIABILITIES

The liabilities side of the balance sheet represents all that the company owes to creditors, plus the shareholders' equity. As much as the asset categories provide enlightenment about business performance, the liabilities side is the real barometer of the firm's credit position and its shareholders' wealth. A discussion of current and long-term liabilities follows.

Current liabilities

Current liabilities are the debts owed to the company's creditors within a year. Although current assets represent the sources of funds to run the business and meet short-term debt, the current liabilities reveal its exposure.

Accounts payable and notes payable: This is the amount the company owes to its suppliers of raw materials as well as to goods and services vendors. The amount owed to banks is included under notes payable.

Accrued expenses payable: These are the cost of salaries and compensation to employees, legal expenses, insurance premiums, pension allocation, rent, heat, advertising expenses, and the like. The amount outstanding to these different parties at the date of issuance of the balance sheet is included under accrued expenses payable.

Federal income taxes: These are the taxes that the company owes to the Internal Revenue Service and are treated the same as any other accrued liability.

Total current liabilities: This is the sum total of all the expenses and obligations due within a year. The usefulness of this category will become apparent when addressing the working capital and financial ratios that measure liquidity.

Long-term Liabilities

Any liability that is not due within one year is included under this section. Excessive long-term debt to total capital can have a devastating impact on the financial health of the firm. The debt service charges constitute a drain on the company's resources. During a business downturn, cash flow may not be sufficient to cover such charges. Leverage in the science of finance is a double-edged sword. On the positive side, it can help boost earnings during periods of economic expansion. But when it exceeds the industry norms or it constitutes a larger percentage of the cash flow from operations, it can have a crippling effect.

Long-term debt: Long-term debt includes deferred income taxes and debentures.

Deferred income taxes: These result from writeoffs of accelerated depreciation. These deductions are taken in the early years of the acquisition of plant equipment and would otherwise have been paid as taxes. Taxes on these properties are deferred to a future date. Companies allocate an amount equivalent to the deferred taxes in their income statement as a long-term liability on their balance sheet.

Debentures: These are promissory notes or bonds that the company issues to investors to raise capital to finance long-term plans.

Total Liabilities: This is the sum total of all the above-mentioned debt categories.

Stockholders' equity

This section of the balance sheet tells a potential investor the real value of his or her equity interest or the true worth of the share he or she is holding. It is divided into three categories: capital stock, capital surplus, and accumulated retained earnings.

Capital stock. This is the true representation of the shareholders' collective interest after paying all moneys owed to the firm's creditors. It can further be subdivided into preferred stock and common stock. Preferred stockholders have some preference over common shareholders as they may be paid dividends and are paid ahead of other owners of the common stock in case of total liquidation. Holders of common stock may or may not receive dividends. Small and fast-growing companies reinvest their net earnings in promising new areas related to their core business or other market opportunities. Holders of common stock are the last to be paid when there is a total liquidation and, hence, they assume the full risk of investing in the fortunes of that corporation.

Capital surplus: This is the amount paid in excess of the common stock legal or par value.

Retained earnings: This item of the balance sheet has a historic meaning more than anything else. It represents the amount of surplus funds earned after paying out the declared dividends that are plowed back into the business to generate internal financing for future growth.

Total liabilities and stockholders' equity: This is the sum total of current and long-term liabilities and stockholders' equity.

THE INCOME STATEMENT

Whereas the balance sheet reports on the firm's financial position on a given date, the income statement gives the necessary details of operations during a certain period. It reports on details of business activity during a defined span of time. It shows what happened in the interval between two dates. Given the differences between the two financial statements, the balance sheet is static whereas the income statement is dynamic. The income statement gives the details of business activities. It matches the sales of goods to the costs and expenses incurred. The following list comprises the many elements included on income statements.

Net sales: The net sales figures represent the firm's net revenues from selling goods and services, taking into consideration returned goods, and allowing for discounts and rebates on prices. While many financial relations describe a company's financial position, sales numbers are the backbone of profitability. Over a number of years, net sales must increase in order for the company's sources of income to grow.

Cost of sales and operating expenses: The cost of goods sold consists of all the costs incurred to convert raw materials into finished products. This includes salaries, bonuses for employees, the cost of purchasing raw materials, rent, heat, electricity, supplies, maintenance, and the like.

Depreciation and amortization: Depreciation, amortization, or depletion of resources is accounted for in this category of the income statement, depending upon the nature of the business. A portion of the value of the companies fixed assets is deducted as part of the expenses.

General selling and administrative expenses: These are the expenses associated with selling the product. They include salesmen's salaries, commissions, advertising, promotion, travel, entertainment, executive compensation, and administrative and office expenses related to sales activities.

Operating income: Operating profits represent the net revenues after deducting all operating costs from net sales. This becomes the new source of cash and liquidity that the firm uses to pay its debts, dividends to stockholders, and interest on long-term obligations.

Dividends and interest: Aside from sales, the company derives income from dividends and interest received on its own investment in stocks and bonds.

Interest expense: The interest paid on the company's obligations is stated under this category. Interest paid to bondholders on debentures, dividends paid to preferred and common stockholders, and so forth are considered as part of the expenses. They are deducted from profits to determine the portion of revenue that is subject to income taxes.

Federal income tax: All corporations pay taxes on their profits after allowing for depreciation, writeoffs, and capital gains items.

Net profit: The net profits figure is arrived at by deducting from net sales all costs incurred in the production and sales of the products as well as taxes, interest expenses, and depreciation.

FINANCIAL RATIOS

Investors do not have to go and visit a company to know how well it is doing. They do not have to see its products to determine how successful is its management team at tapping sources of growth, seizing new opportunities in the market place, or maximizing shareholders' profits. Financial ratios can help investors analyze a company's financial position and its future potential. Bankers may be primarily interested in the firm's near term liquidity. Long-term creditors, as well as investors, may place more emphasis on earnings power and on operating efficiency. Management should be concerned about operations, credit, growth, and the overall financial health of the corporation. Financial ratios provide a great deal of information about the company, its finances, and its overall performance. While they do not tell you where the stock price is heading, financial ratios reveal a great many facts about its profitability, liquidity, leverage position, asset utilization, and growth prospects. Financial ratios can be classified into five types:

> Liquidity ratios: These measure the firm's ability to meet its short-term maturing liabilities, or in otherwords all debts due within a year.

> Profitability ratios: These measure management's effectiveness at maximizing shareholders' equity.

> Leverage ratios: These measure the firm's long-term debt position.

> Asset utilization or activity ratios: These measure the firm's efficiency in using its resources and in channelling them toward exploiting sources of growth.

> Investments ratios: These illustrates the firm's performance and its value as an investment vehicle.

There are two facts to keep in mind about financial ratio analysis. The first is that financial ratios, when analyzed in isolation of industry ratios, can be of little help. The second, and more pertinent, is that financial ratios are best utilized within the context of continuity. Improving or deteriorating financial leverage over a number of years provides much more information than examining a single period. A quick review of these financial ratios and their meaning to investors can help identify the real catalyst behind a trend.

Liquidity

Liquidity ratios address the survival issue of a company and whether it can pay back its short-term debt or not. By studying the relationship between current assets to current obligations, the overall liquidity of the company under study can be assessed.

> Current ratio: The current ratio is calculated by dividing current assets by current liabilities. Current assets consist

of cash, marketable securities, receivables, and inventories. Current liabilities include accounts payable, short-term notes payable, current maturity of long-term debt, accrued expenses, and income taxes. This ratio is the most widely used measure of the firm's solvency as it indicates the extent to which short-term debts are covered by liquid assets.

Normally this ratio exceeds one. But it should not be judged in isolation of its industry current ratio, which may be much higher. The larger the current ratio, the more solvent the company is and the larger the cushion it has to pay its current liabilities. But an excessively large ratio for a long period of time also means that management is unable to use its resources effectively. The company's management may have the expertise to deal with the company's business, but lack the know how to manage growth in other lines. The current ratio should not be analyzed in isolation of the quality of the current assets.

Quick ratio: Also known as the acid test, the quick ratio measures the short-term liquidity excluding inventory, which is the least liquid of all current assets. In other words, the ratio expresses the extent to which the company's most liquid assets cover it current liabilities. It is calculated as

$$\frac{\text{Current Assets} - \text{Inventory}}{\text{Current Liabilities}}$$

The quick ratio does not have to exceed one. When it does, it may mean that the firm could pay off its short-term obligations without having to sell inventories at hand. A figure less than one indicates the company's dependency on inventory sales in order to pay off its short-term debt.

Net working capital: While the net working capital is not a financial ratio, it is a helpful gauge of the firm's liquidity. It is the difference between current assets and current liabilities. It measures the amount of current assets not financed by current liabilities.

Cash-flow liquidity: The cash-flow liquidity ratio is calculated as:

$$\frac{\text{Cash} + \text{marketable securities} + \text{Cash flow from operations}}{\text{current liabilities}}$$

This ratio indicates the extent of cash and cash equivalent assets that cover short-term obligations.

Profitability

Profitability is the result of all policies adopted and decisions made by management to maximize shareholders' equity. Profitability measures reveal the bottom line and are by far the most important criteria available for formulating strategy.

Profit margin. There are several profit margin ratios that could be used to measure the company's profitability, such as:

$$\text{Gross profit margin} = \frac{\text{Gross Profit}}{\text{Net sales}}$$

The gross profit margin measures the company's effectiveness in managing pricing decisions while controlling costs related to sales.

$$\text{Operating profit margin} =$$

$$\frac{\text{Earnings Before Income Taxes (EBIT)}}{\text{Net sales}}$$

EBIT = Net Sales − COGS − General Selling and Administrative Expenses
Where COGS = cost of goods sold

The operating profit margin measures the firm's profitability after all operating expenses.

$$\text{Net profit margin} = \frac{\text{Net Income}}{\text{Net Sales}}$$

Net profit margin measures profitability after all expenses, including taxes, have been considered.

Profit margin ratios are probably among the best indicators of the fundamental dynamics of the company. They reflect the ability of management to control expenses. They tell us a great deal about the company's cost structure, the competitiveness of its products in the marketplace, and how profitable its business is. Profit margins can be calculated from the company's financial statements. They are also provided by the S&P 500, Moody's, and the Value-Line Survey.

A rising trend in margins is positive. A receding profit margin should alert the investor to the possibility of troubles ahead. Upward trending profit margins imply that more earnings are being squeezed out of operations to improve efficiency in cost controls. However, declining profit margins alert us to the possibility that management is unable to control the rising costs of raw material and production. This condition may not necessarily reflect on management's capability to run the business because price competition may lead to declining profitability for all members of an industry group. Stable margins suggest that management is in control of cost and that its products command a competitive position in the marketplace.

Profit margins vary from one industry to another. Analysis of the historic behavior of a company's profit margin should be compared to that of other corporations in the same industry. Profit margins of most industries tend to expand when the economy is expanding and interest rates are declining. Lower interest rates mean lower cost of capital which, in turn, means better profitability. When interest rates rise, they exert pressure on profit margins. Moreover, industries in which competition is intensive should be expected to suffer a squeeze on their profit margins. Food stocks and retailers, for example, are expected to have smaller profit margins than technology or drug companies. Companies with dominant market share positions tend to have a stable and relatively high profit margin.

A company that has stable profit margins during expanding or contracting economic conditions should be appealing as a long-term investment. However, profit margins should be assessed in light of other fundamental criteria. Rising margins without a corresponding rise in sales and operating income may be misleading. Margins may be rising because of lower tax rates or as a result of sales of assets. Cyclical industries tend to have volatile profit margins when compared on a year-to-year basis.

Return on total assets. The return-on-total-assets ratio measures the rate of return on investments (ROI) of the firm. This ratio is the key indicator of profitability. It is calculated as

$$\text{ROI} = \frac{\text{Net Profits after Taxes}}{\text{Total Assets}}$$

The higher the ratio, the more profitable the company is. Here is a barometer of management performance in action. This ratio summarizes the results of all the firm's activities in the marketplace and shows how efficiently run its finances are. Well-run companies earn more on their assets than others.

Return on equity. The return on equity ratio (ROE) measures the ability of the firm to earn adequate returns for its shareholders. It shows what returns owners of shares are realizing on their investment.

The ratio is calculated as:

$$\text{ROE} = \frac{\text{Net profits after taxes}}{\text{Common equity}}$$

Although industry averages are always important in evaluating the firm's financial ratios, the ROI and ROE ratios stand alone in their worth to investors. However, there should be two kinds of comparison to improve the results based on judging these important ratios in isolation of their industries. First, these ratios should be compared over the span of several years, and a stable high return ratio should remain apparent over a period of time. Second, these ratios should be compared with a large number of companies in different industries in order to estimate growth levels.

LEVERAGE

The leverage ratios measure the extent to which debt is used to finance the firm's business. Leverage ratios measure the proportion of funds supplied by creditors relative to those supplied by owners.

From the creditor's perspective, the concern is how much residual equity owners have in the business. If the financing provided by the owners are small, the exposure of the creditors is large, and vice versa. From the shareholders' perspectives, sharing the risk of maintaining operations with funds raised by outside creditors is welcomed. If the company earns returns on the borrowed funds, the shareholders' equity increases and the credit rating of their investment rises.

Long-term debt to total capital and total debt to equity are key ratios in measuring the extent of external debt relative to total capital and shareholder's equity. Here, industry ratios must be relied on since these numbers vary depending upon the nature of the business.

Leverage is a double-edged sword. On the one hand, it can help a company execute its long-term plans and expand into new horizons. Depending upon the capital structure of the firm, debt can help a company introduce new products, develop new technology, or make a promising acquisition. Debt can have a positive impact on earnings as long as profit margins are high.

Highly leveraged companies have more risk of loss in an economic downturn. However, companies with low debt ratios are in a better position to capitalize on market opportunities during phases of economic contraction. Interest rate fluctuations have a direct impact on the cost of capital. Rising rates hurt highly leveraged companies, as they incur rising debt servicing payments. Falling rates, on the other hand, help a company earmark less of its cash flow for debt repayment.

On the other hand, excessive debt can be detrimental to a company's financial position. During phases of economic contraction, highly leveraged companies can experience difficulty servicing their debt obligations. Shaky finances lead to eroding profits and tend to negatively affect earnings. Dividend payouts are less secure and, often, cut as cash flow suffers. Companies with heavy debt are likely to be vulnerable to a profit squeeze in the event of an economic slowdown. In extreme cases, companies with a high debt to equity ratio may face insolvency during an economic recession.

During bear markets, there is a high risk in holding a stock with a high debt to equity ratio. Shrinking consumer demand and declining cash flow can severely affect the balance sheet and, hence, the stock price. Companies with low debt can be more defensive during stock market declines. They can also be in a better position to make smart acquisitions with the excess cash.

Healthy debt ratios differ from one industry to another. What is considered to be high leverage in one industry could be normal for others. For example, utilities, transportation, and heavy industries tend to have high debt to equity ratios. Companies with cyclical earnings should have lower ratios than those in more defensive industries with more stable earnings, such as food and tobacco. Well-managed technology and emerging growth companies tend to have a low long-term to total capital ratio, whereas foods, railroads, restaurants, and airlines stocks may have a much higher leverage ratio.

Although no debt and abundant cash seems to be an ideal situation, it may reflect negatively on the management of the company. It can indicate a shortage of managerial talent and a lack of aggressive plans to use the excess cash to seek new avenues of growth. Companies with low debt and ample cash are often targets for buyout and acquisition.

Times Interest Earned Ratio

The times interest earned (TIE) ratio measures the extent to which interest payments are covered by the firm's current earnings. It involves earnings before taxes (EBIT) and interest expense. It is calculated as:

$$TIE = \frac{EBIT}{Interest\ Expense}$$

While this ratio is incorporated under the leverage heading, it can also serve as a measure of liquidity. A company that earns enough to service its debt evidences a strong financial position.

Fixed-charge coverage. The fixed-charge coverage ratio is calculated as:

$$\frac{\text{EBIT}}{\text{Interest Expenses + Lease Payment}}$$

Here, again, this ratio is a measure of the extent to which a firm can pay all its fixed-charge obligations through its operating income. This ratio can also be considered as a gauge of liquidity and financial soundness.

Asset Utilization or Activity Ratios

Asset utilization, or activity ratios describe the overall efficiency of management in running the day-to-day operations of the company. The ratios pertain to the overall efficiency of the firm as a going concern. They also indicate how well the firm is managing cost, inventory, sales, and assets.

Total assets turnover. The total assets turnover is the ratio of net sales to total assets. It measures the management's effectiveness in utilizing the total resources available to generate sales. A high ratio indicates a conscientious management, prudently managing the firm's assets to enhance shareholders' equity.

Inventory turnover. This ratio measures the firm's efficiency in managing inventory through effective sales strategies. It is the ratio of cost of goods sold to total inventory. Inventory tends to accumulate during periods of slackening consumer demand at the later stage of the business cycle. With the advent of computerized networks and their applications to inventory control techniques, this ratio has improved in many industries and companies. While it can reveal a great deal of information about the effectiveness of selling strategies, its best use is making comparisons within specific industry groups governed by the same economic and consumer patterns.

Fixed-asset turnover. The fixed-asset turnover ratio tells the investor how well the company is using its existing plants and equipment to generate sales. It is calculated by dividing net sales into net fixed assets. Here, again, an industry comparison is the best way to use this ratio, since it varies widely depending upon the nature of the business.

Capital expenditure to fixed assets. The capital expenditure to fixed assets ratio depends to a large extent upon the stage of the business cycle during which it is calculated. Capital expenditure decisions are consumer driven. As demand grows excessive at the latter stages of the business cycle, management tends to adopt aggressive capital expenditure plans. The saturation of capacity utilization to satisfy the rising demand prompts management to lay out capital to increase production capacity. This ratio is also related to the inventory accumulation-liquidation cycle, which has a recognized pattern synchronizing with the cyclical behavior of the economy. This ratio is useful when compared to the industry average and other firms within the same industry group.

Investment Ratios

Investment ratios are used to judge the relative appeal of a stock as an investment compared to the broad market and its own industry group. It's based on comparing a stock price performance to either its own historic valuation or what its potential could be in light of future fundamentals.

Earnings per share (EPS). EPS is by far the most widely watched information about the company's operation. This single number describes how its business has been faring. EPS equals net income divided by the number of shares outstanding. A rising EPS on a year-to-year basis is indicative of improving earnings, which tends to bode favorably for the security in the marketplace. From an investment standpoint, consistency of earnings growth is more important than temporary overinflated quarterly figures. Actually, investors should pay more attention to the earnings per share after excluding extraordinary items. This will ensure that profits were generated from operations and other sources of steady income, instead of being camouflaged by land or property sales or some other historic writeoffs. It is important to realize that rising earnings in a bull market help a stock outperform its own industry group as well as the broad averages. In a bear market, however, improving earnings do not necessarily mean that the stock will go up and defy the major downward pressure of the prevailing trend.

P/E ratio. This is the ratio of the market price divided by earnings per share. It represents the value that investors place on the company's earnings. The P/E ratio is a reflection of the psychological makeup of the investment environment. During bull markets, the ratio tends to expand in anticipation of improving economic conditions and rising earnings momentum. Around major market peaks, the P/E ratio stops expanding as companies are still reporting favorable earnings but their price advance is decelerating. As the bear trend begins, the ratio actually declines.

The P/E ratio differs from one industry to another. For example, the auto companies, or cyclical groups in general, tend to sell at much lower multiples than technology or drug stocks. Fast-growing firms are expected to command a higher P/E ratio than large companies in mature industries. The market's P/E ratio also tends to expand and contract during the business cycle. During the secular bull market (1945–68), optimism about the future drove the market's P/E ratio up 20 times. In the inflationary 1970s, the ratio declined precipitously into the low teens. Even during the great bull market of the 1980s, the market P/E ratio was unable to match its previous record. It is important to keep in mind that, in general, the lower the P/E ratio the more defensive a stock is to market selloffs. High P/E stocks will not tolerate earnings disappointments. Companies selling at a high P/E ratio tumble when they report earnings lower than analysts' expectations. But stocks that are already selling at a low P/E ratio may rally strongly when they announce improving earnings.

Dividends payout ratio. This ratio is the percentage of earnings that the company pays out in dividends. This ratio indicates management's willingness to distribute realized profits back to shareholders. It is calculated by dividing the annual dividends by earnings. The importance of the payout ratio increases when its historical perspectives are considered. Investors who are seeking income should check out this ratio, because it will ascertain expected income in light of projected earnings.

Dividends yield. This is the total cash dividend payment divided by the security's price in the open market at any given time. Income-oriented portfolios should strive at maximizing total return possible from both dividend yield and potential capital appreciation.

Book value per share. This ratio indicates the theoretical dollar amount per common share that investors can expect to receive in case of total company liquidation. One of the oldest methods used in valuing common stocks is their book value. The weakness of this approach is that its validity is dependent upon owning the whole company rather than bing a shareholder. The book value theory becomes totally distorted during periods of high inflation. The number under such circumstances is erroneously understated. The accounting methods used tend to value real estate holdings at acquisition prices rather than at current market value. During periods of runaway inflation, the reported number may be a small fraction of what the true book value of a company is worth. The "mega" takeover mania that swept Wall Street in the 1980s was attributed to the great disparity between the market value of stock compared to its real book value.

Price/book value. This ratio shows the market price relative to its estimated book value. The lower this number is, the cheaper the company is selling relative to its real worth. This, however, may not matter, and a stock may sell at a fraction of its book value for many years. In the 1980s, for example, most of the steel companies' shares sold far below their book value. The only time that this ratio could be of any meaning is in case of takeover. Then it can help estimate how far the stock has to rise, after allowing for a premium for goodwill, until it becomes a reasonable sale in the open market. The price to book value ratio should be analyzed in the context of a number of other fundamental considerations. Investment decisions based on this ratio alone can lead to major losses.

Growth Ratio

The year-to-year net sales growth ratio is an important measure of future fundamentals. When sales are growing at a healthy pace, it should mean that the company's products are in great demand and that the marketing and distribution channels are well structured to deliver the product to the consumer. However, sales may be increasing because of the deep discount offered by the firm, which is allowing it to outsell the competition. A healthy sales growth accompanied by profit margins in line with industry standards is more significant, and should, with some control of the business cost, lead to earnings growth as well.

But declining sales figures can be an early signal of important deterioration in the underlying fundamentals. It may be that the product cycle is reaching maturity or that some other changes have negatively affected demand. Lack of research and development and business diversification slowly lead to decreasing cash flow, high leverage, and severe deterioration in the company's financial position.

As with net sales, the same type of analysis should also be run on the annual rate of growth of operating income, total assets, earnings per share, and book value per share. Growth can be temporarily interrupted by economic downturns, but it should not continue to lag once a recovery starts. Growth figures are key in comparing the investment appeal of different stocks or several industry groups in a well-structured portfolio. The concept of trend analysis applies to financial ratios as well as to the other fundamental considerations. Growing sales, earnings, book value per share, and dividends, when accompanied by reasonable liquidity and leverage, can indicate that future P/E multiples are likely to expand in the future as investors recognize the intrinsic worth of the security.

CONCLUSION

Securities prices in the marketplace are governed by the underlying fundamental position and the earnings power of the corporation. Financial data provided in the balance sheet and income statement could be used to assess the soundness of a company as a going concern. Profitability, liquidity, leverage, and growth ratios could reveal strength or weakness in a firm's financial position that may or may not be reflected in its price. Investment ratios, however, compare the valuation numbers of a company with other members of its own industry group. They could also enable investors to check the stock's performance relative to its historic perspectives in order to determine its current intrinsic worth as an investment. Financial ratio trends could help measure the fundamental background and evaluate future possibilities. While fundamental analysis is considered to be the most important tool available to investors in judging prices on Wall Street, it should be integrated with all the other economic and technical factors that may play an important role in determining the price of the security in the marketplace.

❏ 7

Industry Group Analyses

A lesson taught by panics is that in times of great fear and anxiety values are disregarded and the best stocks go off as much or more than the worst.

Samuel A. Nelson, 1903
The ABC of Stock Speculation

Companies operating within an industry are usually analyzed as a group. They are influenced by common factors that affect their sales and earnings prospects. Their price fluctuations tend to move in sync, whether up or down. Often, just a few stocks may lead the way and outperform the rest of the group. However, in general, although some stocks may lag the initial strength of the group, they eventually catch up and follow the prevailing trend. A careful analysis of industry group behavior during the economic cycle reveals that some recover faster than others at the onset of a new phase of business expansion, may lag and outperform the market at a later stage of the cycle. There are industry groups that are more sensitive to consumers' spending than others and there are those which are most affected by interest rate fluctuations. The trend in some industries may depend upon the rise or fall of commodities prices, while others are influenced most by dollar strength or weakness in the foreign exchange market. But, for all practical purposes, stocks operating in a given industry tend to rise and fall together and, at times, the industry trend progression is separate from the broad market movement. That is why it is important to digest those factors peculiar to an industry group and the fundamental catalysts that govern their performance.

Some stocks may have a faster growth rate than others within the same group. This, in turn, may propel a stronger upward trend in those issues relative to the rest of the group or to the broad market. Each group has its own blue-chip leaders—those well established in that industry. These usually have the economies of scale, the management and human resources, the infrastructure, and the know-how to maintain stable growth over the years. They survive good and bad times, spend on research and development, and are quick to restructure their portfolio of businesses to weather crises and seize market opportunities as they come. This, however, does not imply that they have to outperform the rest of the group or the market all the time to qualify as such. All it means is that blue-chip stocks represent the safest investments in those industries. While such stocks do decline during bear markets, they tend to come back when business recovers. They have established and nurtured their markets and product mixes to capitalize on their vast distribution network. Blue-chip companies' sophisticated research and development facilities enable them to bring to market the fruits of new applications and technologies. Their goals are well stated, and their long-term plans are geared to change with the social and demographic factors to benefit from new evolving trends. They often have a well-established presence in both domestic and international markets.

A blue-chip company's corporate structure has found an identity over the years. Companies differ in their corporate culture and beliefs. Such cultures are based on the norms that were well-established by the founders and have been modified by successive management teams. This corporate culture is what helps giant blue-chip companies maintain the infrastructure, the marketing, and the distribution channels that afford them stable sales and earnings growth.

The chemicals group, for example, consists of Air Products and Chemical, Dow Chemical, DuPont, Ethyl Corp., Hercules, Monsanto, Quantum Chemical, Rohm & Haas, Union Carbide, to name a few. Yet among those companies, probably only DuPont, Monsanto, Union Carbide, and Dow Chemical are considered large. Their sales, capitalization, market share, and size are probably bigger than all the other members of the group combined. Investment strategists classify these leaders as "investment grade" companies, since the risk in them is less than that in other, smaller companies in their industry.

Smaller companies, however, tend to have a sharper rate of earnings and sales growth than large ones. Some of them may rise faster and command a high P/E multiple relative to the market. Beware of disappointments—the market severely punishes emerging growth companies when their earnings are less than expected. Small companies typically come out with new concepts and terrific discoveries. Their resources are often modest and can hardly meet their expanding financial needs. The founders are at the helm and may or may not be aggressive in managing growth. Their lack of financing means and their modest capitalization may prevent them from spending as they should on research and development projects that could help them fuel future growth plans. Some, however, do make it and move up to blue-chip rank. Xerox, Digital Equipment Corporation, and Compaq Computers are just a few examples of companies that have grown at a phenomenal rate in such a short period of time.

The majority of companies, however, tend to grow over the years, at a much slower pace. Some are able to gain market share and increase their capitalization either by acquiring new businesses or establishing a commanding presence in completely new fields. IBM, for example, grew from within, with very few acquisitions. ITT, on the other hand, built a mammoth conglomerate by acquiring many companies in different industries. From an investment standpoint, small emerging growth companies are generally suitable for aggressive portfolio strategies.

THE NATURE OF BUSINESS CATEGORIZATION

Very few companies can be classified under one single industry category. Most companies have a portfolio of interrelated businesses. The classification of a company by industry is a representation of the type of business from which the company derives the bulk of its revenues. There are companies that operate in a given industry for a long time, but over the years, they change the nature of their business. For example, USX Corporation, formerly U.S. Steel, has been and still is the largest steel company in the United States. Yet, over the past few years, it has acquired an oil company in order to diversify its business. Currently, USX is classified as a member of the oil group and has rallied or declined depending upon the trend of oil stocks.

Industry group study can reveal many facts about the forces that have an impact on long-term results. There are sectors of the economy that can be classified as growth-oriented while others may be in a secular declining trend, probably on their way to oblivion. Yet, there are some industry groups that are here to stay and will continue to exist in the future, in one form or another. The soap, food, and soft drink industries are prime examples of industries that are likely to experience little change for many years to come. Their products may have to fit new socioeconomic trends, but their core businesses will remain in high demand. The chemicals, computers, drugs, and aerospace industries are only a few examples of revolutionary and dynamic industries that, while they may substantially change their products, are fast-growing industries that hold great promise for the future.

It is important to note that the steel, auto, and utilities industries were considered the fast-growth industries in the early decades of this century. Nowadays, these industries are stagnant and have average, if not declining, growth rates. The steel industry is faced with intense foreign competition and declining demand. The domestic auto industry is also suffering invasions of overseas car manufacturers. The utilities industry, which was once the beneficiary of the historic transformation from an agricultural to an industrial society, is now highly dependent upon demographics and population movement among states. On top of this less-than-enticing environment, the industry is faced with tremendous environmental challenges that dampen its profitability and long-term growth prospects.

Industry group analysis is scattered throughout the book. The emphasis here is on the classification of the different groups, their natures, and the catalysts that drive them. It is those fundamentals that are responsible for propelling their trend. By focusing on the specific characteristics that are pertinent to a group's internal dynamics, their future price behavior can be anticipated.

COMMON FACTORS AFFECTING ALL INDUSTRY GROUPS

A number of economic factors—home building, cars, and interest rates, demographics, household debt and personal income, and dollar strength—have a direct impact on all industry groups. Such factors influence sales, earnings, and profit margins variably, depending upon the type of industry. Those forces can also enhance potential growth or weaken the financial position of a company within a sector. Some of these factors are the result of the Fed's economic policy in its attempt to keep the economy stable. Other factors emerge from the social, demographic, or political changes that are constantly evolving. Some of the most important factors, which affect most industry group performances, are the following:

Home Building, Cars, and Interest Rates

All industry groups are affected by the monetary policy of the Fed. They are affected by the rise or fall of interest rates. The rise of interest rates implies an increase in the cost of money, which tends to exercise downward pressure on profit margins, sales, and earnings of all industry groups. Some, however, are more sensitive to rate fluctuations than others.

Two economic sectors that are particularly sensitive to interest rate trends are the building and auto industries. These two sectors are of vital importance to the rest of the economy. A rise in interest rates has a direct, dampening effect on the housing market, as households face difficulties qualifying for mortgage loans. Moreover, a number of homeowners may be unable to service their debt. The uncertainty of the employment outlook during periods of economic slowdown also forces prospective home buyers to postpone their spending plans until future dates. Some households may find the cost of maintaining a house prohibitive and may decide to sell. The outcome of all this is that supply exceeds demand during periods of rising rates.

For the same reasons, car sales suffer when rates are high and rising. The excessive cost of servicing loans makes it difficult to purchase new cars. The lack of job security influences

consumers' buying and selling decisions and makes them postpone their purchasing plans. The importance of these two
sectors derives from the dependence of so many other industries upon their financial health. In a typical car, glass, leather,
tires, steel, electronics, fuel, chemicals, and the like are used.
When a house is built, the process employs construction people, engineers, and realtors, and the house needs furniture,
rugs, appliances, and a host of other products. When the
activity in those two sectors contracts, all other industries in the
economy feel the impact. But when rates decline, the housing
market prospers and car sales increase, lifting with them the
rest of the economy. The boom shortly spreads into other
sectors and stimulates the whole economy.

Demographics

All industry groups are affected in varying degrees by
demographics. Beginning in the 1970s, the economy has felt
the impact of the baby boomers—those born between 1945 and
1960. As they flooded the job market, structural unemployment began to rise. As fast as the services sector expanded,
manufacturing lagged and supply shortages resulted. There
was tremendous demand for housing as the baby boomers
sought independence and started families. A period of
"stagflation"—high unemployment and ravaging inflation—
resulted. Supply-side economics came under focus as a possible cure to the rising pressure on prices. The housing market
boom that started in the early 1970s and lasted well into the
1980s drove the prices of both commercial and residential properties to unheard of levels. The main cause of these changes
was shifting demographic factors.

During those years, which were characterized by runaway
inflation, many industries benefited greatly from the coincident
rising demand. Home builders, raw materials producers, energy companies, precious metal stocks, retailers, and the like all
witnessed substantial increases in sales and revenues. Real
assets and, especially, the real estate markets experienced an
era of prosperity and fast-rising prices.

The influence of demographics is likely to continue into
the first quarter of the next century as the baby boomers grow

older. There may be rising demand for such services as health care, banking, investment, insurance, nursing homes, leisure, travel, and so forth. Products and services that cater to the needs of an aging population may prosper. Industry groups positioned to fulfill this demand may experience an accelerated growth phase. Demographics should be factored into the overall investment strategy. Portfolios positioned in those industry groups that are likely to benefit may appreciate over the long term as the market places increased P/E multiples on their earnings prospects.

Household Debt and Personal Income

Household debt relative to personal income is another important determinant of consumption patterns. Consumer spending has a direct impact on sales of goods and services. When debt accelerates relative to personal income gains, future consumer demand may decline and vice versa. The extent of leverage may help foretell of an impending phase of retrenchment in consumer demand as household budgets become strained. The contraction of business helps to reduce consumer debt and to increase savings, which allows the economy to start a new growth cycle.

Dollar Strength

In today's global environment, most industries are influenced by the strength or weakness of the dollar relative to other world currencies. A strong dollar depresses exports, weakens, prices domestically, and leads to rising imports. A soft dollar, however, relieves pressure from abroad, enables domestic products to compete with imports, and helps the full utilization of local domestic capacity which, in turn, lowers the cost structure of production. Most companies have an important stake in the international arena and derive a good percentage of their earnings and sales from trade activities. As much as the strength of the dollar is considered a matter of national pride, a weak dollar enables domestic industries to recapture sales from foreign competitors and boosts sales and earnings derived from overseas operations.

INDUSTRY GROUP CLASSIFICATION

There is no one rigid form of classification that can meet all the categories of industry groups operating in the marketplace. The following analysis is based on broad perspectives of stock characteristics sharing certain criteria that have affected and are likely to continue to affect their earnings in a certain way. Several broad categories describe the majority of sectors of the economy: consumer sensitive, interest-rate sensitive, capital goods, energy, basic industries, transportation, and utilities.

The consumer-sensitive groups are a function of consumer demand and are categorized as growth staples, defensive, or cyclical. Interest-rate sensitive groups are particularly affected by the Fed's monetary policy and the cost of money. This group consists mainly of the financial groups and the building or credit cyclical groups. The capital goods groups depend upon the capital spending cycle and are classified as technology and industrial groups. Basic industry groups are sensitive to commodities and raw materials price fluctuations. The energy sector is vital to all industry groups, the industrial and services sectors, and the economy at large. Both the transportation and utilities sectors serve all the other industry group categories and are capital intensive and asset rich sectors. They are characterized by high leverage and low profit margins.

This study could not possibly encompass detailed discussion of industry group characteristics and earnings behavior. But a number of examples that help the reader understand the multitude of factors that affect an industry and the particular catalysts that help shape its trend during the span of the business cycle have been incorporated.

CONSUMER-SENSITIVE GROUPS

Industries that are highly dependent upon consumer spending are subdivided into three growth pattern categories. The consumer sensitive groups consist of the growth staples groups: drug industry; hospitals and health care; and restaurants, retail, cosmetics, and the media. The growth staples groups are industries with high growth rates. Business cycle after business cycle, companies in this category continue to witness improving sales and revenues. They are highly dependent upon demographics and social trends.

The Drug Industry

This industry is a beneficiary of widespread health awareness and major demographic changes. For many years, this group has had an excellent and stable financial position. During good or bad times, drug companies have solid sales and earnings growth record. Hefty research and development outlays enable them to develop new products. Over the years, the per-capita expenditure on drugs and medical sundries has consistently increased due to the expanding use of drug therapy, the aging of the population, and the introduction of new drugs geared toward improved health care. The strength or weakness of the dollar relative to foreign currencies has an important influence on profits of the drug group. Operations abroad account for a large percentage of the revenues of most pharmaceutical companies, and changes in currency valuations have a material impact on its earnings. On the one hand, when the dollar is strong, sales, earnings, and profits suffer because after currency conversion, revenues are translated to fewer dollars. A weak dollar, on the other hand, helps boost profits and sales, after currency translation. In addition, a soft dollar makes drug company products more competitive in the world market, which increases exports. Figure 7–1 illustrates the behavior of the drug group versus its earnings. Notice how earnings stayed on a rising course during prior business cycles, including past recessions.

Health Care

With regard to health and hospitals, the Health Care Financing Administration (HCFA) projects national health-care expenditures to reach $1.5 trillion by the year 2000, or 15 percent of total GNP. Demographics is one of the most important factors influencing the health-care-related industry groups. People will be treated for illness in good or bad times, and the fundamentals behind these groups are, to a large

Figure 7-1. Drug industry average relative to its earnings.

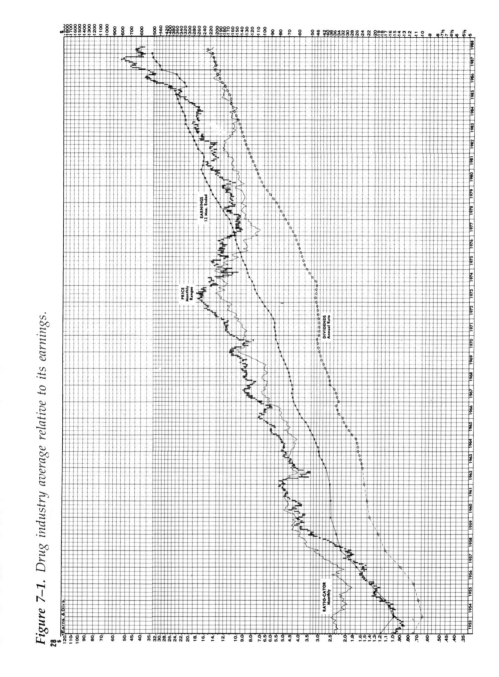

extent, independent of the economic cycle. The need for such services should continue to grow with rising health awareness, especially in an environment of aging populations worldwide.

Yet, for the hospital management group, profitability is dependent on its ability to control the acceleration of its cost structure. The tightening of Medicare reimbursement and fast-rising costs can severely affect earnings. In fact, many hospitals have sustained negative margins from providing inpatient care. Increased competition stems from contracted health maintenance organization facilities, freestanding surgical centers, and physicians' offices. The need for this group's services is expanding, yet its financial position should be closely scrutinized.

The medical supplies group is dependent upon the hospital management industry, but its earnings are more stable. Its growth prospects are influenced more by the rising demand arising from demographics. Diagnostic and therapeutic instruments, surgical appliances, and electromedical equipment aimed at improving the overall level of efficiency of health-care services comprise a key determinant of revenue growth. The application of new technology towards achieving that end is a must for members of this group. Export volume is highly dependent upon the strength or weakness of the dollar and the technological advantage of local versus overseas producers.

Nursing home companies are also dependent upon demographics. Yet, earnings are a function of rate of reimbursement, the availability of nursing help, the facility's costs, and regulatory restrictions.

There is no doubt that the demand for improving health-care conditions will continue to grow for the coming decades. Yet these industry groups have a common enemy, mainly cost control. Investors who wish to position themselves in those lucrative and promising industries should take the time to investigate their financial ratios and fundamentals.

Restaurants, Retail, and the Media

In the same category of consumer-sensitive staple growth industries are restaurants, retail (drugs and specialty convenience stores), cosmetics, entertainment, broadcasting (radio and TV), and publishing (newspapers and printing). Although they differ in nature, they depend, in varying degrees, on the level of consumer spending. Besides the cost control factors, the earnings of the restaurants groups depends upon demographics, geographical locations, and the general economic condition. This industry grew out of social changes that emerged with the two-paycheck family and its tendency to eat out. Drug and specialty retail industries were built on the favorable reception of convenience stores. Location, demographics, cost control, and pricing are important factors that help future growth. Cosmetics are highly dependent upon fashion and fads, improved consumer spending, favorable foreign exchange, and overseas expansion. While considered growth industries, the entertainment, broadcasting, and publishing groups are more sensitive than the rest of the groups in this category to the general business conditions.

CONSUMER-DEFENSIVE INDUSTRIES

The defensive industries are those that, while dependent upon consumer spending, are generally less sensitive to business cycle fluctuations. Household industries (foods, food retailers, soft drinks, beverages) and tobaccos groups constitute the consumer-sensitive defensive sectors. As going concerns, they benefit from an easy monetary policy and lowered interest rates as the cost of capital declines and profit margins increase. Moreover, an improving business outlook and expanding gross national product fuels consumption. Declining commodities prices can also help boost profitability.

The main factor that determines the growth rate of all those industries, however, is population. Per-capita consumption is the most critical factor that helps sales and earnings. Population growth varies considerably on a regional basis, which is a critical factor in analyzing future potential. For example, over the next two decades, Nevada, Florida, and many other southern and western states are expected to experience population growth much faster than the northeast, such as New York, Connecticut, and Massachusetts. Another long-term emerging factor is the acceleration of the globalization of world markets, which could fuel new sources of growth in the international arena.

The consumer-defensive industries are sensitive to socio-economic trends, such as the increase in single or two-person households, the two-paycheck family, and the baby boom and baby bust demographic forces. They are also affected by taste changes in the population and the wave of health self-improvement that is sweeping many parts of the world. The diet food industry is growing, and companies operating in the food, beverages, and tobacco industries are restructuring their businesses to accommodate consumers' preferences. The growing awareness of smoking's health hazards, the strengthening of the antismoking movement, and the rising "sin taxes" are major negative factors facing the tobacco industry. The convenience of food away from home is another factor that is reshaping many segments of the food industry.

The consumer-defensive groups are likely to fare better than other industries during market downturns. They are beneficiaries of disinflationary environments, and their revenues are stable when compared to most other group categories. But, when stocks in any of these industries are analyzed for investment purposes, they should be scrutinized in light of all the above-mentioned factors. Not only should a thorough balance sheet and financial ratio analysis be performed, but a detailed investigation of their product mix and geographic locations of their markets should also be done in order to ascertain potential long-term growth.

Figure 7–2 is an example of historical earnings behavior of a consumer-defensive industry, the foods group. Through the years, this group was able to pass increased cost on to consumers and maintain an upward rising earnings curve. The foods group was a beneficiary of the disinflationary environment of the 1980s. Although its price trend remained dormant during many previous cycles, it became a stellar performer in that decade. Seldom has cyclical leadership persisted for such a long time, yet this group's earnings continue to rise independent of prevailing economic conditions, and that is the ultimate investment criterion.

Figure 7-2. The foods group and its earnings curve over 35 years.

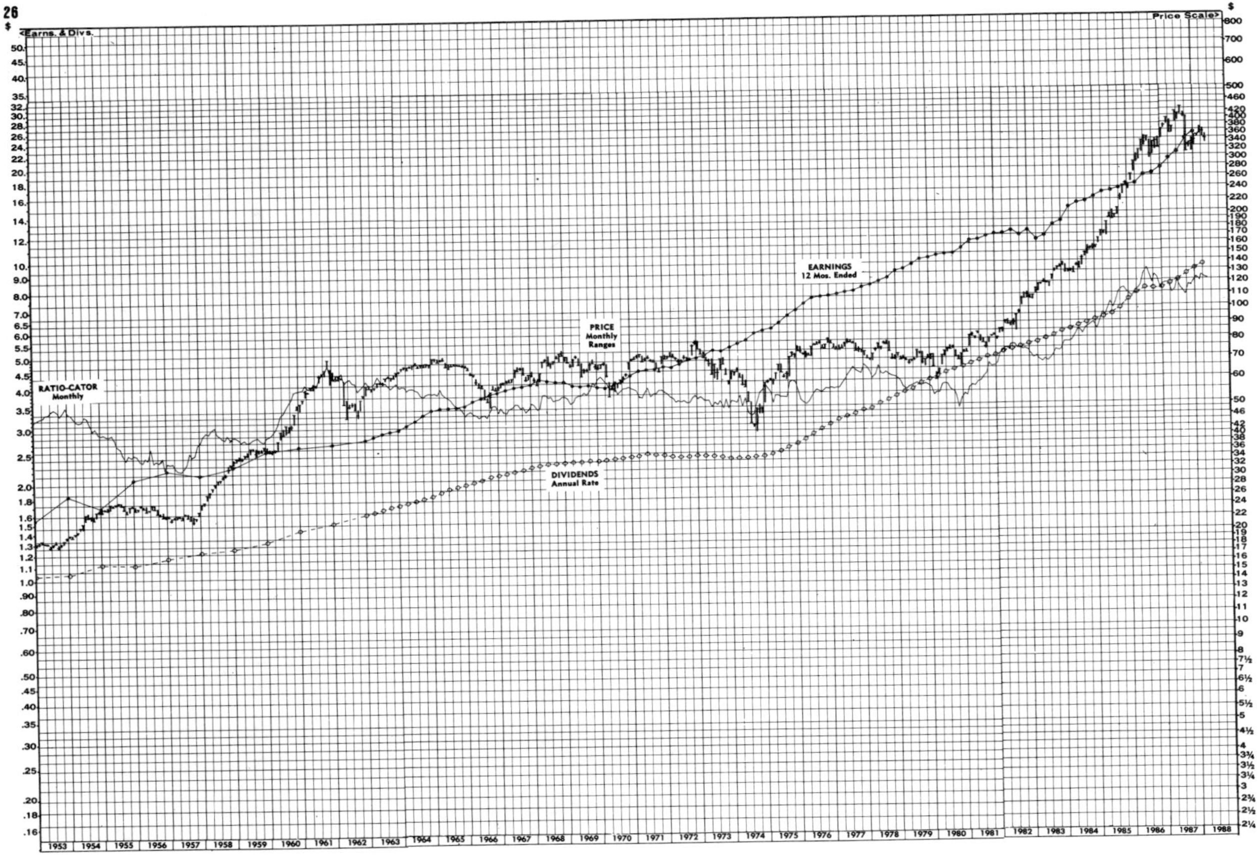

CYCLICAL INDUSTRIES

Industry group behaviors may lead or lag the economic cycle. Toward the end of an economic recession, investors should focus their attention on cyclical stocks. Although during the expansion phase of the economy all stocks benefit, some industry groups tend to have a faster rebound in their sales and earnings than others. These industry groups are tagged as cyclical because their fundamentals are particularly sensitive to the business cycle.

Auto companies, home builders, home furnishing and appliance manufacturers, airlines, papers, tires and rubber, forest products, and retailers are examples of cyclical industry groups. At the end of a bear market, the stock prices in those sectors rise sharply. Because of their operating leverage, their earnings tend to rebound during the early phases of an economic recovery. Moreover, their profit margins also tend to expand rapidly as interest rates decline. In particular, home-building, autos, and airline stocks lead other issues on the way up once a bull market starts. The advance usually takes the shape of a stampede in their equities prices. The extent of the rise in those equities is dependent on their relative intrinsic appeal.

Durable and Nondurable Goods

Industry groups that have cyclical earnings are divided into two categories: the durable goods, and the nondurable goods. In the durable goods category are the autos, auto parts, appliances and furnishings, photography, and leisure time groups. Among the nondurable industry groups are the retail department stores and mass merchandising stores, the textile and apparel industries, air transport, and lodging (hotels/motels) groups. All the durable and nondurable groups are known for their sensitivity to the business cycle. Figure 7–3 illustrates the auto group price history with earnings over 35 years. Notice that earnings have plummeted during recessions and rebounded strongly during the ensuing economic recoveries.

Figure 7–3. The autos group and its cyclical earnings.

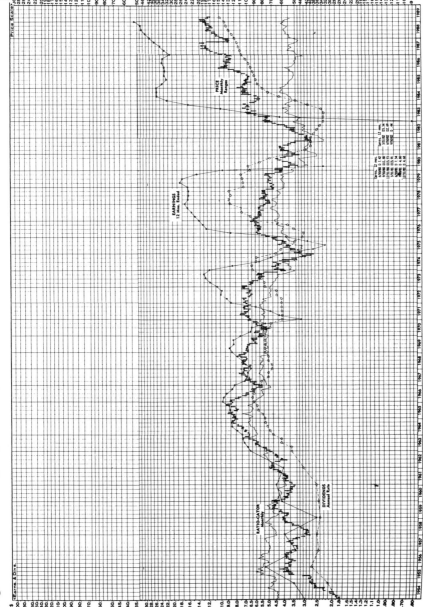

203

From a fundamental perspective, durable goods sales expand rapidly from depressed levels, ahead of other activities in the economy. Being sensitive to interest rates, home buyers try to take advantage of the declining cost of mortgages. The reduced cost of financing automobile purchases encourages consumers to buy cars. As business starts to recover, both commercial and business airline traffic soars. Although other cyclical industry groups benefit from a broad-based economic expansion, the speed of their rise may be affected by the nature of the recovery. There is always the question of whether it will be a consumer-spending recovery or business-investment-led one. The increase in housing starts and automobile sales helps stimulate business activities in a multitude of other sectors that are dependent on these two vital industries. These capital goods sectors provide much impetus to the recovery.

INTEREST-RATE SENSITIVE GROUPS

Interest rate fluctuations have a far-reaching impact on stocks and bonds. Declining rates have been positive catalysts in propelling strong primary uptrends in the fixed-income sector and in the stock market. Although all industry groups are affected by interest rate movements, some sectors are more sensitive to their fluctuations than others. In the past, financial and home-building-related groups have responded quickly to trends in interest rates. At times, they have even reacted in anticipation of new developments on the interest rate front.

Building- and Credit-Sensitive Groups

Home builders, building materials suppliers, the mobile home business, and the savings and loan (S&L) institutions make up this category. They are analyzed here.

Home builders, building materials, and mobile homes: The earnings characteristics of the building related groups are especially sensitive to the trend of interest rates. The group benefits from their declines and suffer from their advances.

Savings and loans institutions: Savings and Loans (S&Ls) institutions benefit from declining interest rates and are adversely affected by their rise. The S&Ls generate profits on the spread between the yield they receive on their mortgage loans and the interest they pay to depositors. When interest rates decline, the interest paid to depositors comes down faster than the yield earned on their loan portfolio, mainly mortgage loans. As a result, the spread between yield on assets and cost of funds widens, which results in improved earnings and profit margins. Moreover, declining interest rates stimulate activities in the housing market and boost the demand for mortgages. When the Fed eases the money supply, the risk of default on mortgage loans declines significantly. And contrariwise, when interest rates rise and the Fed tightens the money supply, housing activities sag, the demand for mortgages declines, the default risk on mortgage loans increases, profit margins are squeezed as the spread shrinks, and earnings suffer. The S&Ls are among the most interest-rate sensitive sectors, and their fortunes are directly dependent upon interest rate trends.

FINANCIAL GROUPS

Money-Center Banks and Regional Banks

The financial groups comprise money center banks and regional banks. Their relationship with interest rates and the economy is elemental. This relationship is described here. Banks lend money to individuals and institutional customers. In return, the banks generate profits on the interest charged on those loans. Banks' net earnings are derived from the difference between the cost of money, or interest they pay to depositors, and the interest they charge borrowers, after accounting for operating expenses. Traditionally, loan growth, improving credit quality, and control of overhead expenses have been the most important factors to influence earnings results. Loan growth is sensitive to both household and corporate borrowing needs. In general, banks' loan portfolios consist of business, consumer, and mortgage loans. Money-center banks, in fact, have a fourth category: international loans to overseas countries (which may carry an increased risk of default, when dealing with economically unstable nations—that is, country risk).

Banks lead the interest rate cycle. They feel the brunt of rising interest rates and benefit from their decline. When interest rates rise, the spread between their cost of capital and their sources of revenue—loans—declines. This, in turn, exercises pressure on profit margins and profitability. In addition, rising interest rates tend to have a negative effect on demand for credit and cause it to slow down. Moreover, at such times, credit quality often deteriorates, and the risk of default often increases. When interest rates fall, however, loan demand expands, profit margins improve, and credit quality is substantially enhanced.

Investors should realize that interest rate fluctuations have a direct bearing on banks' profits. Bank stock prices tended to weaken ahead of cyclical downturns in sync with the early signs of interest rate rises. Banks also tend to rebound sharply when the other economic indicators confirm the business slowdown and the Fed begins to ease.

Recessions adversely affect real estate loans, in addition to industrial capital spending activities. Potential international default is another exposure that banks have to reckon with. A severe global slowdown could cause "mega"-dollar defaults and seriously impair banks' balance sheets. Local economic conditions play a critical role in the loan growth/credit risk cycle. In energy-producing regions, investors have to consider the impact of rising or declining oil prices on banks' clients in those regions. Texas is a clear example of the way local economic conditions can affect the financial position of the banks servicing them. When oil prices plummeted in the early 1980s, banks operating in those regions experienced numerous hardships, and many went under. Agricultural banks, too, were dealt a severe blow during the localized depression that plagued that sector at the time. Hundreds of banks found themselves with a large exposure in questionable loans to farmers during the 1970s.

It is worth noting that the nature of the banking system

has changed a great deal over the past two decades. The increasing interest rate volatility, the dynamic momentum of the financial markets, the invasion of the U.S. market by giant foreign banks free from regulatory and reserve requirements, and the competition of insurance companies, brokerage houses, and credit cards offered by nonfinancial institutions have compelled the banks to seek new avenues of growth and prompted the Fed to deregulate the financial services industry. The 1990s are likely to witness a major fundamental change in banking and finance, characterized by waves of merger, acquisition, and restructuring of banking operations both inter- and intrastate. All these factors are likely to have a mixed impact on the industry and should be approached on a case-by-case basis.

In the 1990s, banking deregulation and interstate banking may present the financial community with new avenues of risk and opportunity. Regional banks, well positioned in growing states and with relatively low exposure to loan defaults may prove to be the real beneficiaries of these sweeping changes.

The globalization of the world's economies and the unification of the European Community in 1992 are also important considerations when analyzing the banking group. Although in the 1970s and 1980s the foreign exchange market soared in an environment of eroding lending profits, the 1990s promise increasingly sophisticated investment banking deals, securities underwriting, and new synthetic financial instruments.

The above analysis, as shown in figure 7–4, is by no means all that could be said about the banking group. It is hoped that this discussion illustrates the micro-analysis process of industry group fundamental considerations. Only after a thorough understanding of the environment and constraints surrounding a specific industry can attention be focused on the individual stock for investment purposes.

Life, Casualty, and Multiline Insurance

Insurance companies are interest-rate sensitive mainly because of the impact of rate fluctuations on the value of such companies' sizable bond portfolios.

During periods of rising rates, policyholders tend to borrow against their policies at lower cost than market rates. The

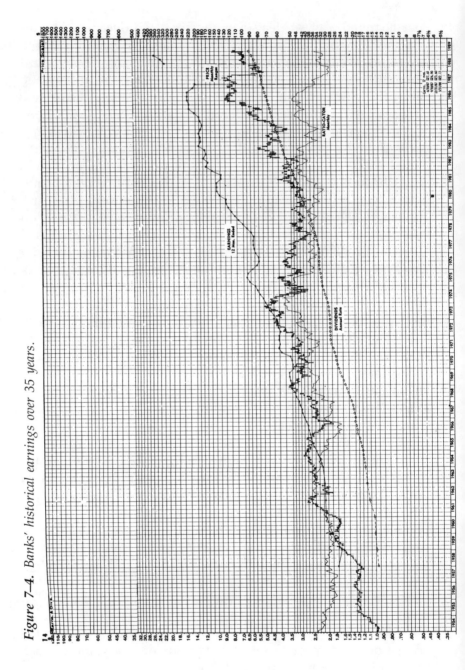

Figure 7–4. Banks' historical earnings over 35 years.

208

drain of liquidity during periods of rising rates raises the risk that insurance companies face in the later stages of the business cycle. In addition, as the general business environment worsens, the rate of growth of new policies declines, as households tend to reassess their spending priorities. So, insurance companies' profit margins are squeezed and the value of their bond portfolios declines. Moreover, insurance policy cancellations run relatively high during periods of rising rates, which results in lost premiums and declining profits.

When the Fed is easing and rates are declining, the bond market rises and so does the value of the bond portfolio. The policy cancellation rate declines, and policyholders' borrowing decreases. All these factors help replenish liquidity and earnings and improve profit margins.

Utilities (Telephone, Electric, and Gas)

The appeal of utilities stocks as an investment vehicle derives from their ability to provide investors with a stream of relatively high dividend income. The companies in this industry group are regulated by local authorities. Utilities firms have to seek approval from state governments before they can raise the rate they charge their customers. Their growth potential is dependent on population increases in the geographic area they serve.

For investors seeking a constant flow of income, these stocks present an alternative to bonds. Because such stocks' dividends tend to increase over the years and because of their potential for capital appreciation, utilities are superior to bonds, which offer fixed coupon rates until maturity. A decline in interest rates makes utilities dividends even more appealing. In addition, because utilities are capital intensive, reduced rates offer them reduced cost of capital, which helps improve their profit margins.

Utilities are a form of oligopoly, in that once they begin to serve a certain geographic area, they stay there, theoretically, forever. As the population grows so does the need for their services. At times, utilities prices have plummeted in the open market because of a temporary decline in earnings or cut in dividends. But very few, if any, have declared bankruptcies.

Utilities are rated high in relative safety among industry groups. Their constant stream of income from electric, telephone, or gas services has always helped them regain financial health and reinstate dividends. Some electric utilities generate a large percentage of their power from nuclear power plants. Those stocks have an increased exposure to nuclear hazards and carry an increased risk. But nuclear energy is the wave of the future; technology faces the challenge of taming that risk.

CAPITAL GOODS GROUPS

The capital goods category comprises the technology groups. This category consists of the semiconductors, instrumentation, electronic equipment, telecommunications, and information-processing groups.

Technology Groups

They represent the areas with the most assured future growth among all sectors of the economy. They are characterized by high volatility and great expectations. Many rise for an extended period of time but suddenly falter and take a long time to come back. Others have the know-how and the established market to maintain steady growth and healthy fundamentals. The technology groups firms' biggest enemy is obsolescence and their greatest challenge is foreign competition. Innovation and research and development are technology groups' lifeblood and most important sources of survival. Yet their high P/E multiples often lead to great disappointments that, at times, are costly to investors. Because technology firms are expected to score an above-average growth rate, they sell at multiples far in excess of the broad market. But this leaves little room for earnings declines disappointment. The high-tech groups are very cyclical in nature. Although these groups follow the capital goods cycle, the biggest danger is that of being caught in an economic slowdown while introducing new products. This often leaves hi-tech firms unable to recapture their research and development expenses and to lose market share.

The semiconductor group is often judged by the book-to-bill ratio. Compiled by the Semiconductor Industry Association, this ratio illustrates the strength or weakness of demand of orders in excess of shipment. When the ratio moves above one, it demonstrates rising demand, typical of periods of expanding economic activities and capital spending. Bear in mind that excessive demand leads to inadequate capacity, firm prices, long lead times, and healthy profit margins. However, when inventory accumulates and demand softens, the book-to-bill ratio slides and the outlook for the industry becomes questionable. Semiconductor firms' hefty P/E multiples usually shrink and stock prices plummet. The demand side is a function of original equipment manufacturers (OEMs), who set the levels of production as deemed necessary by the marketplace. When orders are surging, many semiconductor companies stockpile chips, fearing imminent shortages. When the demand slackens, they are penalized by the overvalued P/E multiples and the hefty inventory they have to liquidate. It is also to be observed that volatility of demand in this industry is caused by the emergence of major new products, such as digital watches, video games, or other electronic gadgets.

With regard to computer stocks and information-processing companies, they also tend to carry premium P/E multiples because of investor perceptions of superior prospects. This leaves little room for earnings disappointments. This industry is dominated by a few mammoth companies that set the trend for technology and storage capacity. That is why many small companies get hurt when an announcement is made that is expected to change the market's technological infrastructure. Finally, as with all high-tech companies, foreign competition—especially from the Japanese and West German companies—has exercised tremendous downward pressure on prices and, hence, on profit margins. Strict cost control measures, special niches, and continuous innovation are important ingredients to look for when investing in high-tech companies. The customer base is also of great importance in ensuring that the company is not dependent upon one single market for its products. Figure 7–5 illustrates this industry group's behavior during past economic cycles. Notice the volatility of their earnings.

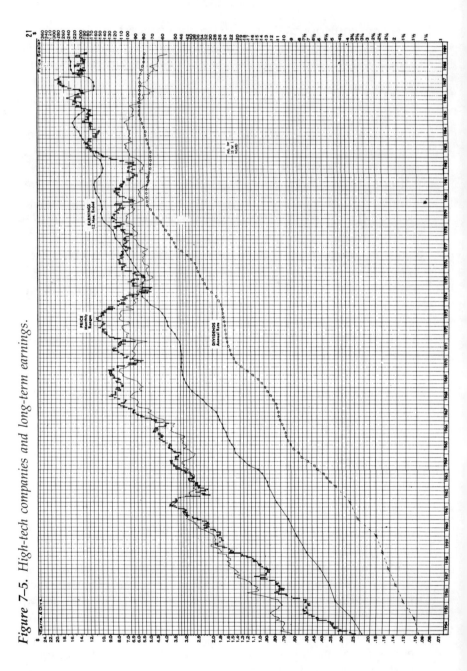

Figure 7-5. High-tech companies and long-term earnings.

212

Aerospace/Defense

The aerospace industry group produces a broad spectrum of defense technologies and equipment, including aircraft, missiles, space systems, military electronics, weapon delivery aids, precision guided weapons, command, control, communications, and intelligence systems. The group is driven by military spending on armaments. It is closely tied to the fiscal policy in place at any given time. When defense expenditures allocated by Congress increase, orders for military hardware increase, which benefits aerospace companies and defense contractors. When federal budgetary restraints are in place, the trend of Pentagon appropriations slows down, which eventually translates to slow order procurements. Revenues, earnings, and profit margins of aerospace companies are severely affected by the defense budget and the fiscal policy.

Other factors that influence the prospects of this industry group are the activities in the airline business and, especially in the future, space research. Vis-à-vis the airlines, the price of oil in the open market may tilt the trend in aircraft manufacturing towards increasingly fuel-efficient airplanes. The invasion of space and the constant research efforts of the National Aeronautics and Space Administration (NASA) to commercialize space travel could be a great source of growth for the defense group. In a unified, peaceful, capitalist world, it seems that this source of growth may replace the role of defense expenditures as the most important fuel of growth in the group.

Figure 7–6 illustrates how the defense group behaved in relation to defense expenditures. The relationship is straightforward. As defense expenditures increase the group's prices on Wall Street go up and vice versa.

INDUSTRIAL GROUPS

This category consists mainly of electrical equipment, machine tools, machinery (agricultural and construction and industrial), heavy duty trucks and parts, pollution control, and conglomerates groups. The industrial groups are beneficiaries of corporate capital spending geared towards expanding exist-

Figure 7–6. The aerospace group and defense expenditures.

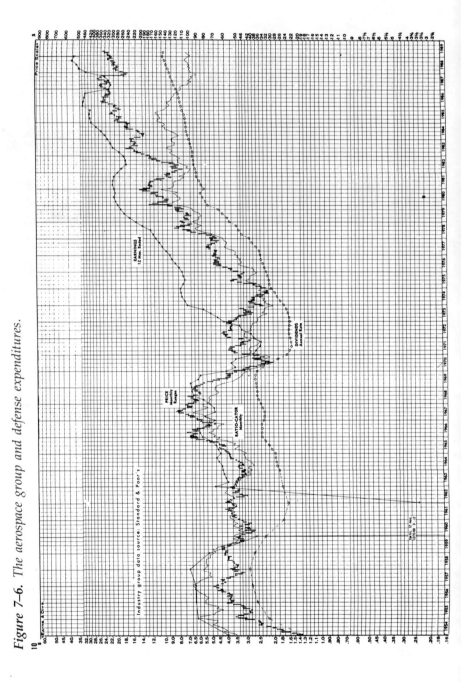

214

ing production capacity. They are back cycle movers since they benefit from the activities of a heating economy as the cycle matures. At the onset of an expansion phase of the economy, there is excess capacity in production in excess of actual demand. As personal income rises and consumers begin to increase their expenditures, supply shortages develop. This leads corporations to allocate funds to build production facilities to meet the surging demand for foods. Companies operating in those industrial groups receive orders to provide the needed production capacity. Their earnings rise as their backlog of contracts expands. These groups tend to benefit from mounting inflationary pressures as congestion occurs in manufacturing plants.

THE ENERGY GROUP

This category includes international and domestic oil, oil services, oil and gas, and refinery companies. The fortunes of these closely related energy groups are dependent, to a large extent, on the price of crude oil. Since the early 1970s, the price of this vital source of energy has been controlled by the oil cartel. However, it should be emphasized that despite the role that oil prices play in determining the financial position and profitability of these industry groups, the relationship between the price of oil and the groups' behavior has been less than homogeneous. Take, for example, refineries: their business could be slightly dependent on production levels. Refineries continue to process and refine crude oil independent of the number of barrels produced. As long as they maintain cost control, their earnings and cash flow levels can hardly be scathed. As to international and domestic oil producers, the fundamentals can remain strong as long as their position in the marketplace is well maintained. The oil and gas companies, too, enjoy a commanding position, and as long as civilization exists, the demand for their output will continue to grow. The only industry group that is heavily influenced by the price of oil in the open market is the oil services group. When the price per barrel shoots up, the economic feasibility of small wells grows, and the demand for such services also rises. And, vice versa, when the price per barrel drops, it becomes too costly and too uneconomical to exploit small oil wells.

The impact of oil price fluctuations on the energy groups is best illustrated by figure 7–7, which illustrates the trend of these groups vis-à-vis the price of crude oil. Notice how both the international and domestic oil groups have completely ignored the plunge in oil prices during the early 1980s. Energy group firms were able to streamline operations and reset priorities in order to maintain profitability. Indeed, the period of shrinking demand allowed many of the domestic and international oil companies to hoard cash, as they could not plow their generated profits back into petroleum-related activities. Also notice that the oil services group has been going through excess capacity as the economic feasibility of hundreds of small oil wells in Texas and other southern regions becomes disadvantageous.

THE BASIC INDUSTRIES AND RAW MATERIALS GROUPS

These comprise chemicals, paper and forest products, metals, glass, coal, precious metals, and the like.

Chemicals

The chemicals group produces: industrial gases such as nitrogen, oxygen, carbon dioxide, and hydrogen; argon and specialty gases; acids, chlorine and alkalines, industrial organic and inorganic materials; synthetic materials such as plastics and manmade fibers; agricultural materials such as pesticides and fertilizers; and many other products, such as adhesives and paints, ingredients for soaps, toiletries, and drugs.

The chemicals group is sensitive to the general state of the economy and the level of consumer spending. Its growth potential is enhanced in an environment of declining oil prices and low interest rates, which help reduce the cost structure. Furthermore, the industry is dependent upon global trade and economic activities and is a beneficiary of a weak dollar. A weak dollar enhances the industry's earnings potential because

Figure 7-7. International and Domestic and Oil Services relative to Crude Oil Prices.

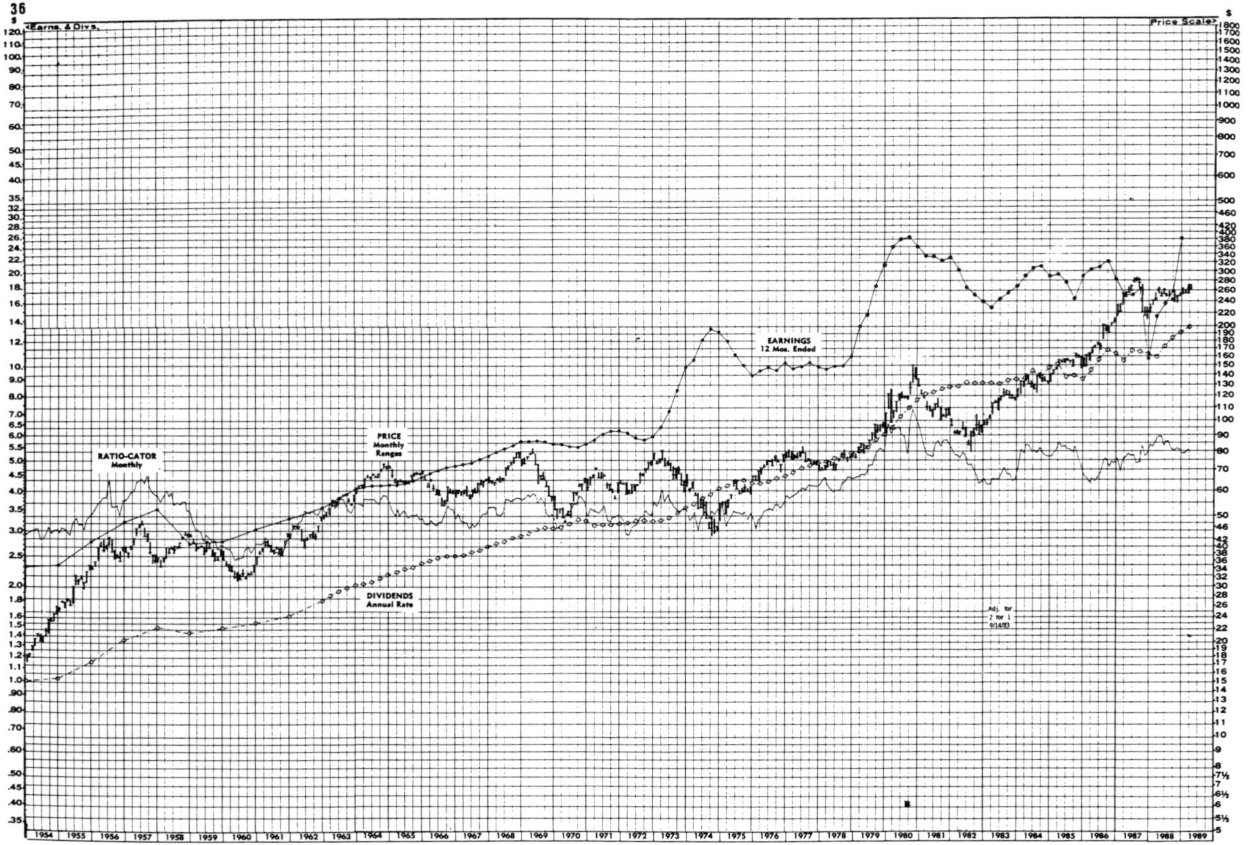

217

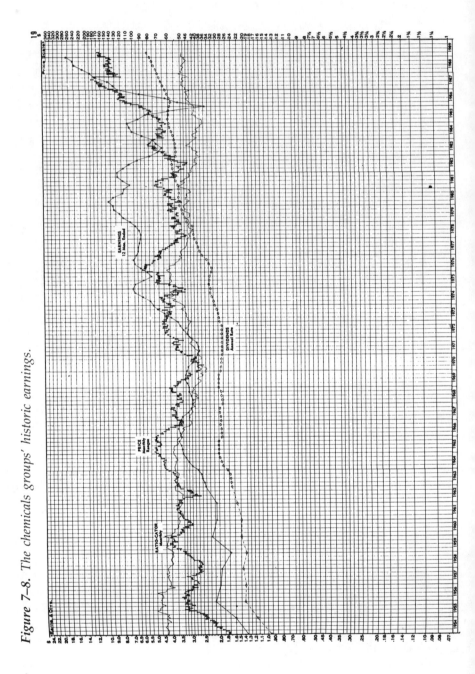

Figure 7–8. The chemicals groups' historic earnings.

218

of the favorable effect of currency translation. The industry outlook is bullish in an environment characterized by strong economic growth, declining interest rates, a soft dollar, a prospering agriculture sector, rising consumer spending, and flourishing international economies. Those are the most important catalysts determining the chemicals industry's long-term trend.

Figure 7–8 illustrates the historic earnings records for the chemicals industry. The graph shows that the group has tended to display cyclical earnings behavior that generally depends on the state of the economy.

Other than the chemicals groups, the paper and forest products, containers, metals and glass, aluminum, copper, coal, steel and precious metals are also classified as basic industries. These groups are heavily dependent upon supply and demand for commodities. Their earnings are cyclical in nature and are prime beneficiaries of inflation. Their sales and revenues fluctuate violently during periods of expansion or contraction of the economy. They are also known for being late cycle movers. Toward the end of an economic boom, when most other industry groups are topping out and on their way to a bear market, these groups may strengthen. In the past they have tended to be in a countertrend to the broad market direction.

TRANSPORTATION INDUSTRY GROUPS

Groups in this category consist of the railroads, truckers, air freight, and the airlines industries. Their earnings are cyclical in nature and highly dependent upon general economic conditions. It is important to note that these groups constitute the Dow Jones Transportation Average. They represent the pulse of business and are considered a true barometer of the economy.

CONCLUSION

The purpose of the foregoing discussion of industry group characteristics is to introduce the reader to some of the peculiarity associated with different sectors. The interest rate sectors, for example, could alert investors to the rising risk when they begin to display weakness. Consumer staples, while growth oriented, are usually analyzed differently as their cyclical fluctuation depends on overall consumption demand in the economy. Raw material sensitive sectors are often a predictor of future inflationary pressures as their earnings tend to be sensitive to commodity price fluctuations. Durable goods stocks, mainly the autos and homebuilders, fluctuate widely during the expansion and contraction phrases of the economic cycle. Some industry groups may lead the way during the early stages of the bull market while others may participate with vengeance as the economy is about to slow down. There are industry groups that are in a long-term secular growth trend while others are having difficulty matching their prior growth measures. Sector analysis is particularly important during the portfolio structuring process. Depending on their growth potential, portfolios could be filled in favor of those that hold the best promise of future growth.

❑ 8

Fundamental Investment Dynamics

The fundamental factors are slow-moving. They are so important that they practically rule the eventual trend of stock prices but, because they generally change slowly and act slowly, their effect upon prices is more in consonance with long-term movements than with the intermediate swings.

Richard W. Schabacker, 1933

Fundamental analysis is the study of a firm's finances, leverage, profitability, and ability to face business challenges and grow. Fundamental analysis is best for projecting long-term earnings performance and for determining the future value of a security. There are several factors that should be considered in order to determine investment appeal—one is whether or not a company is selling far below its intrinsic worth. The question then becomes: How much is the company worth? The firm's book value may be higher or lower than its market price. Simultaneously, it may be laden with cash and little or no debt. But, is hoarding cash a sign of prudence or of an inability to exploit opportunities? Is high book value a guarantee of price appreciation? What is the threshold leverage point beyond which the overall financial position of a company may be jeopardized? Which is more important: sales, earnings, or asset growth? Does the industry group outlook determine the price of companies operating in it? How can industry group characteristics be used in asset allocation and portfolio structuring? There is no single answer to these investment questions, yet sound fundamentals should be the catalyst behind the trend. The more supportive factors there are, the more likely the price will appreciate in the marketplace. The next few pages examine some of the fundamental factors that serve as the catalyst that propels trends in securities markets.

BOOK VALUE

The valuation of common stocks based on their book value is one of the oldest methods used to measure their intrinsic worth. The book value is the difference between the company's total assets and its total liabilities. Stated on a per-share basis, the book value represents what shareholders own after all debts are liquidated.

Over the years, the book value theory has been replaced by the earnings momentum concept. The apparent reason is that the book value only counts in case of total liquidation. In finance, book value can mitigate, along with other factors, the level of risk of a bond issued by a firm. However, in the early 1920s, the investment community became convinced that the book value theory should apply only to cases of takeover. Indeed, a company may sell for many years at a discount vis-à-vis its book value. Fund managers then abandoned the book value theory, which was replaced by the firm foundation that is based on the firm's intrinsic value and its potential for future earnings growth.

Stocks Selling Below Book Value

The book value technique, however, was revived in the wake of the takeover mania of the 1980s. When a stock is selling below its worth, the theory goes, shareholders can benefit if there is a takeover attempt or in case of total liquidation. Seldom has a company been liquidated and the value of its assets distributed to its shareholders. Yet, stocks selling at discounts from book value may offer above-average appreciation potential, provided that they have healthy fundamentals. And this is exactly what happened during the "roaring eighties." After a decade of lingering stock performance and mediocre appreciation, the price of the real corporate assets far outpaced the disclosed value, which was carried at historic acquisition cost. Corporate real estate holdings, in particular, soared in the marketplace although still being reported at low book value prices. This, in turn, led to the takeover mania that

swept the securities markets in that decade and invited corporate raiders. They bid for a company, took it private, stripped
its valuable assets, and recouped all that had been paid for it.
The net result was a new company still operating in the same
field, generating cash flow, and maintaining its market share
position, but without much in the way of real assets.

From a broad investment standpoint, however, the book
value theory offers some help in valuing common stocks. As
mentioned, when a stock is selling below its book value it may
invite takeover. Moreover, this may encourage its management
to invest excess cash to buy back some of its shares from the
open market at less than their net asset value. When the number of shares floating decreases, the stock price may rise, as a
reduced number of shares may enhance the reported earnings
per share and other financial ratios. While investment decisions should not be made based on any single criterion, stocks
selling at a discount from their book value should be carefully
analyzed in order to assess their fundamental position. Should
there be other favorable factors, investors should be alert to the
potential capital appreciation that the stock may have.

The real book value of a company is often understated on
the balance sheet, as assets are reported at their historical cost
instead of their replacement value. The relatively low multiples
during the inflationary 1970s and the swelling values of corporate real estate in the 1980's left behind a large number of
companies selling far below their true worth in the marketplace. Investors were suddenly awakened to the fact that
buying the whole company was more beneficial than buying a
share of its stock.

Not only was corporate real estate value distorted on the
balance sheet, the dollar amount assigned to the firm's good
will was also evaluated at deep discount. Several companies
with established brand-name products were selling in the stock
market at P/E multiples that understated the value of their
market share, historical experience, and marketing know-how.
General Foods, Dart & Craft, RJR-Nabisco, R.H. Macy and
many others were acquired because they commanded great
appeal at their then-current prices on the Exchange.

In general, there are some industry groups in which investors may find many stocks selling at a discount from their real worth. For example, mining stocks and natural resource companies with large reserves tend to sell close to, or at a discount from, their book value. The historical costs of their reserves of raw materials is usually understated on the balance sheet. Paper stocks may carry timber that is reported at a much lower value than its real market price. The same can be said about capital-intensive stocks such as steel, textiles, and railroad companies. For these industries, the natural reserves are reported on the balance sheet at historical costs when they should be reported at their current replacement value in the open market.

Variations on the Book Value Theme

Industry groups tend to sell at different prices relative to their book values. Technology stocks tend to have a relatively modest assets base. But they command historically high good will because of their super growth potential. They usually sell at several times their book value per share. The same can be said about drug companies and, in general, of all emerging growth stocks. The market's discounting mechanism assigns a higher multiple to account for their potential earnings growth.

Although the book value investment approach regained popularity in the 1980s, it continues to be suitable only for institutional investors who can raise the needed money to acquire these bargains. Considering the book value method alone leaves a lot to be desired. Investors who, for one reason or another, cannot buy the whole company, should be advised to rely on other factors. Indeed, companies with high book value per share that cannot generate revenues commensurate with the size of their assets may lack the management skills necessary to generate reasonable returns on these assets. In some instances, the size of the assets may even represent a drain on revenues, as the assets may require more service or maintenance than the returns they produce. The value of the assets of a particular stock is far less important than management's ability to use those assets to increase shareholders' equity.

THE POWER OF EARNINGS

The most important of all the fundamental catalysts is the power of earnings. There is no doubt that when a company is profitable and earns consistent returns that its performance in the marketplace will be enhanced. The power of earnings can be used to lower debt, finance future expansions, generate internal resources for acquisition, increase solvency, invest in research and development for future growth, and improve the overall quality of the balance sheet.

Earnings Variations

Returns may vary from one sector to another and from one company to another. Earnings characteristics of industry groups vary widely during the different stages of the business cycle; they depend upon the economic environment. As a discounting mechanism, the market anticipates future earnings developments. The price of a security may often decline in anticipation of weakening fundamentals and falling earnings prospects. Often the market leads the deterioration in earnings by a few quarters and the price decline in stocks long before poor results are announced. Thus, it pays to examine a number of real-life examples of the behavior of earnings vis-à-vis stock prices.

Case 1. Case 1 illustrates the earnings and securities price behavior of Sara Lee Corporation, a member of the food industry group. As figure 8–1 shows, the relationship here is straightforward: earnings continued to rise over the years and so did the stock price. Also notice that dividends increased over the years. Despite the economic recession of 1981–82, Sara Lee fluctuated within a narrow trading range while its earnings momentum continued to improve unabated. As soon as the bull market started in earnest in 1982, stock price advanced

Figure 8–1. *Monthly stock prices of Sara Lee Corp.*

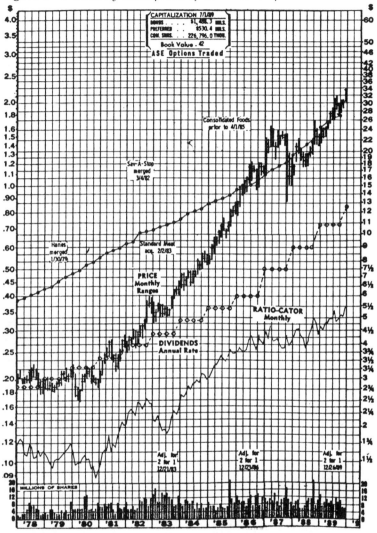

aggressively to reflect those powerful earning trends. The Crash of 1987 briefly interrupted the uptrend, but it resumed its advance afterward when the broad market stabilized.

Case 2. In case 2, price acceleration led earnings improvements. Figure 8–2 illustrates the earnings and price behavior of

Merck, a leading pharmaceutical company. In general and over the years, Merck's earnings performance has been steadily growing. Its upside momentum slowed down during the 1981–82 economic recession. But, as the bull market of 1982 got underway, the stock price accelerated upward in anticipation of a fast rise in earnings. Indeed Merck sold at a healthy premium during most of the 1980s, as its P/E multiple consistently outperformed the market and most of the drug group securities.

Figure 8–2. Merck monthly graph.

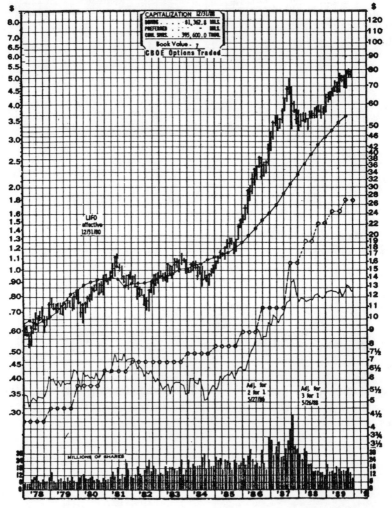

Figure 8–3. *Valhi Inc., ups and downs.*

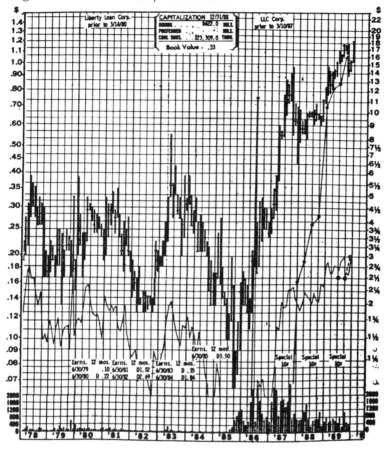

Case 3. In case 3, stocks rose in anticipation of improving earnings. Figure 8–3 illustrates the case of Valhi Inc. For many years, the company has been in the red. In 1985, the stock price declined precipitously to a new all-time low. Just when the outlook appeared bleak the stock then reversed its downward trend and stampeded upward, still in the face of a deficit. The stock continued to rise in the absence of any earnings improvement for two consecutive years. In 1988, the company's earnings rebounded sharply, only to confirm the market's anticipation of this major improvement. Notice that in this example, the stock price behavior was completely divorced from the

broad market action. Its rise occurred at a mature phase of the business cycle.

Case 4.   Case 4 concerns emerging growth and powerful earnings momentum. Figure 8–4 illustrates two examples of stocks that experienced major fundamental improvement and earnings growth: Automatic Data Processing (ADP) and Ennis Business Forms (EBF). In both cases, earnings rose during the 1981–82 economic recession and so did their securities prices.

Notice that in 1981–82, although the Dow Jones Industrial Average declined from around the 1000 mark to below 700, ADP rose from $11 per share to as high as $16 per share. Similarly, EBF held during the 1981–82 bear market and moved marginally higher. It then stampeded upward when the market launched its major uptrend.

Case 5.   In case 5, the stock price anticipates peaks in earnings. Figure 8–5 illustrates the monthly bar chart of Bank of New England (NEB). Since 1978, earnings have been rising. After a shallow decline during the 1981–82 recession, earnings resumed their healthy advance into early 1987.

Because of an extended real estate market in the northeast, the market anticipated that any rebound in earnings would only be temporary. Also, the market focused on mortgage loan vulnerability and the potential default risk. While earnings indeed recovered in 1988, the stock price continued to display loss of upward momentum. As a matter of fact, NEB continued to decline well ahead of the crippling losses that the bank announced late 1989. Apparently, in this case, the price weakness could not have been anticipated, as the subtle deterioration occurred amid healthy earnings announcements. But, because the market looked beyond the rosy picture, it correctly foresaw the end of the real estate speculative bubble and the vulnerability of the Bank of New England to major default risk.

Figure 8–5 also illustrates the example of Cray Research Inc. (CYR), a company that once grew at a fast pace and then started to fade. Here again, after a mild decline during the 1981–82 economic recession, both earnings and the stock price stampeded upward. CYR's peak coincided with the surge in earnings in the first quarter of 1987. The Crash of 1987, broke

Figure 8–4. Automatic Data Processing and Ennis Business Forms.

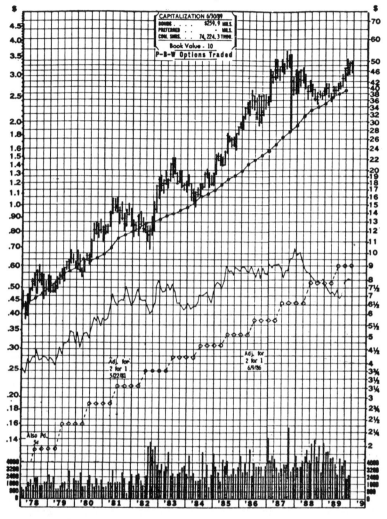

the stock's long-term upward momentum. From that point on, the market failed to respond to the rebound in earnings and became more concerned with future growth potential. The message was that the earnings power of CYR was past its peak and that past performance would be difficult to match.

Case 6. In case 6, the market is shown to anticipate earnings improvements. The example of Walt Disney Productions

Figure 8–4. (continued)

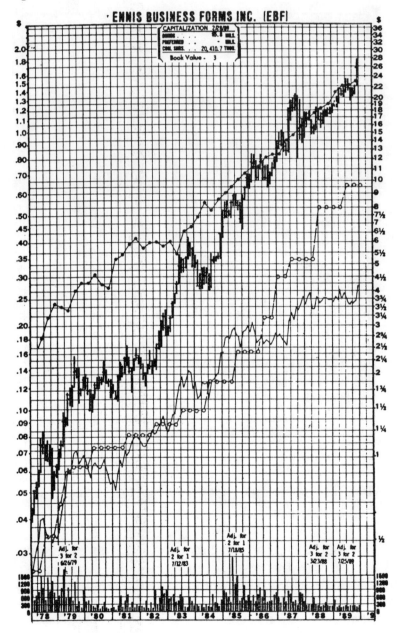

Figure 8–5. Bank of New England and Cray Research Inc., monthly graphs.

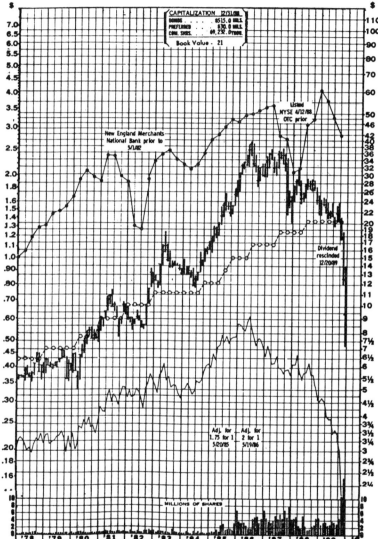

(Disney) demonstrates the market's ability to forecast real long-term growth potential. As illustrated in figure 8–6, Disney had consistent earnings declines from 1981 to first quarter 1984. Yet, the stock price held firm and ignored what the earnings numbers suggested. As soon as the earnings outlook began to show some promise, the stock price advanced aggressively.

Figure 8–5. (continued)

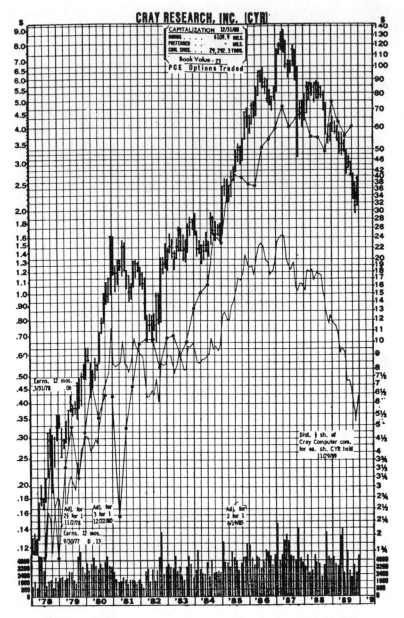

Even the devastating Crash of 1987 did not constitute any serious threat to the overall trend. Earnings continued to grow, and Disney continued to charge to new highs. The market correctly weighed the potential growth of the firm and held during the earnings weakness phase. When promising signs of earnings growth began to be reflected in the quarterly results, the stock price rose rapidly.

Figure 8–6. *Walt Disney Productions.*

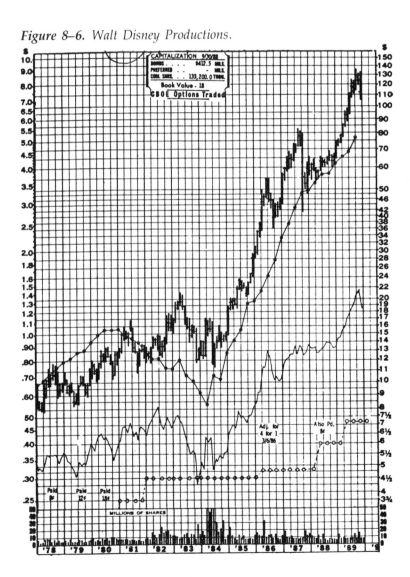

The Price/Earnings Ratio

The price-earnings ratio is an important tool in identifying undervalued securities. In an environment of low inflation and declining interest rates it tends to expand. Under such conditions, stock prices advance in anticipation of an improving economic background. This, in turn, attracts investors to the possibility of realizing capital gains and increases the demand for stocks. And vice versa, when interest rates rise and inflationary pressure builds, the price/earnings ratio contracts in anticipation of lower earnings and a slowdown in business activities.

Studies of many portfolios with low P/E ratios reveal that they outperformed the market over the long term. However, a stock with a low P/E ratio may be selling cheaply in anticipation of lower earnings. It may also be that investors are not optimistic about the stock's growth outlook. Stocks in mature industries usually sell at modest P/E ratios. "Smokestack" industries, such as steel, textiles, and chemicals are good examples of sectors that tend to have modest multiples. Low P/E ratios have a compelling investment appeal as this makes the company less susceptible to disappointments. Subdued expectations limit its vulnerability.

There are some industries that consistently sell at relatively high P/E ratios. Such groups are favored by investors because of their future potential growth. Among those industries are pharmaceuticals, semiconductors, computers, health care, and software companies. There is nothing wrong with investing in stocks with high P/E ratios as long as they show a good track record of earnings acceleration. Moreover, stocks with moderate but consistent growth rates also sell at relatively high P/E ratios.

However, investing in high P/E ratio companies can be dangerous if growth targets are not met or exceeded. Stocks with high P/E multiples tend to be volatile and attract attention. Their rise or fall is usually swift and unrelenting. In most cases they sell far above their book value, because optimism prevails. At the first shadow of disappointing results, however, they plunge, when investors suddenly awaken to their overvaluation. When investing in emerging growth companies, investors should refrain from buying those that are selling at high P/E multiples, especially when the economy is slowing down. Sales should continue to increase independent of the business cycle for a company to be truly considered emerging growth and, hence, deserving of a high P/E multiple.

Thoughts on Earnings and Stock Prices

When judging the market trend in terms of earnings, investors must factor in the waves of optimism and pessimism that sweep the investment arena. There are periods when the market commands high earnings multiples and others when the prices remain subdued for many years. Figure 8–7 illustrates the S&P Composite Index vis-à-vis its earnings since 1953. For almost a quarter of a century, spanning the 1950s, 1960s, and early 1970s, optimism prevailed, and the securities markets witnessed a secular advance that was only briefly interrupted by cyclical declines. In the 1970s, the psychological makeup of the investment arena was overwhelmed by the inflation's devastating impact on earnings quality. The outlook was clouded, and demand for stocks slackened. In the 1980s, when the Fed demonstrated serious intentions to fight inflation, the market enjoyed a terrific advance.

The study of the market price-earnings mechanism may not apply to all industry groups, and certainly not to individual stocks. For example, airline stocks are cyclical; their earnings fluctuate wildly with the business cycle. The aerospace group's performance is highly dependent upon the fiscal policy in place and allocation of defense expenditures. Raw materials prices are subject to shortages and excessive inventory and can influence the price behavior of aluminum, copper, forest products, precious and nonprecious metals, and most other mining stocks. Automobile stocks and the building-related industries tend to reflect the behavior of capital goods sales during the different stages of the business cycle. Banks are often vulnerable to losses and default on both their business and consumer loans. Foods, beverages, and drugs, while stable in their long-term growth potential, can still be faced with unexpected developments concerning product lines and face liabilities that could cripple their balance sheets. Chemical and paper stocks

Figure 8-7. S&P composite versus its earnings.

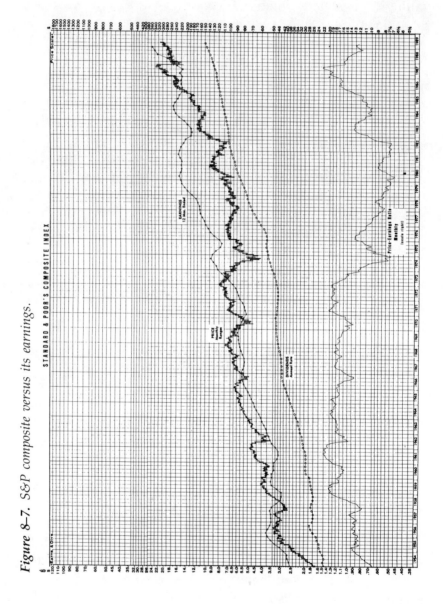

238

are sensitive to business conditions and follow closely the cyclical expansion and contraction of demand. Electronics, computers, semiconductor, and software companies have tremendous growth potential. Yet a case-by-case study may reveal the inability of certain fast-moving candidates to manage growth and cope with the fast pace of new product development. Such firms may soar in one cycle, then fall into oblivion when they fail to bring new products to the marketplace.

COMPREHENSIVE SECURITY ANALYSIS

Predicting earnings is difficult when forecasts are projected without considering the economic environment. A reasonable assessment is possible only when the nature of the industry under study is factored into the final analysis. It is true that the power of earnings is the driving catalyst that propels securities trends, but there are other fundamental factors that can shed light on the potential for future growth. Financial ratios trends, when put in perspective, can reveal improvement or deterioration. A comprehensive analysis of a multitude of fundamental factors and their record over a period of years can help investors gain a comprehensive perspective of the true value of a stock. Furthermore, comparison between the underlying fundamentals of several companies within a particular industry group can help determine relative investment value.

Dynamic Financial Analysis

The balance sheet is like a snapshot of a company's financial data, one which describes the firm's position on the day it closed the books on its fiscal year. The income statement, however, provides details about the company's operating results during the entire year. Both statements are important, but the income statement is the more helpful one in evaluating the quality of earnings. The income statement shows the net proceeds after subtracting the cost of running the business from its net sales or total revenues. The per-share earnings can be inflated by drawing down reserves, capitalizing expenditures, and cutting costs of activities critical to future growth—such as advertising and research and development.

Thorough financial statement analysis can be extremely complicated and tedious. Also, analysis of the company's fundamental position can hardly be of any benefit without a working knowledge of the economic environment in which the company is operating.

Dynamic fundamental analysis is the consistent monitoring of the company's financial position over a period of time. A study of the trend of the liquidity, leverage, profitability, and investment ratios over a number of years reveals the progression of key fundamental factors under varying business conditions. Moreover, comparison of several companies' financial ratios within the same industry group can help identify their value. In order to explain the concept of dynamic fundamental analysis, real-life situations must be studied to see how to incorporate the technique into an overall assessment.

Case 1. Case 1 reviews Phelps Dodge, a leading copper producer. This is a true multidisciplinary analysis of a company that has endured industry difficulties and emerged from severe financial hardships. In the early 1980s, the industry faced hardships because of a glut in copper in the world market. The demand for this commodity plummeted and had an inverse impact on the financial position of companies operating in this industry. Figure 8–8 illustrates the stock price history, spot copper prices, and a number of financial ratios describing Phelps Dodge's financial position.

During the 1983–86 period, the price of Phelps Dodge in the marketplace basically reflected the copper-producing companies' poor and deteriorating fundamentals. Net sales and net income were sagging. The return on equity was negative overall, and the long-term debt to total capital later remained relatively high, at some 40 percent. Spot copper prices kept declining in the open market and exercised pressure on profit margins. Slowly but surely the excess supply of copper was worked out during those years. Also, demand was fueled by the expanding economy. In 1987, the price of copper began to rise, as demand started to exceed supply. Meanwhile, Phelps Dodge's financial position began to improve slowly. Net sales

Figure 8–8. Copper, Phelps Dodge, and its fundamentals.

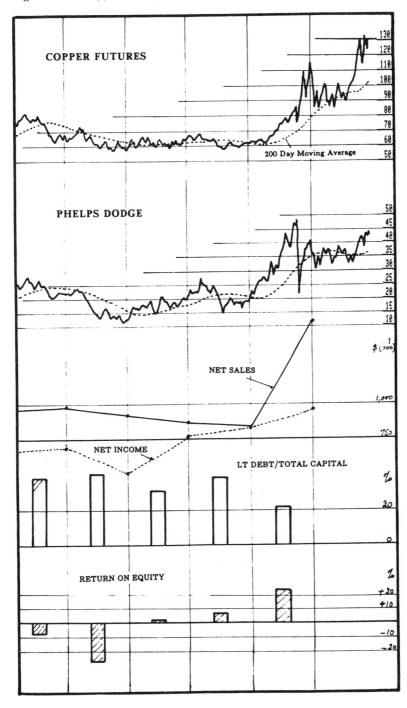

exploded and net income rose. The return on equity rose to a
healthy level and jumped over 20 percent in 1987. Operating
margins improved, and the excess liquidity helped pay a good
part of the outstanding debt. After the temporary but violent
shakeout following the Crash of 1987, the price of Phelps
Dodge stock recovered. But even more important is that, in
1988 as shortages developed for this vital industrial commodity, the price of copper resumed its advance. This was another
indication that the good times for Phelps Dodge were not yet
over. As a matter of fact, the price of the stock, driven by
improving fundamentals and soaring demand for the firm's
products, proceeded in 1989 to sell at some $65 per share. This
example demonstrates that a study of the balance sheet or the
income statement may barely indicate improvement. But a
study of the progression of the fundamental dynamics and the
catalysts that drive an industry or a stock can give investors an
edge in identifying potential. Similarly, a further price rise in
Phelps Dodge stock could have been anticipated independent
of broad market conditions.

Case 2. Case 2 involves a comparative analysis of IBM
and Compaq. Comparison of fundamental perspectives of
stocks in the same industry can reveal causes of weakness or
strength in specific issues or the group at large. In order to
illustrate the power of such a technique, the financial position
of two technology stocks will be examined. The first is IBM, a
giant company in a fast-growing industry. The frontiers of
supertechnology hold a great promise for the future of
mankind—yet IBM, probably because of its size, is considered
by many analysts and investors to be a mature company that
has probably reached the border of diseconomies of scale. Such
diseconomies occur when a company grows to a very large
size—and it becomes exceedingly difficult for it to achieve high
rates of growth. Planning for future growth opportunities in
the marketplace and control of the cost of operations may have
become tedious tasks for management to reckon with. This,
however does not mean that such a blue-chip stock cannot
continue to grow in an orderly manner. All it means is that it
becomes harder to set high rates of growth and profitability the
larger a firm becomes.

The second company chosen for comparison, Compaq Computers, is one of the fastest-growing companies in the history of corporate America. From selling only portable personal computers, the firm was able to soar to an enviable size in only a few years. Obviously, the task of comparing the financial position and growth ratios between these two highly regarded companies is not that simple.

Figure 8–9 is like a snapshot of some of the most important financial ratios vis-à-vis the stock price of IBM. When the great bull market started in 1982, IBM quickly stampeded from below $60 per share to a little over $130 per share. The market correction that ensued in 1984 pulled the price down to the $100 dollar mark. As the bull market resumed its upward rise, IBM soared to the $160 area, in 1986. With the rebound in stock prices in 1987, IBM pushed upward to an even higher level. Then came the Crash of 1987, and the stock declined to close to its lows of 1984. Subsequently, the market overcame the devastating fear of meltdown and proceeded to rise to new highs. Yet IBM lagged and continued to meander around those multi-year lows.

A quick review of IBM's financial ratios reveals some subtle deterioration. The firm's return on equity started to decline, from more than 20 percent per year to around 15 percent. Still an enviable rate of return, yet lower than what the company was able to achieve for many years. While net sales continued to grow in an orderly fashion, IBM's net income peaked in 1985. Its operating margins, too, were squeezed and also declined from more than 20 percent to around the 15-percent mark. Finally, and more serious, is that IBM's leverage position deteriorated as its long-term debt to total capital ratio rose. Given that technology companies are characterized by low leverage ratios, this development may have raised concerns. The slight, yet apparent, deterioration of IBM's fundamental position appears to have been the reason behind the stock's performance in the marketplace. This example is probably the best testimony to the efficiency of financial markets and their ability to discount the true fundamental catalysts governing the future performance of securities.

The second company under study, Compaq Computers, is illustrated in figure 8–10. In 1984, when the stock had just been

Figure 8–9. A "snapshot" of IBM and its financial ratios.

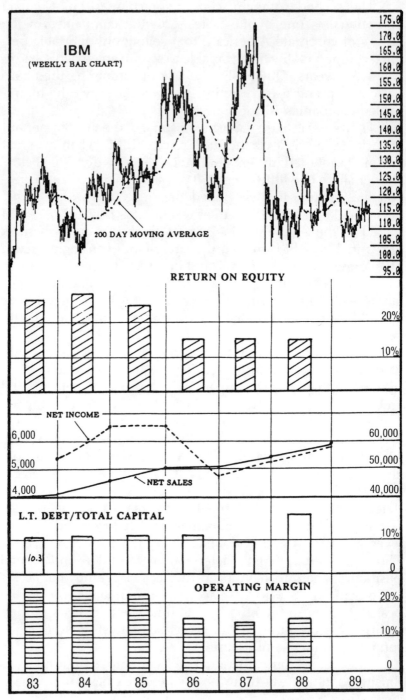

Figure 8–10. *Compaq Computers and its fundamentals.*

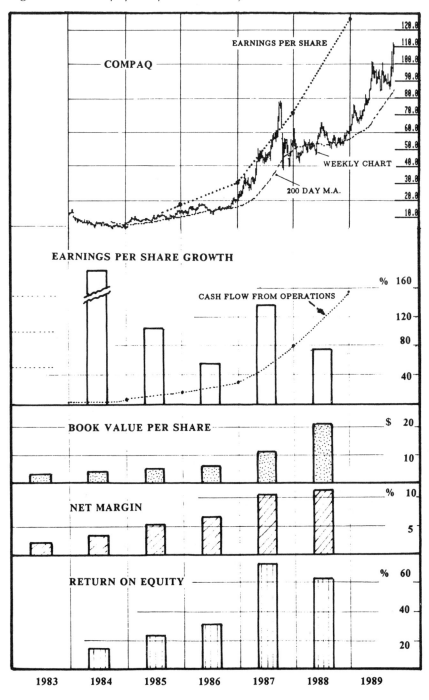

listed on the Exchange, the price plunged swiftly from some
$16 per share to a little below $4 per share. But by early 1985,
the stock regained its upward momentum and started a fascinating long-term uptrend that carried the stock to its all-time
high, more than $100 per share in 1989—more than 25 times
higher than its lows—in only five years.

Earnings per share during those years soared rapidly as
earnings grew at 50 percent or better during that period. The
firm's book value rose from below $5 per share to well over $20
per share in just a few years. Its cash flow from operations
advanced at a meteoric speed. Yet, while the company grew at
this phenomenal rate, its management was able to control the
cost, and its net margins actually expanded to more than 10
percent by 1986. The signs of progress and a promising future
were reflected in all the financial numbers. The end result was
that Compaq Computers generated returns on equity that
could hardly be matched by any other company ever. Here
again the market's ability to discount future growth proved to
be uncanny. The stock price justifiably soared manyfold and,
despite the crash of 1987, Compaq consolidated for awhile and
then charged to further new highs. Not only did the company
make products that were well received in the marketplace, it
also introduced the personal computer business to the wonders
of faster and more efficient chip technologies. Compaq dared to
challenge the dominance of IBM and to compel the industry to
innovate—and the financial markets were there to celebrate
this now legendary success. In both examples, the market's
discounting mechanism was at work.

A comparison between the two companies may bring closer to home the wide difference in performance of IBM and
Compaq. Figure 8–11 illustrates some of the pertinent measures of growth in both cases. Although it bears repeating that
the comparison between the two giant corporations may not be
simple, such comparison still helps visualize the big difference
between their growth rates. Notice, for example, that at 10
percent, sales growth for IBM on some $70 billion in revenues
is much larger than the 80 percent growth rate for Compaq
with only $4 billion in sales. Also, the reinvestment rate of both
companies may not be grounds for comparison because of the

Figure 8–11. *IBM versus Compaq.*

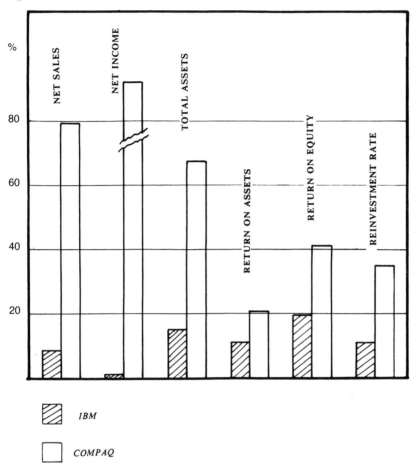

wide difference in size, yet it illustrates how Compaq's management crafted the fast-growing pace of the company.

Finally, if a picture is worth thousands of words, figure 8–12 is a snapshot of the performance of Compaq and IBM stock prices relative to the market. Notice how the two performances were diverging, which can be explained in light of the underlying fundamentals at the time.

Case 3. This example contemplates global analysis of the auto group. An in-depth comparison of the performance of

Figure 8–12. Compaq *versus IBM, relative performance.*

several stocks in the same industry group explains the subdued price performance of General Motors relative to the auto group during the great bull market of the 1980s.

The second leading American auto manufacturer, Ford, and the Japanese auto giant, Honda Motors, both rose several times over at that time. General Motors, meanwhile, although it did rise, did not gain much relative to those two auto manufacturers. The difference in performance between those companies and General Motors is further illustrated in figure 8–13, which shows how Ford and Honda fared relative to GM from 1985–87. Furthermore, the graph also shows how badly General Motors lagged the Dow Jones Industrial Average during the same period. However, the plunge of the broad market and all auto stocks during the Crash of 1987 may have marked the beginning of the end of that disparity.

Why GM behaved as it did during that time may be explained by its loss of worldwide market share, for Ford came out with excellent cars and Honda continued its penetration of the world market. But a look at the relative fundamental positions of a large number of well-known automobile companies around the globe paints a different picture. Figure 8–14 illustrates a broad comparison of some key growth and financial ratios of six auto companies with global presences.

The five-year annual growth rate of auto companies indicates that GM was surpassed only by Ford. The total assets growth rate of GM surpassed all other car manufacturers during 1983–87. Realizing the difference in size between these companies and GM, the dollar amount by which GM actually grew can be appreciated. However, it should be noted here that the reason may have been the tremendous appreciation of corporate real estate value at that time. With regard to returns on assets, GM fared second to Ford, but better than most of the other members of the group. Similarly, the return on equity numbers indicated that GM came third after Ford and Volvo.

This comparison of several key determinants of fundamental performance does not explain why GM underperformed the market and the other auto firms so badly. The question then should be: was it due to some fundamental deficiency with GM stock or was it a case of undervaluation and unwarranted negative psychology? It may have been a combination of both,

Figure 8–13. *Relative performance of GM versus Ford and Honda, and the Dow.*

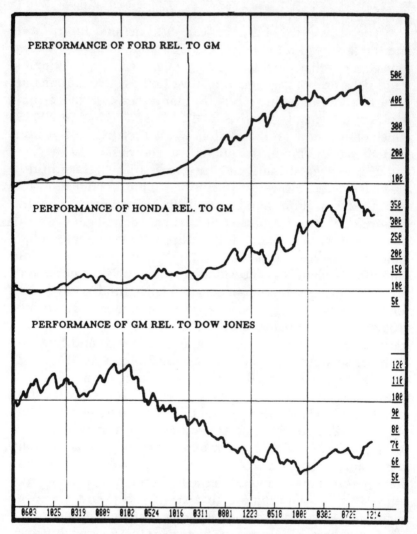

but such a study reveals that the low multiples that GM sold at for most of the 1980s may have been too low, given the overall fundamental perspectives and the low risk that GM represented as an investment.

Case 4. Case 4 comprises a fundamentals comparison among pharmaceutical firms. Food and health-care companies

Figure 8–14. *A broad comparison of the auto group.*

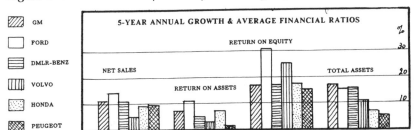

are probably among the most stable industries in the world. They both provide products that sustain life. The food industry is a defensive investment vehicle that, barring unexpected disasters or mismanagement of financial resources, should have stable returns. The drug group, on the other hand, is both defensive and growth oriented. Not only are the demographic factors compelling, but also increasing health awareness has raised the demand for all sorts of personal-care products. For example, figure 8–15 represents a summary of pertinent fundamental factors that are used to value drug companies. The figure illustrates some key financial ratios of six pharmaceutical companies. By looking at the diagram, their financial position can be better visualized and their relative investment appeal compared.

The study covers the 1983–88 period. As the graph demonstrates, the five-year average return on equity has been better than 20 percent for all drug stocks. American Home Products (AHP) led the group with a whopping 34 percent on an annualized basis, followed closely by Merck. Return on assets, too, was healthy for these pharmaceutical companies, with AHP outperforming the group on that score. In the five-year average operating margins and net margins categories, both Merck and AHP held the top two spots. The book value was highest for Pfizer, Merck, and American Home Products. But in five-year annual earnings and annual dividends growth, Merck stood high on the list. In addition, it also exceeded the group average in the five-year annual net sales and net income growth.

Such a comparison may lead investors to invest in Merck if they are in search of the best past fundamental performance in

Figure 8–15. An illustration of a fundamental comparison of stocks in the drug group.

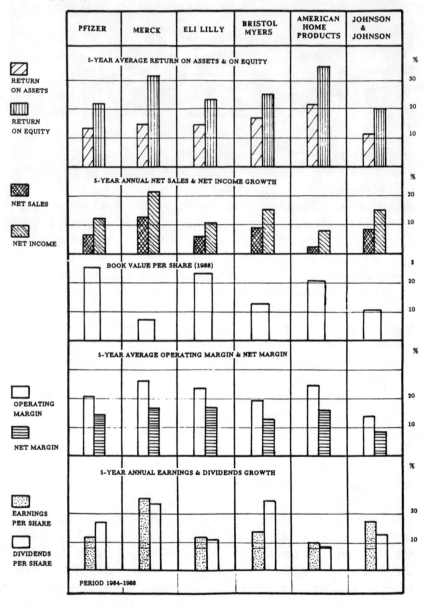

the drug group. However, AHP had little to show for on the earnings and dividends growth. Also, Pfizer may be further assessed as a candidate for long-term commitments, given its healthy track record and high book value.

Such a comparison of the fundamental dynamics of a group can reveal both the state of financial health of the overall industry and the potential winners. At a glance, fundamental comparison illustrates the track record of a number of companies operating under similar circumstances and in unique business environments. Such analysis can also quicken the decision-making process, as it crystallizes the key fundamental catalysts that potentially can affect the price of these stocks. One basis for comparison that has not been incorporated in this study so far is that of relative price-earnings multiples. It is apparent that all members of the group are in a sound financial position. Under such circumstances, it may make sense to choose those companies that are selling at a lower P/E ratio than the rest.

Case 5. This study addresses the multi-industry comparison of fundamentals. Comparing industry group performance over the course of a number of years can simplify investment choices and portfolio selections. For the purpose of this study, the five-year earnings per share growth rate and average return on equity from 1984–88 will be examined. Figure 8–16 illustrates those two key financial ratios.

The graph gives a visual representation of how the different industry groups fared relative to each other. The computer software and information processing groups had the highest earnings per-share growth, followed closely by the forest products, the entertainment, and the papers sectors. Ironically, with the exception of entertainment, the prices of all these groups suffered a decline during 1989. Although forest products scored a respectable earnings per-share growth, they had poor return on equity for the period under study. What is even more surprising is the unusual weakness of the technology-related stocks, which clearly demonstrated excellent growth on both fundamental measures. Moreover, the air transport group underperformed most other industries on either score, but had an excellent rally in 1989 accompanied by rumors of takeovers

Figure 8-16. An inter-industry comparison of earnings growth and return on equity.

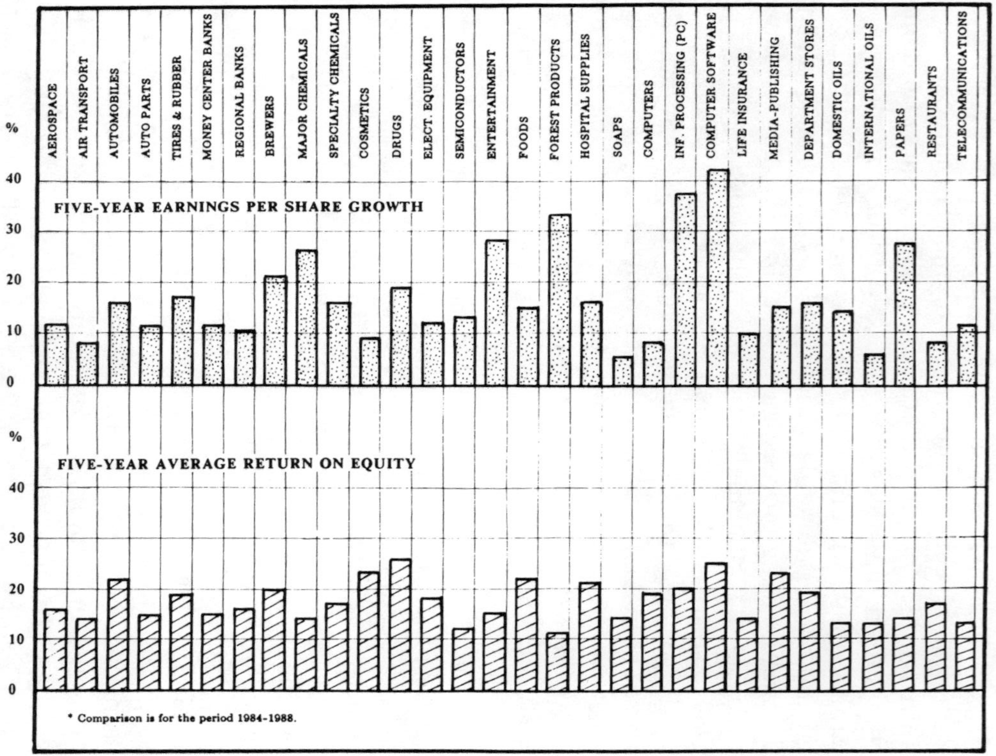

254

by United Airlines and other airline companies. The drug industry had a healthy earnings per-share growth rate and one of the highest returns on equity. Drug companies had the best of both worlds—they staged a strong advance in 1989 that was supported by enticing fundamentals.

The systematic analysis of relative industry group performance serves as an initial study of underlying fundamentals. Although such analysis may not provide much information about the future, it constitutes a preliminary assessment of the positions of the different sectors of the market. It should be considered from a general perspective, to lay the foundation for further detailed studies of the individual groups and specific stocks.

Figure 8–17 illustrates the leverage position of a large number of groups during 1988. The industries with the highest long-term debt to capital ratio at that time were cosmetics, tires and rubber products, restaurants, airlines, oil companies, and department stores. The drug and information-processing groups had the lowest leverage ratio. In light of the study of the three factors discussed, namely return on equity, earnings per-share growth, and leverage, it seems even more justifiable that pharmaceutical companies were the stellar performers in 1989. In this case in particular, the dollar weakness also helped the whole group due to the favorable currency translation. When all these fundamental ratios are considered, however, they still fail to explain the weakness of the technology stocks in 1989. Apparently the cause of the decline had to do with the internal dynamics of the group more than with the prevailing fundamental factors. This at once demonstrates that analysis of fundamentals increases investment success and that, just the same, there are occasional, inexplicable aberrations. These can occur at any time and in any industry group. Overall, however, profitable investing is a direct outgrowth of careful assessment.

SPECIAL SITUATIONS

Certain corporate developments can add to the fundamental appeal of a security and its investment potential. Stock buybacks, restructuring, and splits may attract investors' attention

Figure 8–17. Debt profile of industry groups (1988).

DEBT PROFILE OF INDUSTRY GROUPS (1988)

L.T. DEBT/CAPITAL

256

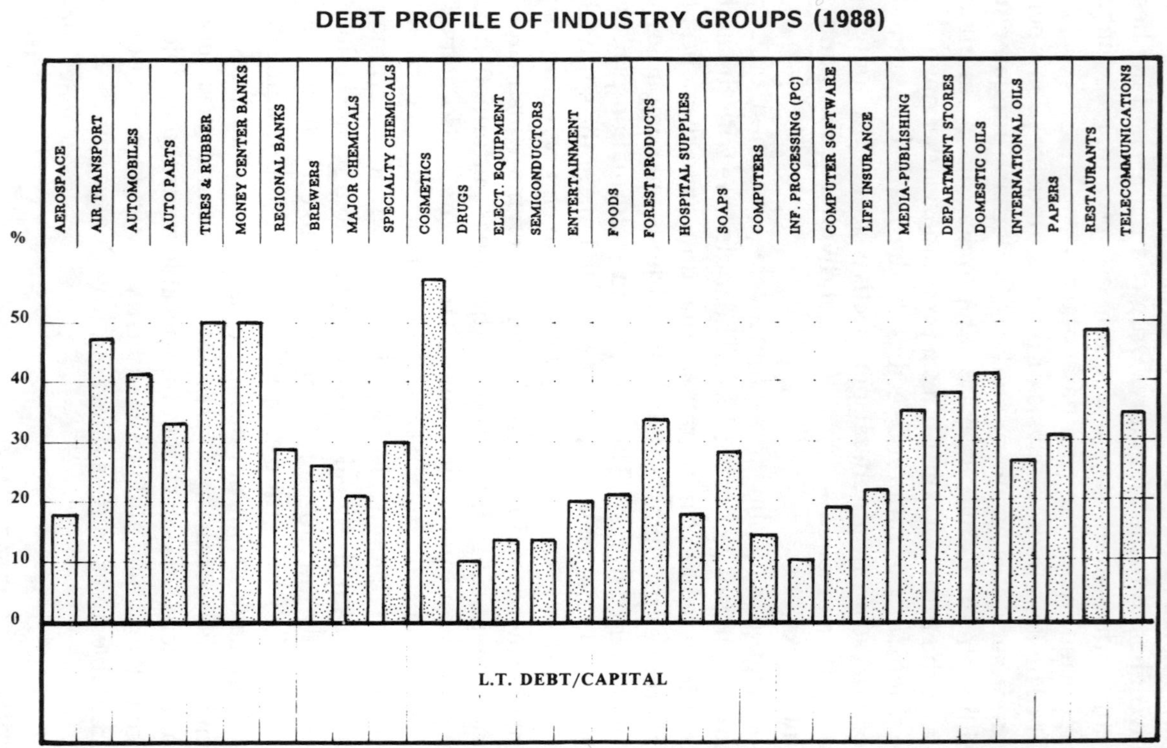

or may indicate potentially promising changes. Such events may also prompt investors to reassess the value of the stock. Divestiture of fixed assets may bring valuable cash to pay debts. Splits bring down the share price and make it more affordable to an increased number of investors. Buybacks can tilt the balance of supply and demand for a company's securities. In order to complement this study of fundamentals, some of these special situations should be examined.

Restructuring

Companies may decide to reposition business operations in the marketplace. This society and economic system are constantly changing. For management to fulfill its duties toward shareholders and maximize shareholders' equity, profit margins have to improve and sales goals have to be achieved. Operations with poor cash flow that restrain earnings growth have to be sold. Unprofitable segments of the company have to be divested. Realignment of operations and consolidation of divisions that serve the same function can save on overhead expenses. Closing out inefficient and antiquated plants is another alternative that management may choose. Layoffs and expense trimming should help improve results. Expanding product lines in the core business while selling marginal operations is strategically important for future growth. Streamlining the corporate structure can yield handsome returns on assets, equity, and net earnings.

As far as investors are concerned, such fundamental improvements can propel a strong upward trend in stock prices. If the divestiture process is timely executed it can enhance long-term value. By focusing on profitable businesses, management may be able to increase profit margins. Instead of spending time, effort, and resources on secondary businesses, corporate planning is focused on fostering those enterprises that are fastest growing and most promising. Proceeds from sales of inefficient subsidiaries can be used to retire debt, buy back stocks, or expand capacity to meet demand. Long-term management objectives can then be better targeted at reshaping operations to cope with decelerating inflation, foreign competition, or new technological advances. In may cases, a new financial structure is created by liquidating or selling segments of the company with large debt financing or marginal returns.

Spinoffs of subsidiaries are another form of restructuring. A company may reorganize its structure, turning it into a holding company. Under such circumstances, the parent company maintains its control, benefits from the flow of equity earnings and decentralizes management decisions, which usually leads to enhanced efficiency. The divestiture of profitable businesses can infuse badly needed cash and be of benefit to stockholders. Investigation of the parent company and the track record of the entity that was "spun off" should be adequately performed. At times, such deals are risky and a thorough study of fundamentals is warranted.

Stock Buyback Programs

Companies may buy back their own shares from the market and retire them as Treasury securities. This reduces the number of shares outstanding. Usually such purchase programs are announced ahead of time. As the number of shares floating decreases, future per-share profits and the shareholders' return on equity are boosted.

Some companies buy back their securities to execute their employees' stock options plans or to meet executives' incentive programs. This is done to prevent the dilution of shareholders' equity which can otherwise result from issuing new shares. The most important of all of the reasons that the company may give for a buyback is that their securities' price is undervalued in the marketplace. Under such circumstances, the company is reinvesting in itself and, hence, enhancing shareholders' equity. Investors have to assess the financial implications of resorting to buyback. If it is achieved through borrowing, then the beneficial impact on earnings and profits per share may only be temporary. Borrowing to buy back its own shares can have a depressing effect on earnings, profit margins, and the overall financial structure of the firm.

Companies are more tempted to implement these programs at times when the price of the stock is selling below the book value stated in the balance sheet. Under such circumstances, the company is acquiring its assets at a discount. Moreover, management may elect to execute such programs when the stock market is low or when alternative investment returns may not be as promising on a comparative basis.

The U.S. Dollar

The strength or weakness of the dollar on the foreign exchange market is important, because most corporations conduct business directly or indirectly with the rest of the world. The position of the dollar has a direct negative impact on earnings. When the dollar is rising, currency translation depresses the reported consolidated earnings. Moreover, export of goods to, and demand for, products from overseas markets declines when the dollar is firm. Most large corporations have a substantial portion of their business overseas. Drug and chemical companies are particularly sensitive to the dollar's position, since a major portion of their earnings is derived from foreign subsidiaries. The fundamental analyst should recognize the trend of the dollar in order to anticipate future earnings.

On the one hand, when the dollar is weak, it negatively affects domestic business because imports become more attractive. On the other hand, it has a beneficial effect on multinational corporations, for it boosts their reported earnings. A stable dollar is the best of both worlds. It helps companies with large overseas operations to profit and plan more effectively; it also retards foreign competition from making inroads into domestic markets.

Financial markets may respond favorably to new concepts or new changes. The prospect of increased earnings growth associated with emerging growth companies is often reflected as a high P/E ratio relative to the broad market—this is the main risk associated with fast-growing companies. The premium that investors could have to pay is a real danger if high expectations do not materialize. Over the years this risk premium has varied; there is no fixed rule as to how high the P/E multiples may go. At the first sign of disappointing financial results, the multiple plummets as the stock tumbles. No matter how high the growth potential of the industry or the company is, unexpected surprises are not tolerated. The price may recover once confidence is reestablished, but often enough the price of the stock remains depressed for a long time.

Emerging growth stocks have appeal for investors. Everyone hopes to detect a fledgling IBM or a baby Xerox. Yet very few emerging growth companies make it to this elite rank. P/E measures have to do with expectations and psychology, so investors should not get carried away with past performance: recessions may adversely affect future growth potential; the company may enter a recession with excessive inventory that cripples its balance sheet or ability to repay debt; moreover obsolescence may quickly cause the company's products to lose their competitive appeal. That is why financial strength and liquidity are key factors to consider when deciding if the company is to survive, let alone continue to grow in the face of a contracting economy. The firm's current ratio and the debt-to-equity proportion bear scrutiny, as they can significantly reduce the company's risk in the business cycle, where exposure equals the risk of bankruptcy during the contraction phase of the business cycle.

CHARACTERISTICS OF GROWTH STOCKS

A sound financial position is the outcome of a number of fundamental factors. Such a position ensures a company's ability to service its debts and generate funds needed to sustain growth and finance future plans. A strong cash position, healthy cash flow, and low debt enable a company to capitalize on market opportunities.

Growth stocks have common characteristics that place them apart from well-managed companies. They may be found in any industry, including mature ones. They tend to have a high profit margin, high return on equity, low dividends payout, and above-average sales growth rate. A high profit margin is the sign of good management, one that keeps cost under control and directs the operation toward promising business. In order to widen the spread between revenues and the costs of operation, a company may restructure its sales mix, expanding those with little or no competition. This maneuver enables the firm to raise prices and pump margins.

Another strategy to help boost margins is that of selling unprofitable operations and maximizing labor and plant capacity. Most fast-growing companies earn above-average returns on shareholders' equity. These returns help them finance rapid expansion without incurring a large amount of debt. Their modest dividend payout is due to the fact that they invest their profits in research and development and other long-term planning purposes. Their sales growth is usually dynamic, as the demand for their products is rising. Cash flow generated from operations should also be growing in order to avoid excessive leverage. A low debt-to-capital ratio is achieved by having the needed liquidity to cover the company's obligation.

Emerging Growth Stocks

New issues are constantly coming into the marketplace. In the first few years, the market tries to assess the long-term potential of the firm based on anticipated growth prospects. There is no rule of thumb that applies to all newly listed companies. The company may have a patent or may be a pioneer in an emerging new industry. The main line of business may hold good promise. Technology, pharmaceuticals, cosmetics, or genetic engineering are some of the fields that may have exciting growth outlooks. Some of the firms may enjoy a fast advance at the beginning, but then fail to manage expansion goals. Such companies rise aggressively for a while, then reverse their trend; and their price falters to levels near to where they came from. Others, which succeed in managing growth either by diversifying their lines of business or expanding their market share, continue on their upward, secular path.

Expectations have a great deal to do with the perception of the company's ultimate potential. Often a stock experiences a decline from the start, as investors realize that they paid more than they should have. Unless management shows an ability to cope with the market risk in their main line of business and effectively handle growth opportunities, the stock may have a limited chance to rise beyond a certain level. Newly listed companies do not necessarily have to be in one of the fast-growing industries. Reebok International and L.A. Gear established their presence in the athletic shoe business, which is a mature but stable industry. Conrail and Federal National Mortgage Association are two examples of large companies in well-established sectors, namely railroads and real estate lending. Home Shopping Network, meanwhile, is a concept company that stampeded upward when it was first listed and plummeted at even greater speed after it reached its peak.

Moreover, emerging growth companies do not have to be new issues. A company may have had a change in management that is perceived by the marketplace as more aggressive than the previous one. The introduction of innovative products or services, or the expansion of established ones may carry the promise of increasing revenues. A company may set an acquisition on course that may help increase its sales base or diversify into new avenues of growth. The firm may increase its expenditures on research and development and may succeed in bringing to market new discoveries or new applications.

One recent example is Walt Disney Productions, which, after gaining a new management, revived its main line of business, planned on overseas expansion, and expanded its entertainment facilities. In general, however, whether new or old, emerging growth companies tend to fare well during economic slowdowns. Often their sales and earnings momentum continue to expand rapidly relative to both other companies within their own industry group and to the broad market.

CONCLUSION

The problem with spotting great investment vehicles is that by the time that they are discovered, the outlook may have become less promising. The important question is the fundamental one, how long can rapid growth continue? The answer to this dilemma has to do with the ability of the management team to steer the company in a promising direction and apply prudent financial controls. But then, how can we evaluate the ability of the executive rank in company to perform such a task? There is no easy answer to that question. And that is because

successful investing is only partly the result of sound fundamentals. The track record is an indication of prior performance;
it has never guaranteed an encore.

In the foregoing discussion, fundamental analysis has
been used to compare the data among different securities and
industry groups. The growth records and financial ratios of a
company could be used to compare its worth relative to another company in the same industry group. Comparison based on
earnings, sales, book value, P/E multiples, leverage, liquidity,
or profitability could reveal the relative worth of a security as
an investment. The same principles could also be used in
assessing the relative appeal of industry groups.

A company or an industry group could be analyzed in
light of development in the commodity futures market or other
demographic factors that may have a pronounced influence on
its future earnings potential. There are no limits to the extent of
analysis that could be performed. Companies or industry
groups could also be compared to other foreign entities around
the world. The globalization of securities markets compels investors to compare the fundamentals of any local company or
industry group to overseas ones of similar characteristics.
Chances are that trends in any foreign market may influence
the price behavior of domestic stocks and industry groups of
similar nature. The purpose of all these comparisons included
above is to illustrate the importance of fundamental dynamics
in the investment process.

PART 4

Quantitative Market Analysis

□ 9

The Market's Internal Dynamics

*To every thing there is a season, and a time to
every purpose under heaven: A time to be born,
and a time to die; a time to plant, and a time to
pluck up that which is planted; a time to keep and
a time to cast away. . . .*

The Book of Ecclesiastes

So far, the value of fundamental and economic analyses in assessing the investment environment and recognizing the catalysts that propel the trends has been explored. The role these methods play in influencing broad market prices, as well as of individual securities, has been investigated. The fundamental and economic perspectives serve as the force behind the direction of price movement in the marketplace and help identify long-term potential opportunities. Such analyses ensure the long-term viability of a company—they describe the company's financial position, its market share, its management's ability to generate profits and maximize its shareholders' equity. Fundamental analysis is of special importance in assessing the business risk associated with a particular security or industry group. The thorough investigation of underlying fundamentals helps control the security risk element and, hence, increases investors' chances of achieving desired objectives. Moreover, the study of the fundamental underpinnings provides an initial feel for the company's intrinsic investment value.

However, while fundamental and economic analyses are conservative and should be at the heart of any investment decision, their predictive value is only valid for long-term commitments. Such commitments are suitable for passive investments—those held for a number of years to give them a chance to reach their full potential. But these types of analyses lack considerations for investors' psychology and cannot be used for timing the purchase or sales of securities. Such methods are superior at identifying the long-term growth of the firm, its earnings, sales, and profitability—but they are inadequate for determining the short- or intermediate-term direction of the stock. By the very nature of financial markets as discounting mechanisms, they tend to reverse direction long before the deterioration in the fundamental background is apparent to the average investor. Although that is why such a method of analysis is best used in positioning one's overall investments, it may at times be harmful for active investors. At any given time, the company's intrinsic value is reflected in the price of the security. Although markets may go through periods of depressed prices, during which the true worth of a stock is understated, most times stock prices are influenced by supply- and-demand forces. The value of a security is governed by all facts known to the informed, as well as to those less informed, who are speculating on future possibilities.

Investment decisions, however, can be enhanced by integrating the best that fundamental analysis offers with some well-known market-timing techniques. Fundamental analysis should be the groundwork for portfolio structuring. But in order effectively to deal with both the market and the security risks, it pays to use both disciplines and seek the best they offer. Just think for a moment—how can fundamentals or even economic statistics explain violent market movements? Severe corrections cannot be anticipated by balance-sheet analysis or by studying the cyclical position of the economic indicators. How can the so-called October Massacres of 1978 and 1979 or the Crash of 1987 be explained using economic or fundamental analysis? How have investors been able to foretell the severe market reactions near options expiration time on the third Friday of the last month of each quarter?

The economic school of trend analysis is vital in forecasting cyclical turns in business. A careful study of the leading, lagging, and coincident indicators can help both investors and business executives make informed investment decisions based on the expected economic outlook. Detailed analysis of help-wanted advertising, consumers' personal incomes, the savings rate, and international trade activities can be used to spot evolving trends in business and industry, as well as to identify major junctures of economic expansion and contraction. The analysis of economic statistics can provide a better handle on timing long-term commitments. But, as is the case with fundamental analysis, economics lacks the ability to forecast short- and intermediate-term trends.

However, although economic analysis can help spot evolving long-term industry trends, it has little value in analyzing specific securities. Here again, the market tends to anticipate economic factors. Bull markets usually end when business is still healthy and the economy is surging upward. Bear markets are born when the recessionary forces are deteriorating and the economic outlook is growing uncertain. Just think about the following question: How could investors have been able to anticipate primary bull market trends in 1948, 1952, 1956, 1962, 1966, 1970, 1974, and 1982 amid a stream of discouraging economic statistics and eroding corporate profits?

Market-timing studies reveal the supply-and-demand forces at work in the marketplace. They detect emerging trends before fundamentals have time to blossom. Quantitative analysis is of great value at major reversal points, when applied properly, and can identify, profitable trading rallies or impending market corrections. Having to deal mostly with prevailing prices and volume numbers, market-timing techniques give early signals of strength or warn of deteriorating internal dynamics. When market-timing techniques are factored into the stock selection process, they greatly enhance investment results.

TENETS OF THE MARKET-TIMING SCHOOL

Market timing was born of observations of repetitive market behavior during the different stages of the economic cycle. In the 1920s, market timers were known as statisticians. They experimented with daily statistics, price, and volume and were able to discover a trend or time its reversal. By carefully studying the internal dynamics of the market, they developed statistical methods, similar to those used in every profession, that forecast the price direction of stocks and bonds.

Over the years, as this school of analysis attracted the

attention of investors, more statistical relationships were discovered and studied. In the computer age, further testing and experimentation with these statistics became possible. The main advantage that market timing offered was that it identified common or repetitive patterns of price behavior during the different stages of the economic cycles. Furthermore, this market analysis discipline investigated the seasonal factors that affect securities prices during major trends. After years of study, it became apparent that there are important characteristics to the market's advance and decline. The study of those repetitive patterns helps anticipate important changes in the prevailing trend.

The lack of convincing fundamental argument to support the market-timing school led many investors to discard its tenets and to discourage its use entirely. Because market-timing techniques are not accurate all of the time and because of their subjective and intuitive nature, market timing was recognized little, if at all, in the halls of academia. For many years, market timing was ignored by both the economic community and proponents of fundamental analysis. However, with the introduction of options as hedging tools, index futures, and the increased volatility of the market in the 1980s, market timing received the attention it deserved from the investing public.

While the worrisome government budget deficit in 1982 dictated caution on both the economic and fundamental fronts, professional market timers maintained an extremely bullish opinion for the global securities markets. The subsequent years witnessed one of the greatest bull markets in history. The more the deficit grew, the higher the market rose, only to prove that economic and fundamental analyses are not the only driving catalysts.

In conjunction with these developments, investors discovered that there are other forces governing price behavior beyond the fundamental and economic perspectives. Buy-and-sell programs near the third Friday of each quarter, when options expired witnessed increased volatility and severe declines that could not be explained by traditional valuation methods. The internal dynamics of the market prevailed, which made the investment community increasingly aware of the importance of market timing. Companies with the most enticing fundamentals weakened when they felt the pressure of the options-selling programs. Passive portfolio managers and mutual funds sponsors, who are judged by their performance, had to pay attention to short- and intermediate-term trading techniques that only market-timing methods could offer. The importance of trend analysis surfaced as more participants started to believe in the wisdom of integrating all these techniques. It was then that the investment community was introduced more and more to terminologies that were once described as witchcraft. Institutions and portfolio managers began to pay attention to such terms as "moving averages," "overbought," "oversold," and other market-timing expressions.

Buying, Selling, and Trends

"Don't confuse me with the facts, just tell me where the trend is going." This is the Golden Rule by which market timers abide. Market timers and trend analysts are a breed apart. They live in their own world of charts. They pay little attention to the details surrounding the company or the economy—they focus on price and volume statistics. They study the internal dynamics of the market and analyze the continuous tug-of-war between the buyers and the sellers, the informed and the speculators, in the marketplace. They are the true believers of the market's ability to discount the future. Market timers are trend followers. They try to anticipate the rational and the irrational aspects of the market. They get so absorbed in their craft that they seldom care to explain the reasons behind their forecasts.

When to buy and when to sell are the most important preoccupations of market timers. "The trend is your friend" is one way market timers defend their craft. They respect the ticker tape and probe into the psychological makeup of the marketplace. Market timers can tell ahead of time that interest rates are going to rise, by citing developing price weakness in the interest-rate sensitive groups and the reversal of the bond market. By watching the trend of commodity futures prices,

they can detect the growing pressures of inflation and anticipate a downtrend in the fixed-income sector. They consider an
overdose of good news to be negative for the future direction of
securities prices, as it may lead to inflation and compel the Fed
to tighten its monetary policy. Market timers believe that a bull
market is healthier when overcoming worries. And when
stocks stop going up on good news, they begin to suspect the
durability of the market advance. They consider the weakness
of the dollar on the foreign exchange market to be a blessing for
drug and chemical stocks and a blessing in disguise for the
overall economy. Market timers respect their indicators and
regard them as true X-ray machines that display the state of
health or sickness of the trend.

Various Techniques

The Dow theory on market trend was never meant to start
a school of trend analysis, though it did. Believers in Dow's
thoughts went many steps further and developed them into a
powerful arsenal of market analysis techniques. R. N. Elliott
took the Dow theory, expanded on it and came out with *The
Elliott Wave Theory*, which became popular in the 1980s. The on-
balance volume technique, helpful in detecting rising or falling
demand for stock also gained fame and became popular in the
1960s. The moving average and relative strength studies received special attention over the years as reliable trend identifiers. Welles Wilder created the Relative Strength Index, an
important momentum indicator helpful in timing intermediate-
term rallies and corrections. Charles Lane discovered the
wonders of stochastics and moved Wall Street closer to realizing the ultimate trader's dream. The market averages were
subject to intense study, as rate-of-change methods revealed
cyclical patterns. Market breadth and oscillators have also
proven their worth as powerful market indicators and have
become permanent tools in the market timers' arsenal.

Most amateurs regard market timing as the ability of the
analyst to detect such price formations as triangles, wedges,
pennants, or the famous head-and-shoulders pattern. These
mechanical methods of trend analysis require a great deal of
experience and practice to recognize. Sometimes they predict

the outcome, but their frequent failure has led many investors to discard the domain of market timing entirely. Modern market analysis is much broader than the simple interpretation of a chart. It is the study of the internal dynamics at work at any time; it constantly strives to analyze the prevailing psychology in the marketplace. Over the years, the discipline has grown more sophisticated, as it has focused on deciphering the interrelationship between the rational and the irrational behavior of the markets.

Because market timing is intuitive, it is bound to misjudge the trend once in a while. No one single school of market analysis is foolproof, and market timing is no exception to the rule. While fundamental and economic analyses deal with rational expectations, market timing deals with the irrational—crowd psychology and emotional considerations are irrational, if not impulsive. Not only do the internal dynamics reveal the balance of supply and demand for stocks but also peoples' expectations, hopes, and dreams.

TOP-DOWN MARKET TIMING

When analyzing stock market trends, market timers usually follow one of two approaches. The first is the top-down approach, which focuses on the big question: where is the market heading? The assumption here is that rising tides lift all ships and that, if the market is advancing, the majority of stocks will follow. The second approach is the bottom-up approach, which is concerned with the trend of individual securities and industry groups. The bottom-up approach is the domain of the stock-pickers. Although they study the broad market actions, they claim that it may not maximize their chances in detecting the winners and spotting the losers. Toward the final stages of an uptrend, and while the market averages are still surging to new highs without corresponding gains by many securities, the stock-picker reigns supreme, as his techniques detect the few winners. During the latter phases of a mature trend, the bottom-up approach is superior in warning about internal imbalances. Moreover, it often happens that the market and a specific stock or industry group move in opposite directions.

The top-down approach is incomplete if it fails to focus on industry group behavior and individual stock trend positions. This is when investing based on the broad market direction can be dangerous. For example, the trend of the oil services group during the 1982–85 period was in a severe bear market when the broad market was a raging bull that carried most industries to all-time highs. Figure 9–1 illustrates the relationship between the market's behavior versus the oil services group at that time.

Figure 9–2 illustrates further the importance of stock selec-

Figure 9–1. *The oil services group versus the market.*

tion and the bottom-up method. The price trend of Advanced
Micro Devices is shown vis-à-vis the S&P 500. Here again,
while the market staged a powerful up move, Advanced Micro
Devices proceeded on a long-term downtrend ignoring the
great bull of the 1980s. When the market rallied strongly, the
stock made a modest advance. But when the market corrected,
the stock plummeted. Then, after the crash of 1987, Advanced
Micro Devices ignored the market's recovery and proceeded on
a downward course.

This is not the only example of a stock that declined amid
impressive market strength. What such an example demonstrates is that stock selection supersedes the determination of

Figure 9–2. *Advanced Micro Devices versus the market.*

the broad market trend in importance. That is why it pays to focus on the trend of the individual security when contemplating adding to a portfolio, rather than depending solely on analysis of the general market trend. Investors probably cannot make money trading the Dow Jones Industrial Average, but they may profit if the stock they own participates in market advances.

MARKET-TIMING INDICATORS

In order for market timers to determine the trend, they rely on a number of indicators. These indicators help them assess the intermediate- and long-term market potential. When the prevailing trend is expected to continue, the market is said to be "in gear." That is when these indicators are confirming the advance or decline. When the indicators are diverging from the market, the trend becomes vulnerable—a reversal may be in the making. Some of the technical indicators are more effective in detecting major long-term trends while others are more helpful in anticipating shorter-term rallies or declines.

The Trend Indicators

In studying the economic indicators, it was seen that interest-rate trends have a direct impact on all sectors of the economy. In terms of business, rising interest rates slow down economic activities and adversely affect earnings, dividends, profit margins, and sales. One of the key areas of analysis for a market is the bond market. The trend of fixed-income securities trend direction is an important leading indicator of future stock prices.

Bonds Lead Stocks

The credit market is especially sensitive to the monetary policy adopted by the Fed. Market-timing techniques recognize the impact of interest-rates on securities prices. Especially from a long-term perspective, the direction of interest rates is inversely related to trends of stocks and bonds. Primary trends in the stock market take their lead from the bond market, which in turn is influenced by interest-rate directions. Figure 9–3 illustrates the leading and lagging relationship between stocks and bonds. The graph shows that the bond market led stocks before each and every important trend reversal, including the one that preceded the Crash of 1987. The decline of the U.S. T-Bond index was a key cautionary signal that warned of a violent reaction in the stock market.

Commodities and Bonds Have Opposite Trends

Moreover, the fixed-income market is sensitive to trends in the commodity futures market. Rising commodities prices tend to lead inflation. In addition, rising commodities prices suggest that it is only a matter of time before the Fed will tighten its monetary policy, which will lead to rising interest rates. When commodities prices rise, bonds decline, and vice versa. Figure 9–4 illustrates this inverse relationship between bonds and commodities prices.

Bonds and Interest Rates

The inverse relationship between interest rates and bonds is illustrated in figure 9–5, which shows how bonds decline when the interest rate rises and advance when it declines. Here again, the uptrend in rates that started in the first quarter of 1987 adversely affected bonds. The T-Bond index reversed its trend in March of 1987, which eventually brought about the severe correction in stocks later that year. Also notice how the decline of interest rates that followed the Crash of 1987, when the Fed infused liquidity into the system, triggered the strong rally in bonds at that time.

INTERMARKET DYNAMICS

So far the relationships between bonds and stocks, bonds and commodities, and bonds and interest rates have been studied. In order to gain perspective on how these markets

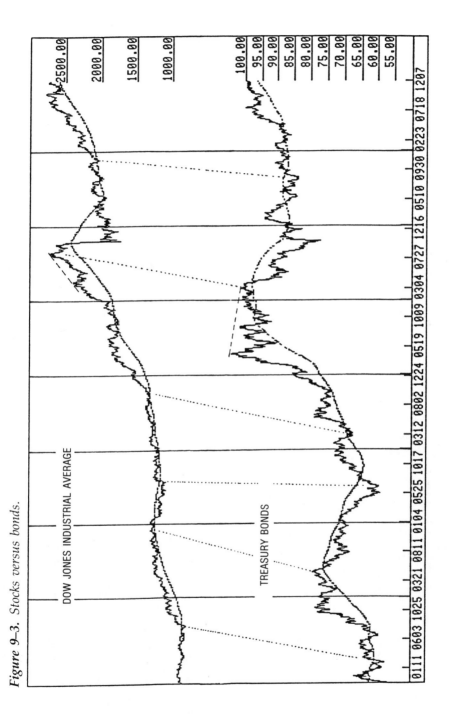

Figure 9–3. Stocks versus bonds.

279

Figure 9–4. The CRB and bonds.

behave relative to each other, let us review their trends during the 1985–89 period. Figure 9–5 illustrates the weekly price range of the S&P 500, T-Bonds, the CRB index and the 3-Month Treasury Bills rate.

During 1985–86, the CRB index was in a decisive downtrend. The Treasury Bills rate was also declining, as fear of inflation was slowly dissipating. The Fed was accommodative, because the economy was growing without the threat of rising inflation. T-Bonds and the fixed-income sector at large were enjoying one of the strongest advances in history. The S&P 500 took the lead from the bond market and marched on to new all-time highs. Near the middle of 1986, the CRB index reversed its trend and started to move upward. Shortly thereafter, the 3-Month Treasury Bills rate began to rise in response to mounting inflationary pressures. The bond market was quick to feel the impact of the rising rates and a downtrend in bonds followed. The decline of the bond market was ignored by the stock market, and the S&P 500 continued its advance to new highs. However, it was only a matter of time before the stock

Figure 9–5. T-Bonds and Federal Funds Rates.

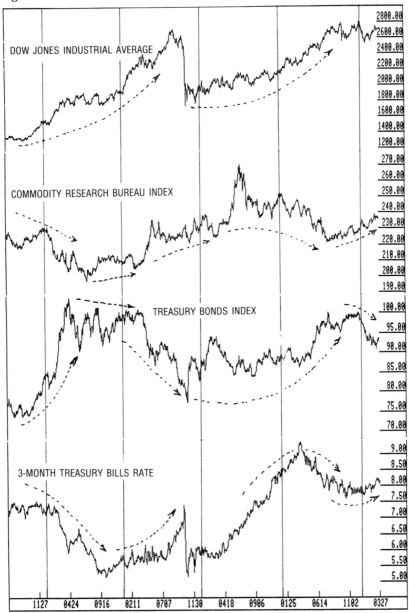

market would decline. The environment of euphoric optimism that prevailed helped the equities market to continue to rise for a while. The investment arena was swept by a wave of takeover activities and great buying demand for stocks. The equities market was on a rendezvous with fate.

The Crash of 1987 prompted the Fed to ease in an effort to save the financial markets from total collapse. This initial decline of interest rates triggered a strong advance in the fixed-income sector. Shortly thereafter, in 1988, the stock market began to recover from its psychological fear of total economic collapse and resumed its pre-1987 advance. Because of the subdued psychological environment and the mass of worries that plagued the investment community at that time, the market advance was met with lack of enthusiasm. This, in turn, prolonged the advance of stocks and supported the defensive behavior of bonds. Meanwhile, the CRB continued to advance until it culminated with the runaway blowoff that coincided with the drought that occurred at that time.

Despite the rise of the Federal Funds and Treasury Bills rate to counteract the strong rise in commodity prices, bonds remained defensive and stocks continued to gain upward ground. Early in 1989, the CRB index showed signs of weakness and started to decline. Shortly after, rates dropped further. A sign of a peak in interest rates was at hand. The economic statistics then indicated to the Fed that business was slowing down and some easing was warranted. As the bond market sensed that the cyclical peak of interest rates was about to materialize, it embarked on another renewed uptrend. The stock market, which was advancing slowly, took its lead from bonds and surpassed its 1987 highs. Until the autumn of 1989, the advance was healthy and on course in both the stock and bond markets. But poor earnings reports and fear of a recession finally took their toll on the market and triggered the bear trend of 1990.

This brief review of the inter-trend dynamics of stocks, bonds, commodities, and interest rates, reveals the real-life relationship between them. Stocks are bullish as long as bonds are trending higher. Bonds weaken when commodity prices rise, which implies tightening by the Fed. When commodity prices are advancing, it is only a matter of time before interest rates begin to move up. This hurts the bond market. When bonds are weak, equities are vulnerable, and so on.

Utilities Lead Stocks

Market timers compare the performance of the various market averages relative to each other. Signs of strength or weakness in any of the averages alert market timers to changes in the market's internal dynamics. Characteristics of a primary bull market mandate that all the averages should confirm each others' action by rising or falling together, allowing for some minor lead and lag time. Confirmation or divergence among the averages holds a special meaning to market timers. For a long-term bull market to continue on track, all the averages should be moving up in unison. When one or more of them fails to reach new highs, market timers will be alert to the negative divergence. This situation often leads to a trend reversal and a market decline. Similarly, when a downtrend has been in progress for some time but one or more market averages resists further weakness, a positive confirmation is signalled. To a market timer, this means that the possibilities are good that the market is likely to reverse its direction and move upward. The longer the divergence persists, the more serious the ensuing trend reversal will be.

Figure 9–6 illustrates the relationship between the Dow industrials and the Dow utilities. This utilities index represents the sum of 15 utility stocks. Known for being interest-rate sensitive, the utilities average tends to lead the Dow both up and down. When the stock market reaches new highs without the utilities average being able to move to higher highs, the advance in stock prices should be suspected, and vice versa. Notice in the figure shown how the Dow utilities failed to confirm the Dow industrials' new highs in the summer of 1987. This nonconfirmation was a warning signal. Notice from the graph how both the T-Bonds index and the Dow Utilities flashed a sell signal in the March–June period, well ahead of the market plunge in October.

Figure 9–6. Bonds, Dow utilities, and Dow industrials.

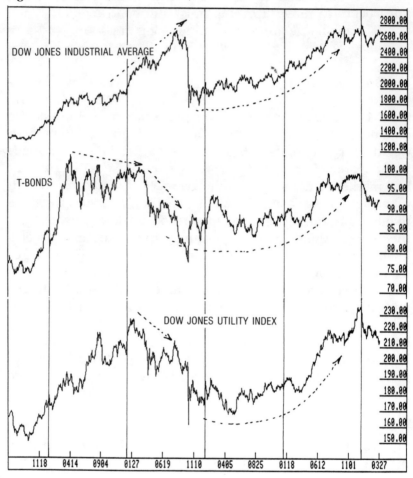

INTEREST-RATE SENSITIVE GROUPS

In the study of fundamental characteristics of industry groups, the reason why some sectors are more sensitive to interest-rate fluctuations than others was explained. Their behavior during periods of rising or declining rates was reviewed. The interest rate trend has a pronounced and direct impact on earnings, profit margins, bond portfolio value, and credit risk. Among these groups are: utilities, banks, S&Ls, homebuilding and insurance stocks. At this stage, their typical behavior during important market turns will be examined.

The interest-rate sensitive groups typically weaken before major cyclical peaks and strengthen before other industry groups near major troughs. Such groups lead the broad market highs and lows, as they take their cue from the interest-rate direction. They are adversely affected by rate advances and benefit from their decline. By monitoring such groups' behavior, the subtle deterioration that often precedes important downturns, or the emerging strength that usually leads bull trends, can be detected.

The bull market that started in 1982 propelled a strong uptrend in most of those groups. However, while the speculative fever in the real estate sector reached its peak in 1986–88, the home building group displayed signs of weakness as early as 1985. When the Crash of 1987 materialized, the home-building group declined to multiyear lows, signalling the end of the real estate boom. The discounting mechanism of the market correctly anticipated the future fundamentals that were to develop in the housing market.

The banks and S&Ls continued their advance into late 1986. But while the broad market exploded to new highs, these groups displayed relative price deterioration. The Crash of 1987 affected them even more severely than the rest of the market. With the benefit of hindsight, the S&Ls crisis could have been anticipated, because the group displayed weakness amid the great bull stampede that preceded the crash. While the broad market resumed its advance in 1988–89, the S&Ls continued to deteriorate until the government had to deal with the agonizing bailout process. As early as 1986, the message was that interest rates were bound to rise and that the credit risk in those groups was about to soar. The extent of the decline among members of those groups varied from the bankruptcy candidates to those institutions whom the market deemed healthy enough to survive and even prosper. Initially, the big money-center banks fared much better than other interest-rate sensitive groups, as the market expected that their well-diversified loan portfolios could pull them through. But as business conditions continued to deteriorate, bond stocks weakened further. By early 1990, they went into a full-fledged bear market of their own, as the housing market seemed to be in a free fall.

In 1987, the interest-rate sensitive groups showed signs of deterioration much sooner than they usually do. While at that time the investment environment was optimistic, and while many analysts, portfolio managers, and sophisticated investors expected the market to move to new record highs as late as September 1987, those industry groups flashed a warning signal that could not be ignored. Notice, in particular, the apparent weakness in the utilities group during most of 1987. The downtrend in both utilities and the bond market warned market timers of the impending collapse.

Figure 9–7 illustrates the trend dynamics of the interest-rate sensitive groups. Notice the subtle deterioration and weak performance of the sectors in early 1987, and which warned about an impending correction in the stock market. Also note the unison of advance and decline of these groups.

Brokerage Stocks as Leading Indicators

In the past, the brokerage group has been a good leading indicator to stock market performance. Behavior of stocks in this industry has often signalled the beginning of a strong bull move or an important reversal. Price behavior provides clues about what Wall Street is likely to do. The reason for such a correlation is that the industry's earnings, profits, and overall financial position depend on the trend of the market. In a bull market, trading is heavy and the volume of transactions is high. This, in turn, translates into commission revenues. The opposite is true in a bear market, as activities decline. The brokerage industry is a precursor to long-term trends and can serve as a leading market indicator.

At the onset of a major bull market, brokerage stocks advance strongly. Their earnings and profits potential increases during rising markets and tend to suffer during bear markets. However, the brokerage group loses its upward momentum as the bull market matures. After the crash, the S&P 500 was able to regain all its losses and proceeded to new highs, but the group barely participated in the advance. The aftermath of the stock market collapse on Wall Street was

Figure 9–7. *S&Ls, banks, homebuilding, and utilities versus the S&P 500.*

devastating. Volume activities sagged as investors remained fearful of the looming shadow of a depression. The brokerage stocks marginally improved amid skepticism and lack of enthusiasm.

In the 1990s, brokerage stocks are likely to assume the characteristics of the interest-rate sensitive groups. The deregulation of the financial services industry will prompt companies in this group to assume many traditional banking functions. The fundamental changes sweeping Wall Street in the 1990s may be affected by both financial deregulation and the globalization of financial markets. Such trends of consolidation have occurred in such other industries as the automobile industry in the 1920s and 1930s, and also the oil services industry in the early 1980s. Deregulation may cause major infrastructural changes in the financial services industry until the end of this decade.

MARKET AVERAGE CONFIRMATION

Most investors focus on the Dow industrials without realizing that it represents only 30 of the mightiest companies of corporate America. The components that enter into this index's calculation are solid, investment-grade, blue-chip companies. Many among them are considered to be the bellwether stocks of their industry group and the market at large. Their typical price behavior during the business cycle is such that they are the first to advance in a bull market and the last to decline during bear markets. The fundamentals of most of them resemble classic textbook case studies. Over the years, they have developed the know-how to manage their internal resources, sell their products, and craft long-term plans to ensure their future growth. While they may not meet the growth ratios of smaller companies, they provide stability. Unless there is a fundamental change in their industry perspectives due to a major socioeconomic trend that threatens their existence, they possess what it takes to seize emerging market opportunities and capitalize on new sources of growth.

Because, in the lexicon of Wall Street, Dow stocks are classified as investment-grade companies, their security risk component is substantially lower than the rest of the market's. Their resilience and strength near major cyclical peaks often camouflage the subtle deterioration that begins to show in the broader-based and secondary market averages. That is why monitoring a number of market averages that encompass the action of a large sample of stocks is always advisable.

The S&P 500 is broader based than the Dow Jones Industrial Average. Its capitalization approximates 70 percent of all NYSE listed stocks. The S&P 500's momentum is a better representation of the overall market trend. While it is heavily weighted by the energy group, it incorporates the price action of 500 stocks of medium- to large-size companies in all industry groups. During primary bull markets, both the Dow industrials, and the S&P 500 should advance in unison, with each new rally's highs scored by either one confirmed by a corresponding advance by the other. When the Dow scores new highs without a corresponding performance by the S&P 500, market timers begin to suspect deterioration in the major trend. They recognize such a divergence in the performance of the two averages as a warning signal of an impending trend reversal. The longer those disparities persist, the more severe the ensuing decline is likely to be.

These are not the only two averages that can provide us with an early alert of a potential trend change, however. The Value-Line index incorporates the prices of some 2000 stocks of all sizes, including some of the Amex and Nasdaq stocks. It is considered by many as the better representation of the market trend. When it fails to confirm the price action of the Dow industrials, it, too, can warn of a potential change in the primary thrust of the market.

INTERNATIONAL MARKET ANALYSIS

Market-timing techniques can be applied to any market in any place around the world. For example, market timing can be used to analyze the performance of a foreign market average, such as the Nikkei, the Dow Jones of Japan, relative to major Japanese stocks. Figure 9–8 illustrates Japan's most widely followed index versus four of Japan's blue-chip stocks, namely Honda Motors, Sony, Matsushita, and Hitachi.

The figure clearly shows that, while the Nikkei was rising to new all time highs, these major Japanese securities were lagging. Starting from the middle of 1988, these blue-chip Japanese companies failed to match the prevailing upward momentum of the Nikkei and rally to new highs. What this divergence demonstrated is that the Nikkei was advancing without corresponding strength from some of its important components. Its unrelenting advance camouflaged the subtle weakness that emerged in the price action of its components. This example proves that the trend of the market average, at times, may not mean much and may even disguise the true nature of the trend in individual securities, no matter what their fundamentals are. Eventually, such divergence lead to a major trend reversal.

MONITORING GLOBAL TRENDS

The globalization of financial markets is a *fait accompli*. The evolution of the information-oriented society, the advancement in technology, and the proliferation of efficient transportation means are bringing the world together. International trade activities are moving us closer every day toward greater international cooperation. Economic policies around the world take into consideration the interdependence of all free economies around the globe. The role of the foreign exchange market is growing to be a self-monitoring mechanism of deficits and surpluses among nations. The world stock markets take their lead from each other. Many American companies are listed on major stock exchanges in Europe and the Far East. Similarly, several European and Japanese stocks are listed on the New York Stock Exchange and the Nasdaq system. In the age of arbitrageurs, who make their livings on disparities in prices among different markets, it is normal to expect global trends to confirm each other unless a trend reversal is signalled. Figure 9–9 illustrates the averages of three major markets. The figure shows that the Nikkei led the recovery of financial markets from their 1987 depressed levels. But the surge of most foreign averages ahead of the Dow industrials signalled optimism, and

Figure 9–8. *The Nikkei Dow Jones versus Honda, Matsushita, Sony, and Hitachi.*

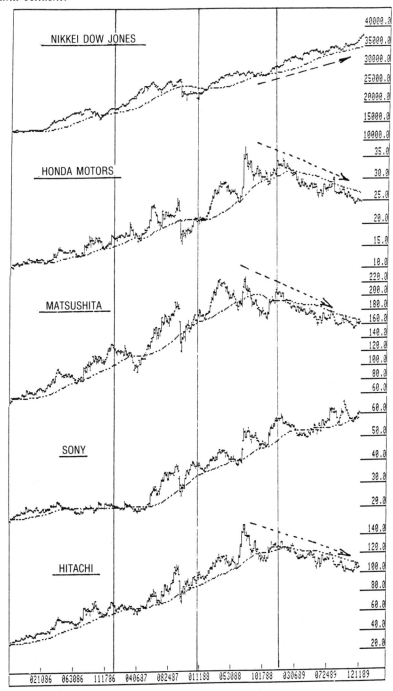

Figure 9–9. Nikkei, Financial Times, and Dow Industrial Indexes.

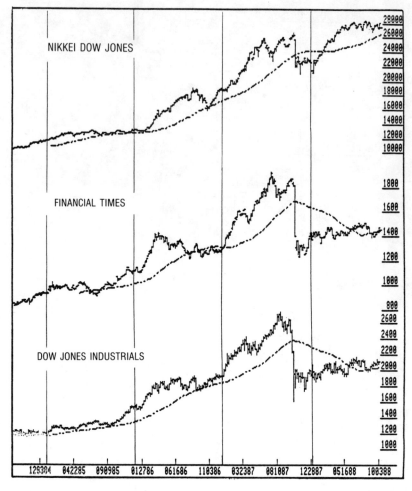

it was only a matter of time before U.S. equities advanced, which they did.

Secondary Markets

Investors should also monitor the AMEX and OTC averages, as they represent the price trend of secondary stocks with much weaker financial positions than their counterparts on the big board. These indexes tend to deteriorate ahead of the Dow Industrials. The security risk in secondary stocks is much high-

er than in those "big-cap" blue-chip industries that compose
the S&P 500 or the Dow. Figure 9–10 illustrates the trends of
the Nasdaq composite versus the S&P 500. By comparing their
relative performance, early weakness or developing strength
can be detected. The constant monitoring of the averages is
particularly important from a long-term perspective. At times,
rallies are dominated by blue-chip stocks, and at others, laggards' catchup moves are to be expected. In a major bull market, the big-cap stocks lead the way, closely followed by sec-

Figure 9–10. *The Nasdaq composite average versus the Dow industrials.*

ondary stocks. After peak momentum is reached during the business cycle, secondary stocks tend to fade away very quickly. Their downtrend usually starts well ahead of the blue-chip stocks. Secondary stock declines are often interrupted by sharp advances—or bear traps—but afterwards they resume their decline. As the bull market matures and the bear market starts, secondary stocks often decline much more than blue-chip stocks.

ANATOMY OF INDUSTRY GROUP BEHAVIOR

Market timers pay a good deal of attention to industry group trends. By comparing their performance relative to the market averages, they can detect changes in leadership and improve their assessment of future potential. The S&P industry group averages are the most widely followed. Their behavior during market rallies and declines portrays investors' opinions of the future fundamentals that will govern prices of industry sectors and the companies they represent.

In bull markets, industry groups with strong upward momentum tend to resist the market corrections and rise strongly during market advances. Similarly, during bear trends, weak groups do not participate in market rallies and decline sharply when the downtrend resumes. In the early stages of a bull market, all industry groups stampede to the upside and score good gains independent of their prevailing or anticipated fundamentals. The sheer upward momentum of the broad market carries all stocks to higher ground. As the bull market progresses, however, some industry groups move up aggressively and clearly assume leadership. However, a number of groups may advance at a much slower pace. A third type may just meander aimlessly. As the bull market matures, fewer and fewer industry groups participate in market rallies. When this happens, investors should be alert to the dangers that usually follow selective markets, as they signal a loss of upward momentum. This process often leads major cyclical highs and then to a full-fledged reversal of the long-term trend.

Similarly, at the onset of a bull market, stocks tend to

follow a similar logic. Initially, there is a stampede, during which blue-chip stocks lead the way. Big investors and fund managers develop an interest in these more stable, financially solvent, and widely held stocks. As the bull market proceeds, attention shifts to secondary issues. Eventually as the advance gains strength, the general public is attracted to the seemingly across-the-board rise, and speculative excesses begin to build in low-priced, poor quality stocks. At this juncture the market grows more selective, and only a few leaders continue to gain. The number of issues advancing grows smaller and smaller until the trend finally reverses. Ironically, however, it is those same speculative issues that lead the decline when the bear market starts. As the downtrend accelerates, the blue chips tumble with the rest of the market. At that stage, the fundamental value of a stock does not help in the face of the fear plaguing declining markets.

In bear markets, industry group behaviors mirror the action of stocks just described. Such behavior usually starts with developing weakness in those groups that lack a fundamental catalyst. The residual strength of some of the leaders distorts the market's deteriorating momentum. But when the downtrend accelerates, all industry groups without exception begin to feel the downward pressure. No matter how sound the fundamental background is or how low the price-earnings ratios are, all industry groups decline. During the final stage of the decline, investor capitulation drives all industry groups to a precipitous selloff. Once an initial climax is reached, a strong rebound sets in. During this initial rebound, the groups that rally fastest are the ones most likely to do well in the next major uptrend.

Following the climax and the rebound, a decline known as "the retesting of the lows" occurs. It is during the retesting phase that leadership changes take place. Those groups that resist the final pullback are likely to be the new bull market leaders. The emerging leaders of the forthcoming advance tend to show improving performance relative to the broad market. After the retesting process is complete, the market is ready to start another bull cycle, during which industry groups stampede upward again and the cycle repeats. The only difference is that those groups that showed the initial strength during the retesting phase are the ones who are likely to move up faster, higher, and for a longer period of time than the others.

In a bull market, some industry groups may move opposite to the major trend. Since improving fundamentals do not affect all sectors to the same degree, the groups that have gone through the slowdown unscathed are the first to advance. Other industries that were caught with high inventories during the economic contraction may miss the initial market strength until inventories are liquidated. Still other industries may be slow to respond until the outlook for capital spending is more promising. Cyclical groups tend to experience the sharpest rebound. Groups sensitive to consumer spending may be influenced by seasonality in their trend behavior. Interest-rate sensitive groups may display early signs of strength in anticipation of a shift in the Fed's monetary policy.

Industry Group Rotation

After the initial stampede of a primary bull market, industry groups stop rising or falling in harmony. Some may lead the way up, while others are preparing for the next move. The leaders soon advance to important resistance areas where they meet selling pressure. At that stage, the dormant groups assume leadership and begin to advance. They, too, run into resistance and begin to correct, while those that stalled strengthen again. This process continues as the bull market runs its course. As the winners consolidate, strength shifts temporarily to the laggards that were dormant during the previous advance. This phenomenon is known among market timers as "group rotation." After the bull market has been in progress for a while, groups that have gone through a prolonged rise reach their maximum profitability. This prompts large investors to focus on laggards in the hope of a catchup advance.

In a bear market, the process is similar but faster. Groups lacking fundamentals decline first. Shortly after, when the bear market accelerates, even the relatively stronger groups start to feel the wave of selling. The downtrend often ends with a massive decline and a climax during which all groups seem to have no support whatsoever. At such junctures, pessimism abounds and investors liquidate out of panic.

Even more important than comparative group performance is the way the group handles successive corrections, however. An ascending line of reactive lows during these intermediate-term declines is a sign of strength. The tendency of an industry group to react only slightly to market corrections is another evidence of a healthy uptrend. The evidence of trend deterioration in a group begins when it suffers a more extensive decline during market consolidation than others. Even more assuring evidence of a trend reversal at hand is that of the group's failure to regain its losses during the subsequent market rally.

The study of industry group behaviors can also help identify those stocks that have the most promising appreciation potential. Stocks in a particular group may not necessarily all weaken when the group is out of favor or undergoing consolidation. Also, those issues that are stronger than the rest of the industry are likely to do even better when the group is ready to advance again. Figure 9–11 illustrates the performance of the drug industry group relative to the S&P 500. Notice how persistent the strength of the group was during that time.

Relative performance ranking among industry groups is vital to the asset allocation process. When a group resists an intermediate-term correction, it is likely to outperform the market in the subsequent advance, and vice versa. Furthermore, the performance of a stock relative to the broad market and to its own industry group are key determinants of its investment appeal. When an issue shows strength relative to other stocks in its own group, the chances are that it will rise more than they do in the long run.

Investors should spend time investigating the performance of industry groups and stocks relative to the general market and to each other. A thorough understanding of the economic and fundamental backgrounds helps determine the selection of the components of a portfolio based on intrinsic value and financial health. Market timing, however, gives perspectives on the internal dynamics of industry groups and individual stocks. By integrating the best of what these schools of market analysis offer, better selections can be made.

Figure 9–11. *The performance of drug groups relative to the S&P 500.*

SUMMARY

The economic indicators are considered good forecasters of the future course of business. The fundamental perspective could help identify sound investments. Yet, the market is irrational at times. Driven by the sum total of all emotions, thoughts, and analyses, the trend of prices on Wall Street may not comply with economic or fundamental forecasting. The Crash of 1987 is an example when the market collapsed without any economic or fundamental justification. As a matter of fact,

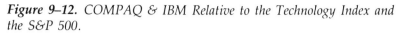

Figure 9–12. COMPAQ & IBM Relative to the Technology Index and the S&P 500.

it was a purely technical reaction that could have hardly been anticipated by any economic or fundamental model.

In this chapter, the technical factors that influence securities prices are introduced. The relative position of the averages and their momentum could reveal subtle weakness or emerging strength.

Commodity prices, and hence inflation, dictate the Fed's monetary policy and the direction of interest rates. Bonds, in turn, are sensitive to interest rate fluctuations and are inversely related to its trend. Bonds lead stocks by a varying period of time both on the way up and on the way down.

The study shows that bonds take their lead from commodity price and interest rate trends. Interest rate sensitive groups and the utility average tend to follow closely the developments in the fixed income market. Monitoring the trend of interest-rate-sensitive groups could warn of an impending credit risk or the onset of an expansion in business conditions.

Finally, global trends are growing in their importance as financial markets around the world are inter-related. By considering the relative positions of international markets and averages, a better understanding is gained which could enhance our forecast of future trends.

The market internal dynamics are helpful in identifying the broad based movement in security prices. When used in conjunction with economic and fundamental analysis, the technical conditions could enhance the portfolio structuring and asset allocation processes.

❑ 10

The Trend Indicators

. . . after all these years, I know one thing for certain: the perfect trading system does not exist and never will. . . .

Jake Bernstein

Market timers study the internal dynamics by assessing the balance of supply-and-demand forces at work at any given time. Their analysis is based on the premise that the market is constantly absorbing and discounting the fundamental and economic factors and their impact on future earnings. Up-trends evolve when the outlook appears promising. Bull markets perform best when they are met with lack of interest and disbelief. Violent reactions occur when emotions, rather than reason, set the pace for trading. Volatility increases when the supply-and-demand factors are out of balance. Short-term trends are temporary reactions to potential positive developments or unexpected surprises. But durable trends concern long-lasting developments that affect the financial prospect of a company or the market at large. Market timing derives its conclusions from the market's action itself. Its practitioners take their signals from financial market activities rather than analyzing the news and theorizing its probable impact.

Among the most helpful tools for market timers are the momentum oscillators. Such indicators as the annual rate of change of the S&P 500, the percentage of stocks trading above their 200-day moving average, the S&P 500 diffusion index, the moving average differentials, the new-highs-to-new-lows ratio, and especially the market breadth can help measure momentum, which represents true latent strength or weakness. Such other momentum indicators as stochastics, the relative strength index, the advance-decline ratio, and other oscillators are more suitable for intermediate-term trading purposes.

Oscillators and rate-of-change methods normalize the trend and indicate the overbought or oversold position of the market. Earnings may be robust and rising, financial ratios may be healthy and improving, and fundamentals may be as sound as can be, yet the market may fluctuate because of the internal dynamics of accumulation and distribution that are constantly at work. With the help of oscillators and rate-of-change techniques, a trader can fine tune entry and exit points. The daily and weekly price action can also reveal the underlying strength or weakness of the trend. Because market timers believe in the ability of the market to discount all future economic and fundamental factors, practitioners respect the tape and try to decipher the internal forces to predict future trends.

MOMENTUM AND THE BUSINESS CYCLE

Momentum studies are concerned with the state of the trend. For instance, in bull markets, the pressure on stock prices is on the upside. At the early stage of a primary uptrend, all stocks move up in sync propelled by the superior momentum that develops around major lows. During such times, the number of stocks reaching new highs far exceeds those receding to new lows. The upside-to-downside volume ratio is also expanding rapidly. The percentage of stocks trading above their 200-day moving average is rising. The moving average differential is also advancing. This stampede tends to strengthen at the early stage of a bull market, as the prospect of economic recovery seems within reach. At such times, however, the effect of the recession may continue to be reflected in the economic statistics. Unemployment may still be rising, consumer confidence may be shaky and investors are bearish in outlook; the Fed then tries to ease interest rates and they trend lower. During the initial stampede typical of the early stages of a primary uptrend, skepticism reigns, as earnings can sometimes continue to be lackluster. As long as the majority of stocks are advancing, however, the trend is healthy. While this strong bullish phase may vary in duration, the upward momentum can persist for six to nine months. As the market advance persists and the economic statistics show early signs of improvement, demand increases, thus adding fuel to market strength.

After a while, the participation of stocks during rallies starts to wane. The gains become more sporadic. Subtle loss of momentum begins to set in. Frequent corrections may interrupt the robust advance. By now, the economy is well on its way to recovery, unemployment is declining, earnings are rebounding, and sales are expanding. During the ensuing phase, the market tends to enjoy a more selective advance, as growth and valuation measures become the driving force behind price performance. Many stocks that have already advanced with the initial stampede mark time in a narrow trading range without appreciable gains. The list of stocks reaching new highs for the year begins to shrink, the ratio of up-to-down volume begins to decline, the annual rate of change reverses direction, and the percentage of stocks trading above their 200-day moving average also declines. From that point on, the momentum *cyclical* peak is at hand and stock selection is more important than market timing.

The determination of momentum during the cycle is crucial, as it indicates the point from which weakness and a major trend reversal should be suspected. Stock prices from here on are likely to be driven by earnings. The market may enter a prolonged phase of group rotation until the final peak is reached. Rotation may dominate the market action as some groups strengthen while others weaken. The market grows more and more selective as the difference between the number of advancing and declining stocks decreases. The loss of momentum becomes apparent as the cumulative breadth fails to confirm the new highs reached on subsequent market rallies.

By the time the cyclical peak is finally reached, momentum oscillators have already signalled the trend's subtle deterioration. The market breadth lags, the list of stocks reaching new highs shrinks, the number of stocks trading at new lows expands, and the annual rate of change trends lower. More stocks and industry groups falter on market pullbacks, and very few advance on market rallies: the bear market is about to start.

Typically, the downtrend starts with a sudden decline that is characterized by abnormal weakness in almost all stocks and that takes the averages below their most recent lows. The number of stocks making new lows expands, and many issues dip below their 200-day moving average. Group after group declines as the downtrend proceeds. During that initial break, many investors are still unwary of the creeping weaknesses and are still driven by hope and greed. The known fundamentals at that juncture are still robust, showing hardly any deterioration. It is typical of such times that inflation rises and economic statistics reach cyclical highs, with capacity utilization near the upper limits—signalling full utilization of production resources. The Fed then tightens and interest rates rise. Housing permits may already have begun to show some softness in demand while retail sales numbers come on strong. The bear market is now in progress, however, as it foresees the declining earnings and the beginning of a contraction phase in the economy.

Momentum analysis is used by market timers to measure the strength or weakness of the prevailing trend during the different stages of the business cycle. Momentum is a barometer of the upside or downside velocity of the broad market. It is the true reflection of the supply-and-demand balance that is constantly governing the price action of financial markets. The message momentum analysis delivers reflects both the known and the potential fundamentals that can affect the position of the market, industry groups, and individual stocks.

To summarize, in a rising market, the price momentum of the broad market is powerful. After a bull market has been in progress for some time, momentum starts to weaken. When the loss of momentum prevails while the market averages are still proceeding to new highs, market timers are alerted to the developing deterioration. A closer analysis is then warranted, as a loss in momentum often signals the early stage of a trend reversal.

Momentum measures focus on studying the rate of

Figure 10–1. *Stages of the business cycle relative to momentum.*

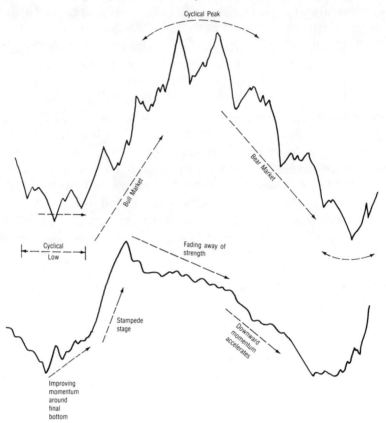

change of the averages, the relationships between advancing and declining issues, the relative position of stocks to their moving averages, the balance of up to down volume, and the comparison of the numbers of stocks reaching new highs to those faltering to new lows.

BREADTH OF THE MARKET

Market breadth reveals the extent of stock participation during market rallies and declines. On any given trading day, some stocks advance, others decline, and a few remain unchanged. From those three numbers published in the financial section of major newspapers, investors can formulate a whole series of intermediate-and long-term indicators. The most important of them is the cumulative advance-decline (A/D) line. This is one indicator that is crucial for following the progression of primary bull and bear markets. Moreover, the A/D line can give an early-warning signal near major turning points. Market timers consider this indicator one of the most reliable for long-term trend identification. In the past, the A/D line warned of a bear market trend ahead of its occurrence and amid euphoria and sound economic conditions. This indicator leads the market at major cyclical highs. Around important cyclical lows, the A/D line either coincides or leads by a very short time which makes it hard to draw decisive conclusions. However, it helps to show the subtle emerging strength in the market as fewer stocks decline during selloffs.

The breadth of the market is the cumulative total of the difference between daily advancing and declining issues on the Exchange. In the early 1930s, the studies of General L. P. Ayres, uncovered a vital relationship between the Dow industrials and the cumulative A/D line.

At the onset of a primary uptrend, both the market averages and the A/D line advance to higher highs in unison. After the bull market has been in progress for a while, it has been noticed that the Dow industrials continue to rise to new highs without a corresponding advance by the A/D line. Market timers call the inability of breadth to confirm the market strength a "negative divergence." History shows that such a development often leads to a major trend reversal. By examining the A/D line's behavior near cyclical peaks it is seen that such divergence has always warned of an important change in the prevailing trend.

Experience shows that when breadth fails to move to new highs on three consecutive rallies, during which time the Dow succeeds to score new highs, that a major trend reversal is near. In the past, breadth divergence signaled the end of bull markets and the beginning of primary bear markets. The lead time between the occurrence of the divergence and the final reversal of the trend varied at previous cyclical peaks. For example, in the late 1920s, breadth revealed the impending

Figure 10–2. Market breadth relative to the Dow industrials.

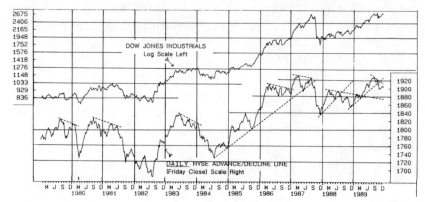

decline in the averages by almost three years before the Crash of 1929 finally materialized. In general, however, breadth divergence takes place six to nine months before the final market peak.

One explanation of the divergence between the Dow Industrials and the cumulative A/D line is the strong performance of blue-chip stocks relative to the broader market. As the primary trend is maturing, the Dow components, which are known to be of superior quality, continue to advance—while smaller stocks lag in momentum. This lack of participation of medium and small capitalization stocks leads to breadth divergence and, hence, gives an early signal of trend deterioration. When the blue-chip stocks are leading without secondary stocks' participating, the trend's direction becomes questionable. As a matter of fact, in the latter stages of a bull market, there is often a camouflaging effect created from the rise of the Dow components to new highs without corresponding action from industry groups and stocks. It is the breadth of the market that usually reveals the subtle weakness that precedes major peaks.

Figure 10-2 illustrates market breadth versus the averages near major cyclical peaks. Note how the apparent weakness in the advance/decline line led the severe market corrections in 1980-81, 1983-84, and 1987. The fading breadth momentum warned about the onset of a broad market weakness well before the imminent decline.

RATE-OF-CHANGE OSCILLATORS

Market timers rely heavily on rate-of-change oscillators to assess market momentum. These indicators are often charted against the major averages in order to analyze the short, intermediate-or long-term trend potential. The rate-of-change indicators tend to fluctuate between two extreme readings that coincide with peaks or troughs of the market. These boundaries are commonly known as "overbought" and "oversold" levels. The market is considered overbought when a rally drives the rate-of-change oscillators to the upper range. Overbought levels are cautionary signals that the advance is extended and that a correction may ensue. The market is considered oversold when a decline pushes the oscillator to the lower range. Oversold levels are bullish since they indicate that the market has reached an area of significant support from which it can rally.

Rate-of-change oscillators are calculated by substracting the price of the market average "x" number of days ago from its current value. The outcome is then divided by the number of days used as a basis for comparison. Market timers often use a large number of rate-of-change oscillators when studying the position of the averages. For short-term purposes, ten-day rate-of-change oscillators are common. For intermediate-term purposes, the 30-day rate-of-change oscillators are used. For long-term trend studies, 150-to 250-day rate-of-change oscillators are preferred.

Rate-of-change oscillators can be used in analyzing market averages, industry groups, or individual stock momentum. They are of universal value, as they also help measure the momentum of the dollar index, commodity prices, foreign securities, and market averages—even economic statistics and fundamental data.

It is worth mentioning at this stage that overbought markets do not necessarily mean that a plunge is imminent. Extremes in overbought levels have often suggested a very strong upward momentum that is likely to resume after short-term hesitation. Similarly, an excessively oversold position may mean that the market or the stock is very weak and that the downward pressure is likely to resume after some sideways consolidation. Oscillators are most useful in a market in which the averages are fluctuating within a trading range. At the onset of a primary bull market, the oscillators are expected to remain in an overbought position for an extensive period of time. Also, in a bear market, their oversold position may persist and should not be interpreted as a reason for bargain hunting. Oscillators in general should be used with the major trend in mind and should be interpreted in light of the cyclical position of the broad market.

Among the most useful and widely known oscillators are the annual S&P 500 rate of change, the nine-month diffusion index, and the 25-day and the 13-day NYSE index rate of change.

The Annual Rate of Change

This is one indicator that has consistently forecasted cyclical peaks and troughs. The S&P 500 annual rate of change is probably one of the best long-term indicators known to market timers. The following formula is used to calculate it:

$$\text{Annual Rate of Change} = \frac{X\text{-}Z}{Z}$$

where X = The value of the S&P 500 for a given month
Z = The value of the S&P 500 for the same month a year ago

For example: if one wants to calculate the annual rate of change at the end of August of 1987, one substracts the value of the S&P 500 at the end of August 1986 from its value at the end of August 1987. Then divide the outcome by its value at the end of August 1986. Figure 10–3 illustrates the history of this indicator since 1952.

The annual rate of change is more consistent at major cyclical lows than at market peaks. In the past, when it declined to -10 percent or below and then changed direction from down to up, it signaled the lows that preceded a primary bull market. A better confirmation would be to wait until the indicator crosses the "zero" line. Remember that the slope of

Figure 10–3. S&P 500 annual rate of change.

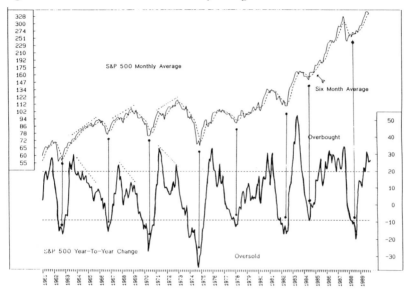

the annual rate of change has to reverse itself from down to up from below the −10 percent mark. Major cyclical lows are indicated on the graph. It is important to note that there is nothing magical about the −10 percent mark—it may have been coincidental during previous major troughs.

The annual rate of change has seldom signaled a major peak. However, it can help determine the peak momentum during a primary uptrend. At the start of a new bull market, this indicator stampedes upward. After it reaches +30 percent or higher and changes direction, it usually confirms the point of peak momentum. Past that point, the market may continue to rise but the advance is likely to be selective, characterized by rotation. A major divergence usually follows, as the market may continue to reach new highs at a slower rate on a year-to-year basis. Finally, when the annual rate of change declines to below roughly +20 percent, a bear market is likely to start shortly thereafter. During primary downtrends, even the best fundamentally situated industry group decline with a vengeance. When the annual rate of change reverses its direction

Figure 10–4. The S&P and the nine-month diffusion index.

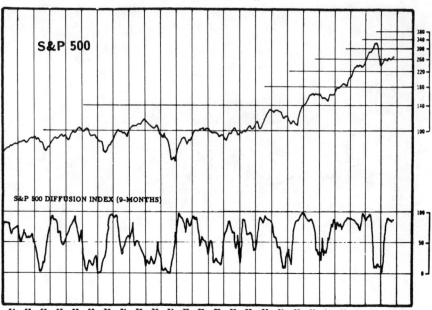

from up to down, it is an important cautionary signal and raising cash should be considered.

Peaks are part of a process and take time to develop. The decline of the annual rate of change to −10 percent or lower should alert the investor to start looking for stocks and industry groups that may soon start bottoming out. By the same token, the peak momentum point is important because it tells the investor that he or she should pay more attention to individual stocks and industry group trends. It is from that point on that stock selection becomes much more important than market timing. Seldom have industry groups made their final peaks or troughs in unison. They tend to diverge in their performance near cyclical highs and lows. Some reach their cyclical highs or lows ahead of the broad market, while others lag the market troughs. Since the S&P 500 represents the performance of all industry groups, it tends to reach new highs after the peak momentum has been seen. At major cyclical troughs, the averages have often declined to new lows after several industry groups had already bottomed out. The process of industry group rotation has to be kept in mind when this indicator reverses direction.

The Diffusion Index

A diffusion index measures the breadth of the advance of all stocks. It is calculated by dividing advancing stocks by the total number of issues traded on the NYSE. The diffusion index can be estimated for five weeks, three months, or a longer period of time. The nine-month diffusion index is another consistent long-term indicator that has signalled major stock market cyclical lows. Figure 10–4 illustrates the S&P 500 versus this important indicator. Notice how the nine-month diffusion index led important market troughs by a few months. The best way to use this indicator is that of watching for a reading of 10 percent or lower and then watching for the market trough in the next few months. This indicator can also be used as an alert to the bottoming out process of some industry groups ahead of the market averages.

The 13-Day Rate of Change of the NYSE Composite

This rate-of-change oscillator is helpful in timing short-term market rallies and declines. The NYSE Composite is by far the best market average representing all the stocks listed on the New York Stock Exchange. Figure 10–5 illustrates the relationship between the index and the 13-day rate of change. The overbought-oversold levels are indicated to show the levels from which the market rallies and declines started. Notice that despite the rising major trend at that time, the rate-of-change oscillator was still helpful to traders in providing them with buy and sell signals. A word of caution, however—while the oscillator may anticipate market strength or weakness, it does not necessarily mean that all stocks will follow the market trend and rise or fall with it. When combined with other short-term indicators, the predictability value of the 13-day rate-of-change oscillator can be substantially enhanced.

Figure 10–5. The 13-day rate of change relative to the NYSE composite.

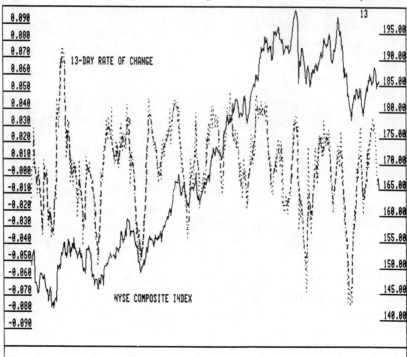

The 30-Day Rate of Change

This indicator is more useful in timing the intermediate-term trend. Here again, the indicator should be interpreted in light of the major trend. Also, as the span of time under study is expanded, market timers can detect divergence of the oscillator better from the action of the averages. When divergences develop between the market averages and the rate-of-change oscillators, they can only indicate a loss of upward momentum. This weakening price action often leads to a more serious consolidation phase. Because long-term downtrends emerge from loss of intermediate-term momentum, any divergenc should be analyzed carefully, remembering that this may be the starting point of a longer-term trend reversal. Figure 10–6 illustrates the behavior of the 30-day rate-of-change oscillator versus the NYSE Composite, The overbought and oversold levels are also shown.

Figure 10–6. 30-Day rate of change relative to the NYSE composite.

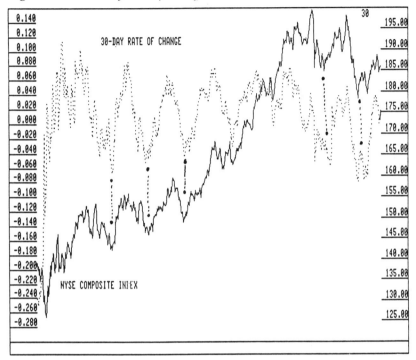

Percentage of Stocks Above Their 200-Day Moving Average

Trend analysts consider that a stock that is trading above its 200-day moving average is bullish. When a stock declines below its moving average, it is considered weak and is likely to decline further. During bull markets, stocks tend to advance above their 200-day moving average and move higher. The broad market momentum could be better assessed by monitoring the percentage of stocks trading above the 200-day moving average. Typically, during primary bull markets the number of stocks trading above their 200-day moving average expands as more and more stocks advance on rallies. Consequently, this ratio keeps rising. When the percentage of stocks above their 200-day moving average reaches 80 percent or higher and reverses direction, the peak momentum of the advance for the cycle may have occurred. If the market averages continue to score new highs without a corresponding rise in this indicator,

Figure 10–7. *The percentage of stocks over 200-day moving average and the S&P 500.*

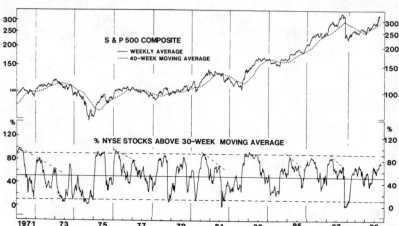

it indicates that fewer and fewer stocks are participating during market rallies. Typically, at such a stage of the cycle, the averages are camouflaging the subtle weakness in the broader market. During bear markets, this ratio is usually less than 50 percent. Around cyclical lows, the number of stocks that are still trading above their 200-day moving average may dip below 20 percent for a few months. It is worth mentioning that in extreme cases, such as the Crash of 1987, this indicator went as low as 4 percent.

Figure 10–7 illustrates the percentage of stocks above their 200-day moving average versus the S&P 500. Notice that a decline in this ratio indicates a loss of momentum in many stocks and often precedes important market setbacks.

Stocks Making New Highs or New Lows

At the close of any trading day, a number of stocks advance to new 52-week highs while others fall to new 52-week lows. When the number of those making new highs is larger than those making new lows, the major trend is likely to be up, since more stocks are showing strength than weakness. In a typical bull market, the new highs far exceed the new lows. As long as the number of new highs is increasing relative to the new lows, the market advance is likely to continue. When the number of new lows outpace the number of new highs, it is to be assumed that the decline is in progress.

While this indicator helps confirm the market strength or weakness, its real value is in determining the peak momentum juncture of the cyclical advance or decline. When the number of new highs, for example, keeps rising day after day and week after week, far outpacing the new lows, there comes a point of climax. After a short-term pause, the market resumes its advance, but the number of stocks scoring new highs does not exceed those made on previous rallies. This is the point at which the peak momentum is assumed to have occurred. Determining that point is important because it tells the investor that a period of rotation may have started and that the bull market has entered a mature stage characterized by a selective environment. The reverse is also true. It becomes crucial to monitor the number of stocks making new lows on any subsequent decline, since if the number shrinks and fails to exceed previous levels, it has to be assumed that the downward market momentum has been exhausted and a bottoming process has started.

The new highs/new lows list can be further analyzed for overwhelming strength or weakness in a particular industry group or stock. When the stocks making new highs for the year are evenly distributed among many industry groups, the market is in a healthy trend and the long-term advance may be assumed intact. When the list of new highs is selective, investors have to be skeptical of the advance and investigate the many other indicators. In addition, when a stock appears on the new-highs list, this could mean that it has excellent upward momentum and further fundamental research should be performed for a possible buy. On the other hand, when a stock declines to new lows for several weeks in a row, it should mean that the stock is very weak and that reassessment of its fundamentals may lead to a decision to sell.

An important observation is that when the list of new highs is dominated by preferred stocks, the market is strong and is likely to advance. When the new lows list contains many preferred issues, weakness ahead must be suspected. The reason is that preferred stocks are sensitive to interest-rate trends and credit conditions. An expanding number of new highs among preferred stocks may indicate that interest rates are likely to ease. And vice versa, when the averages are moving to new highs while the new lows list is dominated by preferred issues, the likelihood of rising interest rates is high and prices in the equities market may be vulnerable to a correction.

Up-to-Down Volume Ratio

The ratio of the daily volume of advancing stocks to declining stocks is another useful momentum indicator. When this ratio is high—ten to one—it may mean that a substantial market advance lies ahead and contrariwise, when the averages are reaching new highs without the up/down volume ratio expanding, it may indicate a loss of the trend's upward momentum. This can be an alert for a period of selective advance or decline in the future.

The true value of this indicator is in confirming rather than timing the trend. Standing alone, this indicator is practically useless, since it is neither related to price momentum nor to the average volume per stock, and it can easily be distorted if the bulk of up volume has been concentrated in only a few issues, especially near dividend recapturing time. The 10-day moving average of the up/down volume ratio can be used to spot divergences between this indicator and the major market averages leading to anticipation of intermediate-term trend reversal.

Stochastics

Stochastics is an oscillator that helps traders and market timers determine entry and exit points. It is particularly helpful for short-and intermediate-term analysis of momentum. Stochastics has been widely used by professional commodity traders. However, its forecasting ability can be applied to the analysis of stocks, industry groups, or the averages. It is hard to tell how long this indicator has been used, but C. Ralph Dysant was among the early observers of its behavior. Thanks to Dr. George C. Lane this valuable trading tool was popularized and is now established as an important oscillator in computerized trading systems.

Stochastics is based on the observation that at the top of a rally prices tend to close at the lower end of the price range and at the bottom of declines prices tend to close at the higher end of the price range. Stochastics consist of the K&D lines. The K line is calculated as follows:

$$(K) = \frac{\text{Last closing price} - \text{closing low of x-\{day or week\} ago}}{\text{x-\{day or week high\}} - \text{x-\{day or week low\}}}$$

In order to smooth out the movement of the K line, a moving average, known as the D line, is calculated and superimposed on the chart. The calculation can be based on daily or weekly closing prices. Any number of days or weeks can be used; this author prefers to work with the 14-day closing prices for short-

Figure 10–8. *The 14-day stochastics of the S&P 500.*

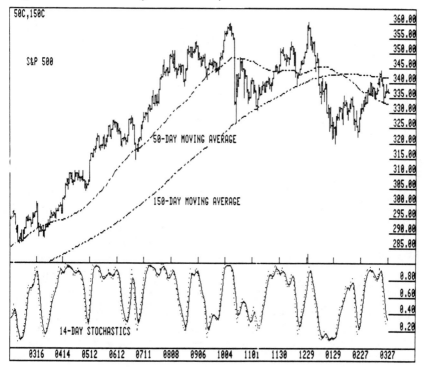

Figure 10–9. 14-day Stochastics of The Nikkei Dow Jones.

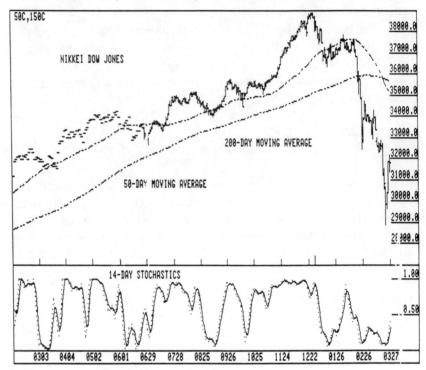

term trading. For the intermediate-term, the 14-week stochastics seem most valuable.

In order to illustrate the behavior of this indicator, Figures 10–8, 10–9, 10–10, and 10–11 will be used. Figure 10–8 illustrates the S&P 500 with 14–day stochastics. Notice the buy signals around the oversold levels. Also notice how the overbought level may not necessarily trigger a sell signal in the case of strong uptrends. In fact, stochastics are best used to initiate buying in a bull market. Overbought levels can only indicate that a slowdown in the upward momentum may be due.

Figure 10–9 illustrates the 14-day stochastics as applied to the Nikkei. The reason the Japanese index is used is because it demonstrates the behavior of daily stochastics under conditions of very strong upward momentum. It is also worth noting that stochastics oscillators are generic in nature and can be used to analyze any market, industry group, or stock. Notice that in

Figure 10–10. *The 14-week stochastics of EXXON.*

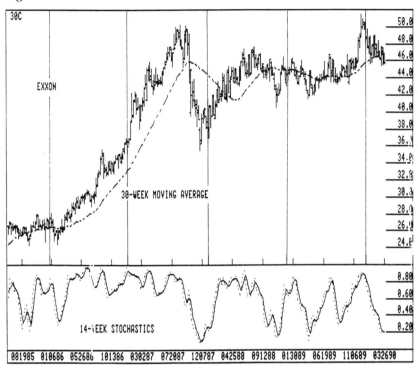

the case of the Japanese market, daily stochastics remained overbought for a long period of time. This example also reveals the inherent weakness of stochastics, as it could have triggered false sell signals around overbought levels.

Figure 10–10 illustrates the 14-week stochastics. Notice again the price behavior near overbought and oversold levels.

Figure 10–11 illustrates the 14-week stochastics versus the Treasury Bonds Index. Notice that the overbought levels did not mean much during the stampeding price action and that stochastic oscillators worked best during the trading range that prevailed during most of 1988 and early 1989.

Working with stochastics may require familiarization of its behavior in many different situations. Its biggest weakness appears to occur during periods of sustained market advance or severe downturn. No single indicator should be used alone, and this one is no different. Awareness of its position relative

Figure 10–11. The 14-week stochastics of Treasury Bonds.

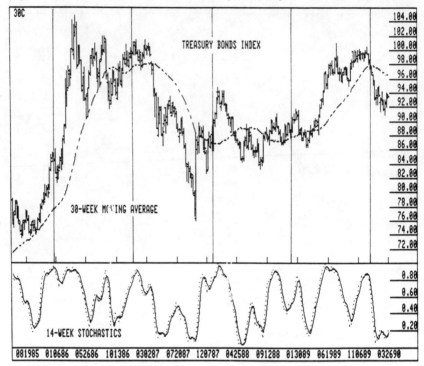

to other indicators and understanding its limitations are crucial to using it profitably.

Relative Strength Index

In 1976, J. Welles Wilder, Jr., discovered the Relative Strength Index (RSI). Soon after, many professional traders and market timers incorporated it in their arsenal of momentum indicators. The RSI measures both the price volatility and the rate of change. It can be used for all markets, industry groups, and individual stocks. It is based on the fact that price elasticity prevents securities from rising or falling without any countertrend reaction or period of consolidation during which future fundamentals are thoroughly assessed. The RSI is calculated as:

$$RSI = \frac{\text{amount of gains over the past (N) days}}{\text{amount of losses over the past (N) days}} \times 100$$

Like any other oscillator, the RSI fluctuates between over-bought and oversold levels. But its real advantage is its ability to generate good divergence measures. Higher highs in the market averages should be confirmed by corresponding higher highs in the oscillator. If not, bearish divergences occur, following which major trend reversals could follow. Similarly, in a downtrend, when the RSI holds above prior selloff lows as the market plummets, a bullish divergence is triggered, suggesting the potential for a trough.

Figure 10–12 illustrates the daily Dow industrials versus the 14-day RSI. Notice that overbought and oversold levels can enable the trader to anticipate corrections. But the real value of

Figure 10–12. *The Dow versus its 14-day stochastics.*

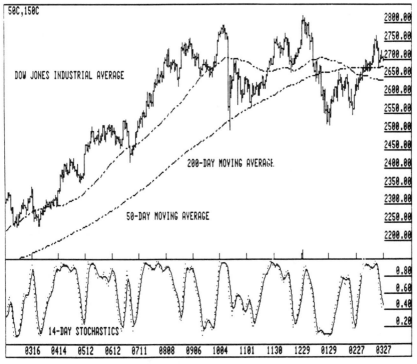

Figure 10–13. The Nikkei versus the 14-day RSI.

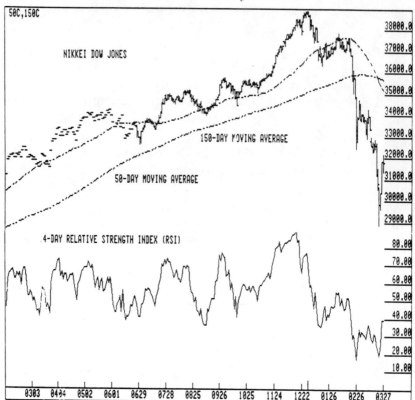

the indicator is in its confirmation and divergence signals, which often precede important market reactions.

Under normal circumstances, the short-term RSI oscillator fluctuates between 70 percent at overbought boundaries and 30 percent near oversold levels. However, during an exceptionally powerful rally or decline, it could soar above 90 percent or plummet below 10 percent. Such extreme readings indicate a strong momentum that can carry prices much higher or much lower. Under such circumstances, it may be too early to sell or to buy. The best way to handle such extremes is to wait for a clear divergence before initiating a trade. Figure 10–13 illustrates an example of an excessive overbought or oversold case. Notice how the Nikkei scored high RSI readings during its

Figure 10–14. *T Bond Index versus the 14-week RSI.*

prolonged advance and how, when it reversed in early 1990, it moved with the same intensity in the opposite direction.

A better indicator for intermediate-term trend analysis is the 14-week RSI. Significant advances or declines can result from overbought or oversold positions. Figure 10–14 illustrates the Treasury Bond Index versus the 14-week RSI. From the graph, notice the negative divergences that developed in 1986-87 and late in 1989. Both were followed by sizable declines in bond prices.

In summary, the RSI is an application of momentum oscillators. It is one of the most helpful tools used by traders to measure the rate of change of prices. The curve of the RSI is directly proportional to the velocity of the movement. When it reaches extreme highs, an overbought situation develops from which the price reacts downward, and vice versa. The RSI is a generic statistical technique that can be applied to any market average, industry group, or individual stock. Its best use, however, is in alerting investors to exhaustion of upward or downward momentum. When divergences develop, they signal the possibility of an important trend reversal.

Moving Average Differential

The moving average of any market, industry group or stock reveals the trend's direction at any point in time. The smaller the number of days used in its calculation, the more sensitive the moving average is to price fluctuations. Commodity traders rely on the 5-day moving average in order to catch the fast swings that characterize commodity movements. Commodity traders cannot afford to use long-term measures, as any minor price reaction represents a high risk in relationship to the leverage associated with such transactions. For equities traders, however, a 30- or 50-day moving average is more commonly used in order to detect intermediate-term price swings. Volatility is much lower for stocks than it is for commodities. In order to focus on the long-term trend, investors can ignore the minor price corrections and are better off relying on the 150- or 200-day moving average. This long-term trend identifier can enable traders to reap the profits that result from consistent price advance, usually accompanied by improving fundamental and economic factors.

The use of the moving average indicators is not restricted to analyzing trend direction. Such indicators, short-, intermediate-, and long-term position relative to the price of the market or security under study can reveal a great deal of information about the trend. The short-term movements are temporary phenomena driven by supply-and-demand imbalances between the buyers and sellers. But in a healthy uptrend, the price tends to maintain a relatively large distance from the 5-day moving average that indicates the power of the prevailing momentum. This short-term strength, however, leads to intermediate-term rallies, which are the result of favorable fun-

Figure 10–15. *The daily Dow industrials relative to its 30-day moving average.*

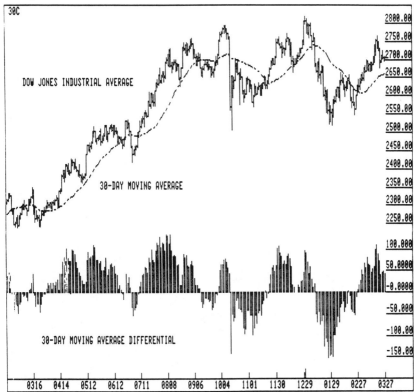

damentals. Such rallies can last for a few months, unless the news indicates renewed weakness in the company's financial position. Longer-term trends tend to persist for many years and can carry the stock or market prices severalfold higher or lower. The strength of the intermediate-term fuels the long-term price trend. A crossing of the short-term and intermediate-term moving averages warns of a temporary reversal, or a correction, in the price. However, a crossing of the intermediate-term and long-term moving averages is more serious, as it may signal the onset of a major trend reversal.

The differential between the price and the moving average is a helpful indicator that can reveal the direction of the trend. This can be used to forecast countertrend reactions. Figure 10–15

Figure 10–16. *The daily Dow Jones industrials index relative to its 150-day moving average.*

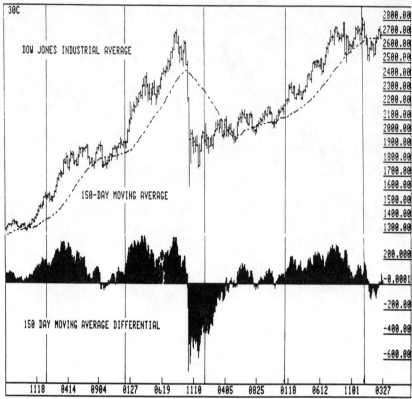

illustrates the moving average differential concept as applied to the daily bar chart of the Dow industrials. The principles of this indicator can apply to the short-, intermediate-, and long-term trend. In the case at hand, the difference between the market price and its 30-day moving average is plotted. As the figure demonstrates, this difference widens up or down depending upon the price direction. Peaks and lows can be identified after considering the longer-term prospects. During bull markets, this indicator is likely to spend more time in the positive half, as the price continues to break out to new highs on every consecutive rally, and vice versa. As far as the indicators are concerned, uptrends are characterized by consistent overbought levels interrupted by some short-term countertrend movements. In the case of a downtrend, the price reaches an oversold position and remains in there for an extended period of time until the decline runs its course.

Figure 10–16 illustrates the difference between the price of the daily Dow industrials and its 150-day moving average. This indicator can be used to analyze the long-term market momentum. Notice that the differential in this case is larger, and the volatility of the indicator is less than in the case of the 30-day moving average. More reliable signals can be obtained from this longer-term indicator than from the shorter-term one.

Figure 10–17. *The 45 and 15-day moving average differentials applied to the market.*

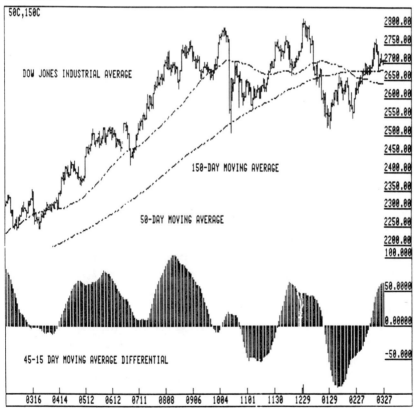

Figure 10–18. *The Dow industrials index and the 150- and 50-day moving averages differential.*

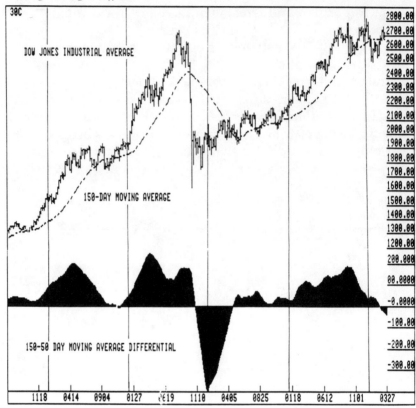

Another way that the moving average technique can be used is that of measuring the difference between two moving averages and relating them to the price movement. The average with the larger number of days is substracted from the shorter-term one. This means that the long-term average will be the zero line with the other oscillating above and below it. In a trendless market, the departure between the two moving averages is likely to be locked in a narrow range. But when a strong rally or decline develops in a specific direction, the difference between them will expand. An uptrend will result in positive values and a downtrend will produce negative ones. The departure of two moving averages from each other could be used to detect overbought and oversold conditions as well as important intermediate- and long-term turning points. The moving average differential technique is based on the fact that short-term price direction cannot stray far away from the securities or market price without some kind of correction. For the short-term, the departure between the 21 and nine-day moving averages proves to be effective. Figure 10–17 illustrates the concept of the moving average differential technique using the 45 and 15-day combinations. Notice the pyramids that develop around the market tops and bottoms.

The departure between the 150- and 50-day moving average makes an excellent long-term momentum indicator. This trend identifier demonstrates the relative weakness or strength of the corrections that interrupt a major advance or decline. Sometimes these setbacks retrace a good percentage of the gains or losses. However, they may also signal a maturing stage of the trend, which is usually followed by a major peak or trough.

Figure 10–18 illustrates the Dow industrials weekly bar chart versus the difference between the 150- and 50-day moving averages. First observe that this indicator is smooth and consistent. When it is rising, it tends to continue as long as the bull trend is intact, and vice versa. In addition, this indicator also gives warning signals when it diverges from the market. When the market makes new highs without a corresponding new high from the moving average differential, an important trend reversal is likely to follow. Notice the divergence that developed in 1987, signalling a serious change in momentum. While most investors and speculators hoped for further advance, the nonconfirmation of this indicator should have cautioned them about the impending weakness.

THE DRAWBACKS OF OSCILLATORS

The momentum oscillators are indicators designed to move up or down with prices to signal extended positions, known as overbought and oversold. Experience has shown that price changes follow momentum changes. Before any mar-

ket rally or correction, momentum oscillators are likely to reveal some price resistance and hesitation in the prevailing
trend. A reversal then follows, which often is accompanied by
overbought or oversold positions. The real problem with the
oscillators, however, is in properly interpreting their meaning
during the different stages of the cycle. In bull markets, overbought conditions occur and remain there for extended periods
of time. Indeed, the stampede of prices at the start of a primary
uptrend is characterized by a consistent and almost uninterrupted rise, which pushes the oscillators above their normal
overbought boundary. Similarly, in a bear market, oversold
conditions persist for a while and carry prices to new extreme
lows. If oscillators are used mechanically based on established
overbought and oversold positions, then they may make the
investor sell too early in a bull market or buy long before the
bear market runs its course.

Even the reliable divergence signals generated by the momentum oscillators can be false and misleading. The best way
to deal with this deficiency is by relying on several indicators at
the same time. If the weight of the evidence suggests exhaustion of momentum in either direction, then corresponding
portfolio adjustment should be warranted. Any trader who
wishes to use momentum oscillators has to study their relationship relative to market prices and digest their behavior at tops
and bottoms. One final word about oscillators: experience
shows that improved results can be realized by monitoring the
intermediate- and long-term oscillators simultaneously and
comparing their relative positions.

SENTIMENT INDICATORS

Most books on investments approach the subject of market forecasting from a rational expectation perspective. This
myth led to disappointing results, which supported the efficient market theory. When the price trend diverged from fundamental expectations, advocates of this theory were quick to
explain that the market's efficiency factor in all known facts at
any point in time. Yet, what most market thinkers fail to con-

sider in their overall analysis is the impact of crowd behavior and sentiment measures.

Market timers recognize the irrational behavior of the market at important reversal points. In the past, waves of euphoria and excessive optimism have coincided with market declines and downtrends. Also, subdued prices, lack of interest from the investing public and panic selling have characterized major cyclical lows and the beginning of primary bull trends.

In the 1930s, contrarian thinking had been popularized by the writings of Humphrey Neil (the father of the contrarian discipline). Ticker tape reading, at that time, was the most viable way of monitoring the market's action. Professional traders tended to sell amid waves of public buying and buy back on precipitous declines that scared the ardent optimists. Yet, during all those years, it was only tape reading and guesswork that enabled speculators to time and execute their contrarian strategies. Rising trade volume characterized by a large number of small orders revealed those period of excessive buying by the average investors.

In the 1940s, the odd-lot theory emerged as a quantitative tool with which to measure public sentiment. Garfield Drew was the first to popularize that technique. His theory focused on the odd-lot buying and selling activities. When the odd-lot orders expanded substantially for a long period of time, it was time to take a contrary view to the prevailing trend and vice versa.

The odd-lot theory reigned supreme until the advent of the options market. In the 1970s and 1980s, the odd-lot statistics offered little help as investors' income rose and with it their ability to buy round lots. Another development was that of the development of index and stock options that could be used to measure the extent of speculators' bullishness or bearishness. These quickly became the most widely followed sentiment indicators by market timers. Another indicator that proved to be of great value in applying contrarian thinking is that of studying the level of conviction of the advisory services. This indicator was created by Investors' Intelligence in Larchmont, New York. Tracking the opinion of professional market analysts gave another dimension to trend forecasting.

The problem with sentiment indicators is in their application. Major signals may be few and far apart, and the greatest danger is to be indiscriminately a contrarian. The investing public is right most of the time. It is only during those periods dominated by sweeping crowd behavior without much left of reasoning that the theory works best. The tendency of most students of sentiment indicators is to react prematurely and miss on the big moves. It is as losing a proposition to be a perpetual contrarian as it is to always be an optimist or a pessimist. The sentiment indicators work best when they confirm the deterioration of the economic, fundamental, market-timing, and other trend indicators. Sentiment indicators should never be used in isolation from all of the other theories and market analysis techniques.

The Put-to-Call Ratio

When speculators are bullish they buy "call" options. When they are bearish they buy "put" options. A call option is a contract that entitles the buyer to purchase a specified number of shares at a fixed price. If the price appreciates, the call buyer will make money by exercising the option, and vice versa—the speculator will lose if the option expires below its exercise value. The reverse applies to put options. Puts are equivalent to short selling when the speculator is betting on a decline. The options market is very speculative. It is the action of those speculative activities that market timers use to measure the overall sentiment in the market.

This ratio is more suitable for traders than for investors. It does not match the other momentum or trend indicators in importance. When call buying is excessive and put buying is low, the market may be vulnerable to a correction. If this condition occurs in sync with a major momentum divergence, indicating the loss of upward momentum, then it may serve as a confirmation of an impending reversal, and contrariwise.

The put-to-call ratio all by itself is meaningless and of little value. Only when it displays excessive optimism in the face of waning upward momentum or gloomy pessimism in conjunction with a precipitous market decline may the put-to-call ratio foretell an oncoming change. An important criterion to watch for is whether the ratio is consistent for a long period of time. Its meaning on a day-to-day basis gives no help in forecasting.

Advisory Services

Investors' Intelligence of Larchmont, New York, publishes a weekly survey of sentiment of the advisory services. The survey represents the opinion of professional market newsletter writers and "gurus" who earn their living forecasting the market direction. The survey gives the percentage of those among them who are bullish, bearish, or expecting a correction.

These advisory services are widely followed by the investment community. Their followers tend to act on their advice. The advisors themselves are mostly trend followers. That is why they often fail to recognize major tops or bottoms as they are developing. In the past, when the percentage of bullish advisory services was overwhelmingly convinced of an uptrend, the market either corrected or reversed its major thrust, and vice versa.

This sentiment indicator is meaningless in isolation from all the other economic, fundamental, and quantitative factors. The advisory services may be justifiably bullish for a long period of time. They may become bearish when it is appropriate to do so. This indicator, however, is important when the momentum and trend indicators are flashing warning signals and the economic indicators are fluctuating at or near previous cyclical peaks or troughs. Such services may then confirm that the oncoming change is of major dimension and should be taken seriously. For example, in September 1987, the advisory services were about 60 percent bullish for several weeks as the gurus predicted that the Dow would top 3000. In line with that, the bond market and the Dow utilities were in a downtrend. In conjunction with these developments, all momentum oscillators displayed major price divergences as they failed to confirm the new highs scored by the averages. The excessive bullishness by major advisors demonstrated that even professionals can be susceptible to emotional reactions rather than logical ones. As a matter of fact, most of the trend indicators revealed above-average vulnerability that should not have been ignored.

Media Focus

The sentiment indicators, in general, are not strictly quantitative. They display the mood of the speculators as well as the professionals toward the market. Such indicators may not give a worthwhile signal for a long time—but when they do, they add an extra level of confirmation to trend projections. Most market timers monitor them on a daily basis, though it is better to be detached, as they may lead to premature conclusions.

A negative or positive psychology tends to propagate quickly among investors. The news media reports on the subject by the hour. But they can also be used to detect deep-rooted convictions and perceptions of certain aspects of the market. When equities prices failed to advance in the 1970s, the market trend was described as "the death of equity" at the close of that decade. A few years later, the stock market embarked on the great bull market of the 1980s. When the copper industry encountered a depression and severe fundamental deterioration in the 1980s, the media tagged it as "the bygone days of mining stocks," just in time for the great advance in Phelps Dodge, a major copper producer. In the same manner, discouraging reports about utilities stocks and gold appeared on the front page of major business publications right before a major change took place.

Such pessimistic perceptions of a market or an industry group can leave room for contrarian thinking. It is when things look their best that they are vulnerable, and when the masses completely ignore potential that they may be about to stage a strong come back. However, the media indicators and most other sentiment indicators fail to provide the exact element of time. They are best used by passive and long-term trend followers.

SUMMARY

The market's internal dynamics are important when trying to judge the likely future direction of prices. The market-timing theory is based on the repetitive nature of market fluctuations under similar circumstances. There have been common patterns throughout history that coincided with the occurance of highs and lows. Such indicators can be monitored in order to compare their behavior relative to past performance. There are a number of statistical tools that can help identify trend reversals and extreme deviations from the trend. Among those are sentiment indicators, momentum oscillators, and trend identifiers.

The supply-and-demand factors are driven by the psychological makeup of the investment arena. Overenthusiasm leads to highs and masses of worries trigger important reversals. The market has reacted sharply to its own internal imbalances more often and more violently than to any fundamental or economic factors.

Market timers rely on sentiment indicators in order to measure crowd psychology. The put-to-call ratio, the percentage of bullish and bearish advisory services, and the overall picture portrayed by the media are key in deciphering the emotional underpinnings governing the purchasing or sale of securities in the marketplace. The meaning of these indicators is crucial at major junctures. When they indicate excessive enthusiasm or despair, the time is ripe to behave like a contrarian. The importance of market psychology and internal dynamics cannot be underestimated. The clearest example was the series of market collapses late in 1978 and 1979 that could not be explained by the business background. The most traumatic of them all, however, was the Crash of 1987, which could not be explained by either the prevailing economic or fundamental environments at that time.

The upside or downside movement is limited by the extended position of momentum oscillators. At major lows, prices stampede upward with a rapid increase in velocity. When the acceleration phase runs its course, a slowdown in the rate of increase sets in during the continuation of the upward trend. Prices finally stop gaining and a trend reversal materializes. The cycle is then repeated in the opposite direction. Oscillators are rate-of-change indicators that can help uncover price levels at which the market or a stock encounters significant resistance. Rate-of-change indicators measure the extent by which a stock has made an unusual deviation from its trend. Experience shows, under such circumstances, that securities tend to move back toward their trend line, which results in rallies or corrections. The trading index, advance decline oscillators, stochastics, and relative strength index can help identify overbought and oversold levels from which reactions are likely to occur.

Moving averages, are helpful as trend identifiers. Their smoothing action of erratic price fluctuations add clarity to price paths and have the ability to display loss of momentum. A stock trading above its moving average, which is slanting upward, is considered to be in an uptrend. Chances are that it will continue to climb for a long period of time before a major reversal occurs. At that juncture, the stock is likely to pierce the moving average, which will be flattening out. When the price continues to decline, the moving average will change direction and confirm the downtrend's impact. Moving average differentials are also helpful in determining the loss of upward or downward momentum. In addition, the crossing of two moving averages can signal an important trend reversal of intermediate or long-term proportions.

No one single technique is infallible in the marketplace. It pays to monitor more than one indicator and compare oscillators at different junctures of an advance or a decline. Furthermore, it is crucial to analyze thoroughly the underlying fundamental and economic backgrounds and fit all these factors into a unified business cycle framework.

❑ 11

Intermarket Relationships

*Ancient Chinese mythology relates the charming
tale of the flexible bamboo and the defiant oak.
During the Monsoon season strong winds assaulted
these plants. The stubborn oak was broken in half,
but the resilient bamboo bending to a superior force
survived to stand straight when the winds
changed. While thoughtful people can easily see
many applications of this moral, the one
concerning us here is the maxim of not fighting
the ticker tape.*

James Dines

A study of the economic and fundamental factors reveals the forces at work that shape the long-term direction of prices. The internal dynamics, as verified by momentum oscillators and sentiment indicators, explain the market's irrational behavior. Such indicators cannot be ignored, because when they occur, they tend to have a varying impact on different industry groups and individual stocks. Quantitative techniques help anticipate intermediate-term corrections or emerging strength. They provide signs of price exhaustion near major trend reversal junctures long before they are reflected in the published economic and fundamental statistics. Yet, it is the sum total of all these indicators that eventually reveals the weight of the evidence indicating the future course of prices. A thorough investigation of the economic, fundamental, and market-timing factors should be the guide in determining trends and in formulating appropriate investment strategies. No assessment of the market outlook is complete if the inter-market relationships are not examined.

MARKET LINKS

Market trends are interrelated and tend to feed on each other. There are links between the different sectors of the financial markets. Awareness of these links can enhance an investor's ability to forecast future possibilities. The commodities market, for example, influences the trend of interest rates, which affect the bond market, which, in turn, impacts securities prices. These intertrend relationships cannot be ignored, as they shape final investment decisions.

Each market is sensitive to a set of specific fundamental factors. Yet, each one's rise or fall may influence other sectors and serve as a catalyst that strengthens or weakens their positions. A trend in a specific market has consequences on others; there is a domino-like relationship. Financial markets may lead or lag each other. At any given time, they may be at a specific phase of their own cyclical behavior. A study of these intertrend dynamics can help anticipate future developments before they are recognized by participants in any specific market. Two sectors may have a positive correlation. An uptrend in one of them fuels the prices in the other or simply confirms its advance. Or, two markets may have an inverse relationship such that the strength in one of them may indicate weakness in the other. Sometimes the trend in one sector may warn of a potential trend reversal in another. The trend may also confirm and support the major trend in progress in other markets.

As discounting mechanisms, financial markets are not only influenced by their own unique fundamental environment but also by the behavior of all other markets. Financial markets are interrelated, as they constantly affect each other's performance. In the process of discounting future economic events, they move in concert. These intermarket relationships forewarn of important trend changes. By understanding their influence on each other, investors can anticipate peaks, troughs, and trend perspectives.

What Market Links Reveal

Markets are often dormant and trendless when investors lack conviction about the future. During such times, the indicators are likely to be nonconclusive. But when there is consistent improvement or deterioration in the fundamental background, the prevailing trend may be expected to prevail. When the market stops rising on favorable news or resists falling in the face of negative developments, a major trend reversal may be in the making. It is at such junctures that it pays to monitor other markets' behavior, as it may give early warning signals. In addition, intermarket relationships can reveal emerging secular trends that can last for a decade or more and that are triggered by powerful fundamental changes.

For example, in the 1970s, the commodities market became very active as speculators sensed accelerating inflation. The gold and silver markets, in particular, witnessed explosive advances. Most commodities stampeded, as demand far exceeded supply for all kinds of goods and services. The baby boomers invaded the job market, earned income, settled in their own houses, and went on a spending spree consuming everything in sight. The surging need for shelter, furniture, transportation, financial services, and all sorts of goods exercised pressures on prices and fueled inflation. Analysis of the potential impact of inflation on financial markets might have led investors to realize that real assets were going to outperform stocks and bonds. The rising commodities prices were signalling the changing environment and may have prompted adjustments in the asset mix. In the early 1980s, however, the high real interest rates put a dent on inflation, and commodities markets subsided. The price of grains, soybeans, and other food components plummeted and the agricultural sector suffered a depression under the burden of debt. The fixed-income sector experienced one of its best advances in history. This, in turn, triggered the raging bull market in equities.

The early 1980s also witnessed a speculative binge in the real estate market that carried prices to unsustainable heights. The rise of prices in the housing sector, however, was driven by the events of the 1970s that had left behind a generation that thought inflation would continue to soar forever. Although the speculative excesses took hold for a few years in favor of real-assets investing, it had to end as household debt reached historic highs. The bubble of the real estate mania was finally pierced during the Crash of 1987 and the long protracted decline of prices began.

Globalization-Intercountry and Interrelated

There is always one market or another that is active at any given time. In the 1970s, it was the commodities and real estate markets. In the 1980s, the place to be was in equities and fixed-income securities. As favorable trends emerge in a certain market, activity rises and transaction volume expands. In the 1990s, it seems that the wave of globalization will gain further upward momentum; its consequences cannot be underestimated. The position of the dollar in the foreign exchange arena should become a key trend determinant in many financial markets. The dollar's strength or weakness can have a domino effect on the economy, commodities prices, interest rates, the fixed-income sector, industry groups, and, particularly, on multinational companies. Investors cannot afford to close their eyes on the growing interdependence of the world economies and the multilateral trade activities that can affect earnings, sales, and the financial health of corporations. Securities markets around the world move in unison, as demonstrated by their simultaneous collapse in October 1987, and their ensuing recovery. Globalization is taking hold, and no nation can afford to operate in isolation of the rest of the world.

Inflation and interest rate fluctuations travel across national borders around the globe. The continuation or reversal of a major trend in any market is a function of other trends emerging in other sectors of the economy. With the advance in information processing and exchange of financial data around the world, the full integration of financial markets is a dawning reality. Without proper assessment of the implications, of changes in any market on the others, volatility may increase and surprises may result. The purpose of this chapter is that of examining some of the most important intermarket relationships. This will be further integrated in the multidisciplinary analysis of the subsequent chapters.

BOND MARKET INTERRELATIONSHIPS

The bond market attracts investors who are looking for a steady stream of income with reasonable but low risk for the principal. These bonds are issued by the government and the public sector to finance future budgetary and long-range planning needs. They carry a certain coupon rate that is paid at regular intervals and have a maturity date at which time the principal is paid back to the bond holder.

Interest Rates and the Bond Market

Because of the coupon rate, a bond's appeal is highly dependent on the general level of interest rates. During periods of rising inflation and soaring interest rates, the value of fixed-income securities declines in the open market. And vice versa, when inflation is under control and rates are declining, bonds rise as the appeal of safety and income entice investors to buy them. Hence, the relationship between the trend of interest rates and the bond market is inverse.

Figure 11–1 illustrates the inverse relationship between the bond market and interest rates. The 3-months Treasury Bill rate was chosen because it mirrors the fluctuations of the Fed-

Figure 11–1. *3-months Treasure Bills and the Bond Market.*

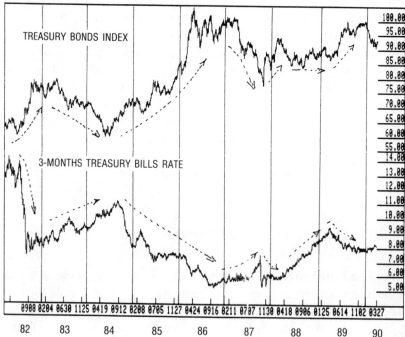

eral Funds rate while being less volatile. Notice that the mild rise in rates in 1986 prompted a precipitous decline in 1987. The weakness in bonds eventually led to the meltdown in equities in October of that year. This relationship is so important that it should be monitored constantly. Bonds lead stocks both up and down. Rising interest rates propel a decline in bonds that is usually followed by a fall in stock prices. But the question remains: how does the fixed income market anticipate the rise or fall of interest rates? Rates fluctuate depending upon the Federal Reserve Board's policy. A tight policy is usually implemented when the Fed wants to fight inflation and an accommodative one reflects its effort to prompt a business recovery and stimulate the economy. Hence, the trend of interest rates can be determined if one can tell where inflation is heading.

The commodities markets and raw materials prices can give an early indication of the future direction of prices. Rising demand for industrial and agricultural commodities can reveal a heating economy and mounting inflationary pressures. This rise in commodities prices is the leading indicator of a rise in rates. Therefore, for the bond market to discount rate rises, it must take its lead from commodities trends. One of the most important commodities, with above-average impact, is crude oil prices. Energy is used in almost all economic activities and its rise or fall determines, to a great extent, the general level of inflation. Any price fluctuation in the cost of a barrel of oil is quickly reflected in the price of almost all goods and services.

Crude Oil Prices and the Bond Market

The rise or fall of oil prices has a broad impact on the cost structure of business in all sectors of the economy. It is one of the most important commodities to monitor, as it plays a vital role in determining the outlook for inflation. Crude oil is a key component of the economic output, because it enters into the process of production of a wide variety of goods and services. The price fluctuation of crude oil adds to or substracts from the price structure of so many final products. In the 1970s, the quadrupling of oil prices triggered the acceleration of an inflation that reached almost out-of-control proportions. In addition, the price of this important commodity has shaped the monetary policy for the past two decades. When the price rises, the Fed tightens and interest rates rise. This, in the past, has caused recessions to follow which, in turn, led to a slowdown in consumption and a subsequent stabilization process.

The strength of crude oil prices has an inverse relationship with the fixed-income sector. Rising oil prices are perceived by investors as inflationary. Under such circumstances, the Fed tends to tighten its monetary policy, which implies higher interest rates. The bond market suffers in an environment of rising inflation and high interest rates. This relationship between bonds and crude oil prices is crucial, because it determines the trend of interest rates, the behavior of interest-rate sensitive sectors of the economy, and the equities market overall.

Figure 11–2 illustrates the relationship between crude oil prices and the T Bonds index. As can be seen, the two markets tend to move in opposite directions. When crude oil prices rise bonds fall, and vice versa. When the price of crude oil plummeted in 1985, the bond market stampeded upward. The Treasury Bonds Index subsequently reached an all-time high. The stock market took its lead from the bond market, following suit and surging during the first half of 1987. Also notice that the firmness of crude oil prices in late 1989 led to the bond market's decline in January 1990.

Bonds, Crude Oil, and Interest Rates

The inverse trend relationship between oil and bonds is not foolproof, however. In figure 11–3 the 3-Months Treasury Bills rate is included with crude oil and bonds. Notice that the rise of crude oil prices near March 1989 was not accompanied by a decline in the fixed-income market. As a matter of fact, bonds rallied with strength in the energy sector.

The 3-Months Treasury Bills rate peaked at that time, however. It seems that the bond market at that time was more influenced by the prospect of declining rates than by rising crude oil prices. This three-way relationship can hardly be ignored. Investors should always monitor the relative trend

Figure 11–2. *Crude oil versus bonds.*

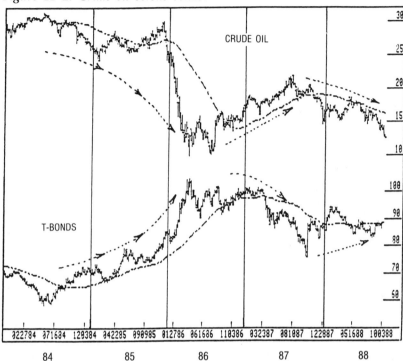

relationships between these three markets, as this can determine inflationary expectations, the interest rate's likely direction, and the outlook for bonds.

COMMODITIES TRENDS

Commodities prices are sensitive to inflation and interest rates. The commodities market is a discounting mechanism of future prices of raw materials used in manufacturing, as well as agricultural and food products, and precious metals. Producers of such commodities hedge their position against future increases or decreases by selling contracts at the current market prices. The buyer of these contracts speculate on the trend that is likely to develop in these commodities. If the buyer expects that inflation is gaining upward momentum, then he or she

Figure 11–3. Crude Oil, Bonds, and the 3-Months Treasury Bills Rate.

will go long. If the rate of inflation is declining, he or she may initiate short positions in anticipation of a fall in raw materials prices.

By selling contracts against their crop or prized, mined material, hedgers transfer the risk of price fluctuations to the speculator. They are willing to deliver their commodities at the specified prices they agreed to. This way, they can improve planning for production and increase efficiency with their internal finances. Speculators, on the other hand, come to futures markets with hopes of beating the game, allured by the hefty leverage. The excitement of the game and the dreams of making a killing drive them to participate in predicting the future course of prices. In their pursuit of profits, they analyze the known and potential fundamentals that are likely to affect their future.

The balance of supply and demand for commodities eventually determines their price and their trends. As consumer demand expands during phases of economic recovery, the pressure mounts on raw materials prices. Aluminum and copper are industrial metals that enter into the manufacturing process of many goods. Lumber is a vital ingredient for the housing market, manufacturing of furniture, and other wood products. Gold is a commodity that has long been recognized as a store of value and a hedge against the devaluation of paper money. Moreover, gold is an effective tool with which to deal with political uncertainty. Other precious metals such as platinum and silver have important applications in the industrial sector. Prices of agricultural products are also traded on the commodity futures exchanges, and their trends are impacted by increases or decreases in consumption levels. Upward trends in these commodities prices indicate a heating up of the economy; when commodities prices are on the rise, inflation gains upward momentum. If the Fed adopts an accommodative and expansionary policy, the rise in raw materials prices is then likely to accelerate with inflationary consequences. But, if the Fed tightens its monetary policy, which is more likely to happen, interest rates rise and commodities prices subside. Eventually, the high rates put a dent in the trend of inflation, as measured by both the wholesale price index and the consumer price index. The weaker the real supply-and-demand balance for goods and services in the economy is, the more severe the ensuing downtrend in commodities becomes, which is all part of the business cycle.

The CRB Index

The Commodities Research Bureau Index (CRB) reflects the future trend of the Consumer Price Index (CPI) and closely correlates to it. The CPI compares the current prices of a fixed basket of consumer goods with their levels in a given base year.

This basket consists of food, clothing, transportation, raw materials that are used in manufacturing, transportation, and other services. Both the CPI and the Producer Price Index (PPI) are reported once a month, whereas the CRB is a daily index that provides information about future price trends. Moreover, starting from 1984, gold, which is a good barometer of inflation, was included in the calculation of the CRB index. That is vital to monitor the commodity futures prices. Because of their high sensitivity to inflation, commodities tend to have a direct effect on other markets. They provide clues about the likely future trend of inflation, interest rates, bonds, and the stock market. Another reason why the CRB should be monitored is that the CPI and PPI project what has already happened, whereas the CRB gives a daily and weekly assessment of the direction of prices and the outlook for inflation.

Figure 11–4 illustrates the CRB index versus some of its components. Notice how commodities prices may not move in unison at all times. This has been helpful in interpreting the trend. For example, in the wake of the drought of 1988, agricultural commodities prices soared as markets anticipated future shortages. Corn, soybeans, wheat, and other grain prices rose sharply. Their advance was immediately reflected in a corresponding advance in the CRB index. Yet, an analysis of the trend of gold and crude oil revealed that these two commodities were receding. Their decline, at that time, indicated that the rise of the CRB was only temporary and that the drought was not likely to trigger a wave of inflation all across the board. Indeed, once it rained, grain prices fell and the CRB index also declined. That is why it is important to analyze futures markets in relationship to each other, as such analyses may reveal whether inflationary pressures are reflected in the trend of a large number of commodities or are limited to only a few particular cases.

Commodities and the Bond Market

The CRB index is the equivalent of the Dow industrials for speculators in the commodity futures markets. More importantly, its fluctuations bear directly on movements in other markets. A rise in commodities prices spells trouble for the

Figure 11–4. *The CRB index and some of its components.*

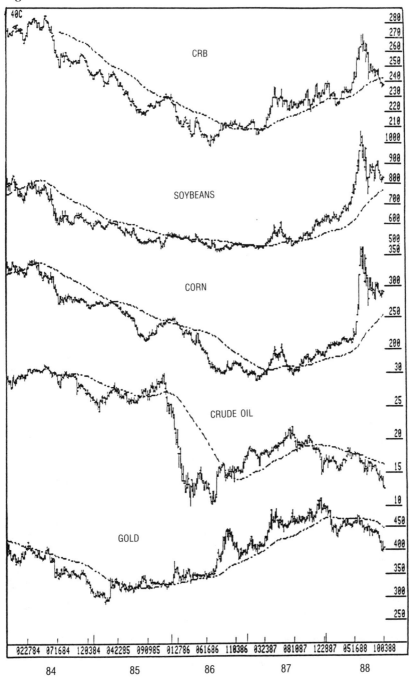

fixed-income sector. It is an early indication of a broad advance in interest rates, which directly affects the values of fixed-income securities. Figure 11–5 illustrates the relationship between bonds and the CRB index. Notice that the two markets are inversely correlated—their trends are opposite to each other. When the CRB index moves up, T-Bonds move down and vice versa. The fixed-income investor should recognize the influence of a rising or declining trend on bonds' investments. Notice also the slight lead in timing that commodities markets have when compared to T-Bonds.

Commodities Prices and Interest Rates

Interest rates have a positive correlation with commodities prices. When the cost of money rises, it discourages borrowing and causes economic activities to slow down. On the corporate

Figure 11–5. *The CRB index and Bonds.*

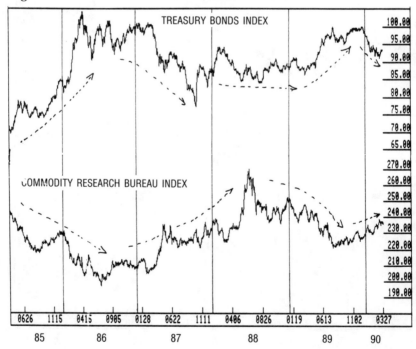

level, profit margins fall and demand for products and services decline. This prompts cuts in the labor force and curtailment of capital spending. At the consumer end, rising rates compel households to save and make them postpone their buying plans. The result is a decline in both consumption and production and a contraction in business activities. This cycle repeats itself over and over again.

Figure 11–6 illustrates the relationship between commodities prices as represented by the CRB and interest rates. It is important to note at this stage that the initial rise of interest rates may not affect commodities prices. It is their persistence that eventually leads to the slowdown in demand and the broad containment of the inflationary forces. Not only does it matter how high rates go, but also how long they stay relatively high in real terms. In the late 1970s, it took a huge advance in rates, to almost 20 percent, and a very tight policy to get prices

Figure 11–6. *The CRB index and the Three-months T Bond.*

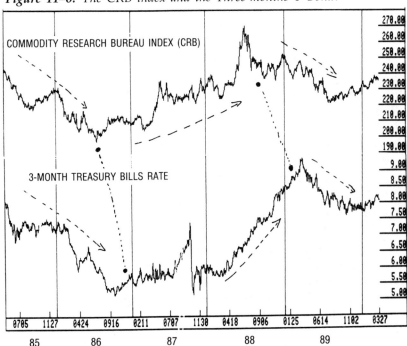

under control. After that period of runaway inflation and for most of the 1980s, rates barely reached double digits. Their mild rise in the absence of the demographic factors and oil shocks enabled the Fed to control rising prices without having to be too stringent.

Commodities Prices, Crude Oil and Bonds

Commodities prices have an inverse relationship with bonds. Their rise implies mounting pressures on the Fed to tighten money and an advance in interest rates, which negatively affect bond prices. The reverse is also true.

The trend of the crude oil market is a good indicator of future inflation. Because it is used in the manufacturing of all goods, it plays a crucial role in determining the amount of pressure on prices in the economy. If the CRB is rising, it may be premature to deem such strength as indicative of resurging inflationary pressures. An analysis of the price progression of crude oil is as important. When both the CRB and crude oil are rising, it may be justifiable to get concerned about the outlook for inflation and interest rates. But if the CRB is rising while crude prices are subdued or falling, then it may not necessarily be that inflation will accelerate. Examining the trends of these three markets can reveal a great deal about the outlook for inflation and the likely monetary policy that the Fed will choose to adopt.

Figure 11–7 illustrates the relationship between the fixed-income market as represented by the Treasury Bonds Index, the CRB index, and crude oil. The bond market is sensitive to commodities price trends, especially crude oil, as they often determine the future direction of interest rates. Since the rise or fall of raw material and agricultural products leads rates, the bond market reacts inversely to their trends. The arrows show the inverse relationship between the three markets. When the CRB index rises, T-Bonds fall, and vice versa. Note how in 1984 and 1985, the bond market rallied strongly as commodities prices trended lower. Furthermore, in early 1986, the Treasury Bonds index accelerated upward when crude oil prices plummeted. When the downside decline of both the CRB index and

Figure 11–7. *The CRB index, T Bonds, and crude oil.*

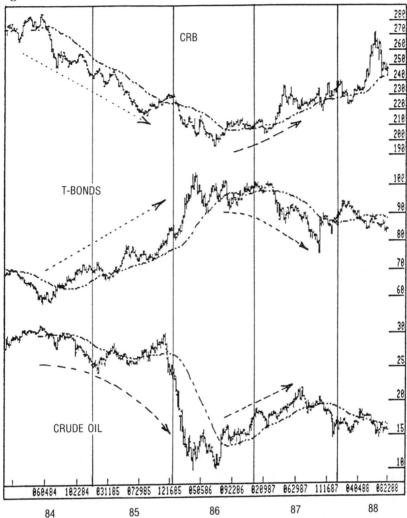

crude oil was exhausted in 1986, the bond market stopped making new highs. As commodities were bottoming out, bonds were topping out. Notice how the drought of 1988 did not severely affect the bond market, as crude prices were falling at that time. Despite the rise in grains and the food components of the CRB, it was the crude oil market that delivered an unequivocal message that any rise in inflation is likely to be temporary in nature and may end as soon as the drought ends.

Interest Rates, Commodities Prices, and the Bond Market

In order to integrate thoughts and digest interrelationships between bonds, interest rates, and commodities prices, figure 11–8 may be of help. It demonstrates how in a real-life environment, these markets behaved and how they influenced each other. Starting from 1984, commodities prices were declining and the CRB index was trending lower. The Fed eased, as it felt that inflation was indeed under control. By mid-1986, however, the CRB index bottomed out and commodities prices reversed into an uptrend. Notice that rates lagged behind the rising CRB index. It was only a matter of time, however before the Fed adopted a more restrictive monetary policy. When it finally did, rates began to firm up and the bond market went into a tailspin. The precipitous decline of the bond market eventually led to the plunge of the stock market in late 1987. As the Fed became more concerned with the aftermath of the crash, it eased temporarily into the first quarter of 1988. As rates declined, the bond market rebounded sharply.

But the CRB index continued to rise and the threat of inflation loomed. The drought of 1988 further aggravated the commodities situation, and fueled the upward momentum of the CRB index. The Fed, once again, began to tighten and rates soared. But the subdued psychological mood of the fixed-income sector led the market to remain locked in a trading range awaiting the cyclical peak in rates. By March 1989, the upward momentum in rates displayed upward exhaustion. Meanwhile, the CRB index was also subsiding, the economic environment at that time signaled a slowdown. This was accompanied by the crisis of the savings and loan industry and the shaky outlook for real estate. The initial decline in rates in 1989 led to a strong rally in bonds. In early 1990, crude oil and gold prices began to strengthen.

At that point, the bond market became worried about the future course of inflation and entered a corrective phase. This explains what happened between 1985–89. It focuses on the

Figure 11–8. The CRB index, T Bonds and the Federal Funds rate.

intermarket relationships and serves to illustrate the dynamics of bonds, commodities prices, and interest rates. Although there is no assurance that this exact example is going to be duplicated in the future, it approximates what may be expected under the set of circumstances given at that time. Remember that all markets go through periods of aberration once in a while. They tend to deal with extremes—the pendulum swings from excesses to shortages and back.

THE IMPACT OF UTILITIES

Utilities stocks have special appeal for investors who are seeking a steady stream of income without much risk to the principal. The dividends payout ratio is usually high and the yield is often competitive with government bonds. Income-oriented portfolio managers diversify their holdings in utilities stocks, which not only provide income but also the potential for capital appreciation. The industry is considered mature. It is highly regulated by local government authorities and its future growth is highly dependent on demographics and geographic location. The migration of business and people among states helps increase sales.

Interest Rates and the Utilities Index

The risk in utilities stocks depends upon earnings and especially on the amount of dividends paid to investors. During periods of accelerating inflation, the fast rise in interest rates diminishes utilities' investment appeal when they fail to increase their dividends commensurately. In order for utilities to pay higher dividends, they have to increase the fees charged for their services. Local authorities' approval or denial of rate hikes restricts utilities' ability to raise dividends.

Another risk associated with investing in utilities stocks is related to nuclear plants. Most utilities companies have a number of plants that generate electricity from nuclear sources. Leaks, environmental threats, and increased public perception of the dangers of nuclear energy could be a cause of their modest valuation in the marketplace.

Figure 11–9 illustrates the Dow utilities and the Three-Months Treasury Bills rate. The relationship between them is inverse.

OTHER LINKAGE INDICATORS

There remain several key indicators with which inter-market relationships can be isolated and measured. The TED spread, bonds, the Federal Funds Rate, the Dow utilities, gold, crude oil and a number of other factors reveal the relative strength or weakness of markets at critical junctures. When rates rise, utilities stocks decline, and when they fall, utilities advance. The utilities group is known for being interest-rate sensitive. The graph also demonstrates how the group displayed weakness in 1987 and signalled the onset of a correction in the equities market. The decline of both utilities stocks and the bond market flashed a sell signal that, if abided by, would have saved investors the subsequent trauma.

Figure 11–9. *Dow utilities versus the Three-Months Treasury Bills Rate.*

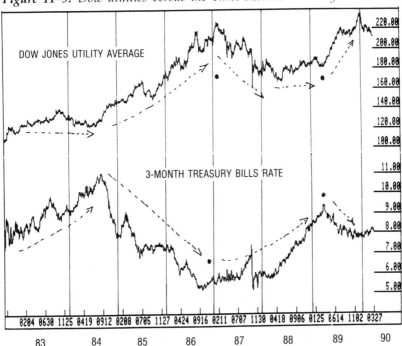

The Ted Spread

The spread between Treasury Bills and Eurodollar rates is another key indicator that can help project the trend of bond prices. When this spread is expanding, *i.e.*, the TED spread line is rising, bonds are vulnerable to a decline. When the TED spread is falling, bonds are likely to be bullish. This inverse relationship is worth monitoring, since it can confirm or diverge from the other indicators—its message is important to reckon with. When the Fed is tightening, the TED spread expands as rates on short-term Treasury Bills rise faster than those paid in the international markets on Eurodollars. And vice versa, when the FED is easing to stimulate the economy, rates fall in the United States faster than in foreign markets. There is no threshold level at which a buy or a sell signal is triggered. It is the direction of the TED spread line that is more important than its value. In an environment of skyrocketing interest rates, such as was the case in the late 1970s; the spread was much higher than when rates subsided worldwide in the 1980s.

Figure 11–10 illustrates the relationship between the TED spread and the Treasury Bonds index. The arrows clearly show the inverse relationship between the two. In 1982, the bond market stampeded upward in late July and was shortly followed by the major cyclical low in the market in August. The spike in the TED spread that occurred coincided with the low in the Treasury Bonds index. The precipitous decline in the TED spread that followed confirmed the trend of interest rates and the bullishness in both the equities and fixed-income markets. Late 1983 and early 1984, the TED spread rose again as the Fed decided to slow down the pace of economic recovery. The bond market weakened, which propelled an intermediate-term correction in stocks. From mid-1984 to mid-1986, the TED spread kept narrowing as rates declined. This, accompanied by a plummet in crude oil prices and a broad decline in commodities, gave a jolt to the fixed-income market. In late 1986, the spread expanded again, and bonds endured a severe setback that culminated with the Crash of 1987. The arrows indicate the points at which important reversals in the bond market coincided with a change in direction of the TED spread.

Figure 11–10. *T Bonds versus the TED spread.*

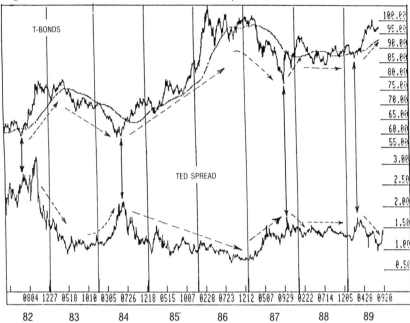

Bonds, TED Spread, Federal Funds Rate, and the Dow Utilities

Once the intertrend relationship between bonds, the TED spread, the Federal Funds Rate, and the utilities stocks is understood, their behavior relative to each other can be monitored. While all these markets are influenced by a multitude of economic and fundamental factors, and while they seemingly operate under different circumstances, their trends confirm the type of monetary policy adopted by the Fed in its effort to manage the economy. Figure 11–11 is an illustration of the Bonds index, the TED spread, the Federal Funds Rate, and the Dow utilities. Here again, the figure demonstrates the behavior these markets show relative to each other. When the TED spread and the Federal Funds Rate decline, both bonds and utilities strengthen and rally. And vice versa, when they change direction and rise, the interest-rate sensitive sectors of the economy suffer and fall. When the outlook is clear to everybody and the crowd is able to forecast the direction of prices correctly, the tendency of these markets is to proceed as expected but to exceed downside or upside targets. In other words, when the vision of the majority of participants is clear and unanimous about the outlook for the economy, interest rates, or the bond market, aberrations tend to prevail as excesses build and trends exacerbate. However, history shows that when the conviction is high about a certain event, a contrarian alternative takes hold. The consensus has seldom been able to predict the future with great accuracy.

GOLD AND INTEREST RATES

Gold has long been known as a store of value and a hedge against inflation. Investors have always sought the yellow metal as an alternative to paper money. The gold standard has been abandoned in the early 1970s and the world monetary system has since been governed by the "floating" of international currencies in the foreign exchange market. Yet, gold continues to represent the best investment when inflationary expectations are high. In the late 1970s, gold prices and gold-mining stocks stampeded to all-time highs in the face of the runaway inflation of the time. In addition, gold is a good defense against political risk, being the equivalent of an international currency, and accepted all over the world. When political unrest erupts in any country, investors and people of that country change their currency into bullion.

Gold has a rather loose relationship with interest rate direction, at least in the short-term. The two have been inversely correlated with a lag. When rates have peaked, gold prices begin to rise, and when they firm up and are about to rise, gold prices subside. There is a time lag that is difficult to quantify between the action of the two.

Figure 11–12 illustrates the relationship between gold prices and the Federal Funds Rate. Peaks in interest rates lead uptrends in gold prices and troughs of rates lead downtrends in gold. This relationship, however, should be treated carefully, as gold prices are influenced by many factors and some of

Figure 11–11. *T-Bonds, the Ted spread, the Federal Funds rate and the Dow utilities index.*

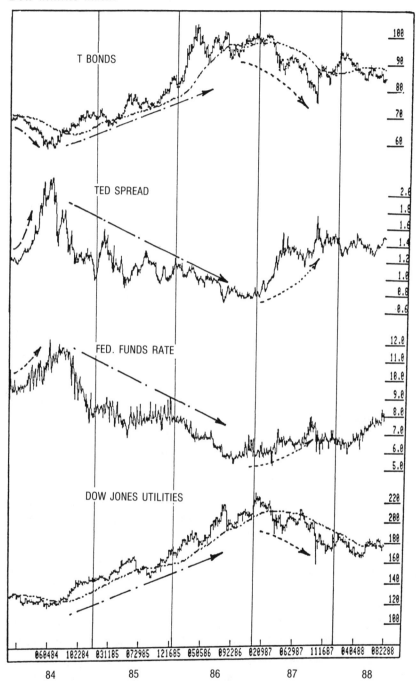

Figure 11–12. *Gold and the Federal Funds rate.*

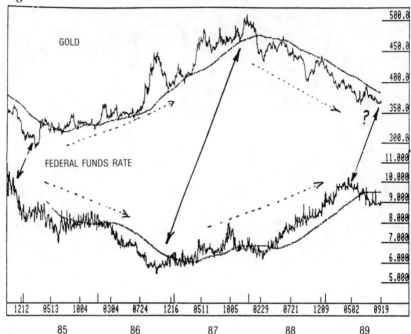

them may prevail at a certain juncture such that they negate any relationship between the precious metal and interest rates. The above relationship can be explained by the fact that after a peak is reached in interest rates, the economy is likely to be either entering or is in the middle of a contraction phase. This, in turn, raises the credit risk for most corporations and negatively affects their cash flow and earnings. The result is most likely a decline in securities prices, leaving gold as one of a few investment alternatives that provides safety in the face of an economic recession.

When rates reach an important low and start rising, gold prices decline because investors know that the Fed is tightening and that it is only a matter of time before inflation subsides. The high rates entice investors to high-yield, risk-free money market rates. So gold gains in appeal when rates peak and declines when rates rise. But, again, this relationship has not proven to be one that has a high percentage of reliability, as gold is influenced by a variety of other factors that may influence its trend despite the rise or fall of interest rates.

CRUDE OIL FUTURES VERSUS OIL STOCKS

Crude oil prices are vital for almost all sectors of the economy. The relationship between energy prices and companies that operate in this business is of particular interest. The trend of three key groups has been examined relative to the major swings of oil price per barrel. Figure 11–13 illustrates the S&P international oil group index, domestic oil group, and the oil services group vis-á-vis the price of crude oil. As history demonstrates, the international oil group was not affected by the decline in crude oil prices. As going concerns and by virtue of being an oligopoly, the group continued to prosper as it trimmed its expenses.

The domestic oil group also ignored the meltdown of crude oil prices and continued to be valued in the marketplace based upon its earnings and cash flow outlook. Only the oil services group closely mirrored the crude oil trend. The overcrowding in the industry hurt sales and earnings. The excessive capacity led to price competition, which exercised severe downward pressures on margins. The end result was a precipitous decline in oil services companies in the open market. However, while the relationship between the energy-related groups and oil prices has not been apparent, it must be stressed that a rise in crude oil prices has an instant, positive impact on oil-producing companies. Without having to do anything, their underground holdings of crude oil and natural gas rise, causing a boost in the value of their unused and untapped inventory of natural resources.

THE DOLLAR AND INDUSTRY GROUPS

Almost all large companies derive a substantial percentage of their revenues from overseas business. The chemical and drug industries, in particular, are sensitive to the dollar fluctua-

Figure 11–13. *Crude oil versus domestic and international oil groups and the oil services group.*

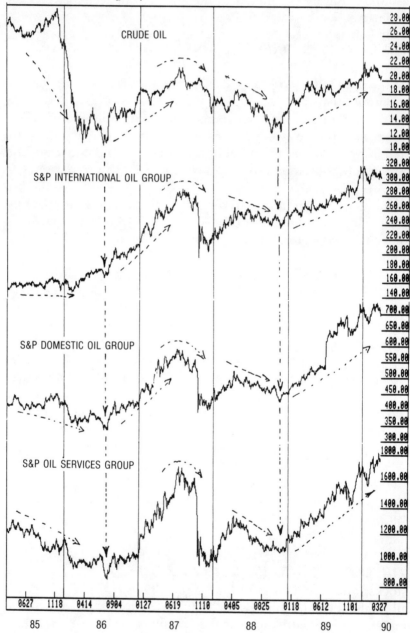

tions in the foreign exchange market. The trend in those two groups is highly correlated to the strength or weakness of the dollar relative to international currencies. The reason is that their substantial sales and earnings from offshore operations tend to be positively or negatively affected by currency translation. A strong dollar can adversely affect financial results and their advance if the broad market trend is bullish. If the dollar strength coincides with a bear market, the price decline of those two groups may intensify. Similarly, when the broad market is bullish and the dollar is weak, the advance of those two groups may accelerate. And if the general market trend is bearish, but the dollar is weak, both groups may resist the downside pressure and outperform the other sectors. So, besides all the other factors that influence the trend of these industry groups, investors have to take the effect of the dollar's position into account. Figure 11–14 illustrates the dollar index versus the drug and chemical industry groups. Both groups have been beneficiaries of the dollar's weakness during the 1987–89 period.

COMMODITIES PRICES VERSUS INDUSTRY GROUP TRENDS

Commodities prices have a particular impact on certain industry groups. For example, when the future or spot price of aluminum rises, it may imply that the demand for that commodity is expanding. Under such circumstances, the stocks operating in those industry groups, the bulk of whose business depends upon this commodity, may also rise as the demand for their products is expected to expand. Experience shows that aluminum stocks tend to advance when the price of the raw material rises.

The same intertrend relationship exits between lumber and the forest products group, between copper and the copper stocks, and between gold and goldmining stocks. In general, all stocks that are highly sensitive to the fluctuations of raw material prices in their business operation tend to follow their trends.

Figure 11–14. The dollar, chemicals, and drugs.

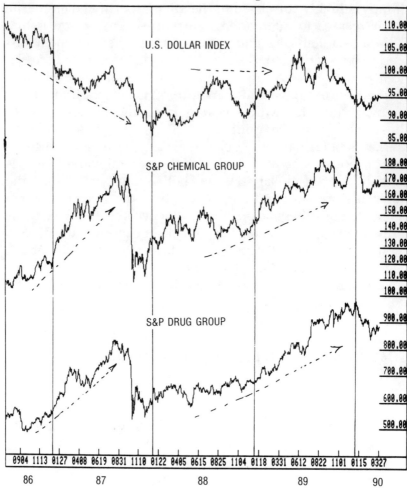

However, aluminum, copper, and forest stock companies do always benefit from a rise in commodities prices. A company is a going concern whose fortunes depend upon its management's business knowhow. The extent of the relationship with commodities prices is no more than a potential positive or negative development that can help the trend in those industry groups. It should be considered another catalyst in addition to all the other fundamental catalysts that studied earlier.

The relationship between raw materials prices and stocks in industry groups that are sensitive to commodities fluctuations holds true during the different stages of the business cycle. Mining stocks are late-cycle movers, as their earnings and sales accelerate with the expanding consumption of a heating economy. Figure 11–15 illustrates the prices of the CRB Raw Material Industrials Spot index and four different securities that are beneficiaries of commodities price rises. Notice that the low of the industrials spot price index in late 1986 was the trigger point for most of the stocks shown. The accelerating commodities prices propelled a strong upward trend in 1987. The crash, while severe, was only a temporary interruption to the rising prices. In fact, all these stocks eclipsed their pre-crash highs.

To summarize, commodities trends play an important role in determining the future price direction of several other markets. Not only do they affect the Fed and, therefore, the outlook for interest rates, but they also affect the trend of securities prices in both the equities and fixed-income markets. In addition, they have a direct influence on mining stocks and basic industries.

THE DOW TRANSPORTATION INDEX AND ITS COMPONENTS

Four industry groups enter into the calculation of the Dow Jones Transportation average, namely the airlines, the railroads, the air freight firms, and the truckers. It is important to monitor the average itself as its confirmation or divergence affects the overall trend of the market.

When analyzing a trend's price action at any given time, it pays to assess the perspective of these industry groups that influence its behavior. At times, the airlines may lead the way and add considerably to the advance or decline in the averages. Following that stage, the airline stocks may reach an extended or overbought position and may start to correct. Afterwards

Figure 11–15. CRB raw industrials Spot index and four mining stocks.

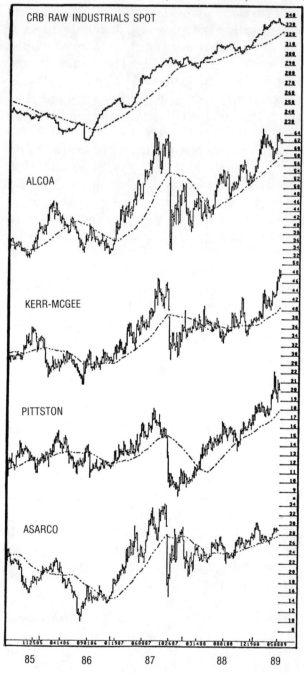

Figure 11–16. The Dow Transportation and its components.

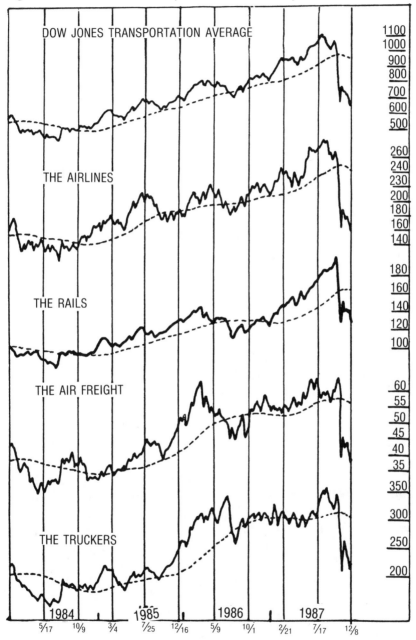

their trend may go sideways or may retrace part of the gains achieved in the previous rally. While this group remains dormant or consolidates, another transportation group may strengthen and compensate for the airlines loss of momentum. The railroads, for example may assume the leadership for some time, such that the trend of the Dow Transportation average continues to rise.

The intertrend relationships of these four groups at any given time is vital for spotting emerging opportunities. The rotating nature of this market is best detected in such a situation as this widely followed Dow average has only four groups whose action determines its trend direction. Moreover, when weakness sets in in the majority of the transportation groups, it may signal an important trend reversal with negative consequences for the overall market. Figure 11–16 illustrates the Dow Transportation average, with its four components. Notice the rotation of strength and weakness and the oscillation of leadership among the different transportation groups.

COMBINING THE INDICATORS

The momentum oscillators could signal important price levels where some reversal may be expected. However, in bear markets, the indicators tend to reach oversold conditions and remain in such a position for a long period of time as prices continue to plummet. And vice versa, in a bull market, overbought readings may mean a little as the upward thrust may propel prices higher. A better perspective of the internal dynamics could be achieved by examining the trend in light of several momentum indicators. Figure 11–17 illustrates the weekly bar chart of the Dollar Index versus three momentum indicators. Bottoms and tops are designated by arrows.

Two of the indicators shown are geared to analyzing the intermediate-term prospect, whereas the last one is used for the short-term. The first indicator is the 14-week stochastics. The middle indicator is the difference between the 150 and 50 day moving averages. The last one is another moving average differential indicator that is calculated based on the differences between the 45 and 15-day moving averages. In the summer of 1987, the stochastics indicator reached an extreme oversold position, it was not yet the time to anticipate a major trend reversal as the moving average differential of 150 and 50-days was trending lower. It was clear then that any strength in the

Figure 11–17. *The Dollar Index versus the momentum indicators.*

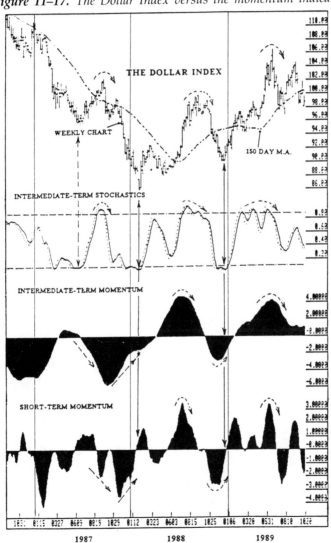

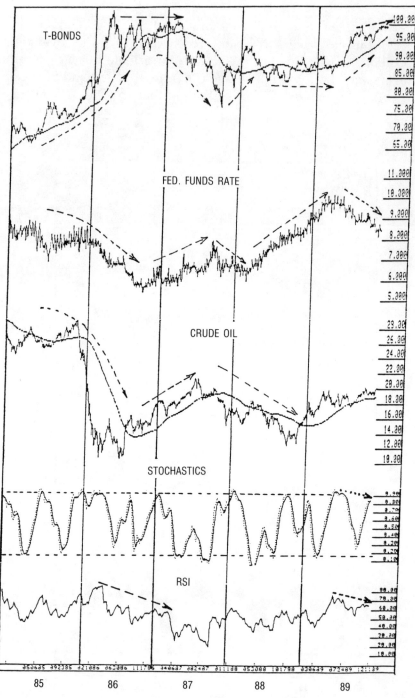

Figure 11–18. *Bonds, rates, crude oil, stochastics and RSI.*

Dollar Index is likely to be temporary as the downside momentum was still intact. In early 1988, however, the deep oversold condition in stochastics was being accompanied by rising lows in the other momentum oscillators. The upward slanting moving average differentials signalled a positive divergence with the price as it kept rising when the index was reaching for new lows. That oversold position was to be followed by a trend reversal in the index. Notice also how tops coincided with overbought stochastics and a reversal in the intermediate-term momentum clearly showed in the behavior of the moving average differentials.

A study of several indicators at the same time could reveal more than any single one would. By superimposing those indicators, we can get better informed expectations of the potential of the next phase of price fluctuation. The same principle could be applied to a stock, an industry group or any market average. An even stronger level of conviction of the future outlook could be realized when the surrounding economic factors are used to support the momentum figures.

Multi-indicator Analysis

A more complex way of analyzing the trend is by using the multi-indicators and multi-relationships techniques. This is an advanced method that could give investors an added dimension in understanding the intermarket relationships as well as the momentum oscillators.

Figure 11–18 delineates a price chart of T-Bonds, the Federal Funds rate, crude oil, the 14-week stochastics, and the 14-week RSI. The fixed-income market is inversely related to the trend of both the Federal Funds rate and crude oil prices. The arrow drawn on the graph shows that this relationship held from 1985 to early 1988. However, as 1988 progressed, the interest rate advance was accompanied by a decline in crude oil prices. Although the monetary policy was tight, as indicated by firmness in the Federal Funds rate, the behavior of energy prices actually signaled that inflation was under control and that it was a matter of time before rates would come down. These two opposite trends in the two indicators left the bond market in a trading range as investors felt that in the absence of inflation, the Fed was likely to ease. Meanwhile, rallies and corrections were signaled by the overbought-oversold position of the stochastics oscillator. The RSI, usually considered a trend indicator, showed two negative divergences in 1986–87, and late 1989. Both nonconfirmations brought about a serious decline in the fixed-income sector. In early 1989, the Federal Funds rate peaked, and the bond market rallied strongly. But as the firmness in crude oil prices persisted, and the momentum became oversold, the T-Bonds index started to show signs of deterioration. This deterioration eventually led to the serious correction in bonds and stocks in 1990. Such multidisciplinary analysis is difficult to perform for each market and every situation. But this example demonstrates the power of such a technique and how it can be used to anticipate trends.

Comparing Bonds to Industry Groups

Several industry groups may be classified as interest-rate sensitive. The homebuilding and forest products industries are among them. Like bonds, the housing market is inversely related to interest rate trends. Depending upon the monetary policy adopted by the Fed, mortgage rates rise or fall—and so go busts or booms in the real estate market. The forest products group is dependent, to a large extent, on the activities in the housing market. But although wood is used to build houses, it is also used to manufacture paper. That is why the forest products group is less sensitive to bond market fluctuations than the home building group.

Figure 11–19 illustrates the relationship between T-Bonds and both the home building and forest products industry groups. The bond market advanced sharply from 1984 to early 1986. The home building industry group also rose, at a slower pace. Forest products, meanwhile, had an overall upward bias. As interest rates started rising, the bond market achieved a peak that culminated in a nasty decline in early 1987. The home building group followed a similar pattern, and while the stock market in general stampeded in 1987, the home building group proceeded on a downward course. The forest products group accelerated to the upside into early 1987. Despite the above-average strength in most equities, however, this group saw its

peak several months before the broad market. The Crash of
1987 caused prices in both industry groups to plummet. Although the bond market was able to stage a comeback, both
groups continued to display weakness. Remember that bonds
have little credit risk. But stocks in those groups represent risk
as an investment at a late stage of an economic recovery and in
an environment of rising interest rates. This example shows us

Figure 11–19. *Bonds, home building, and forest products.*

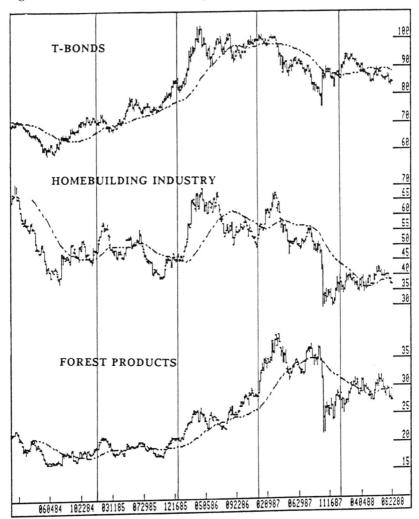

that it pays to compare markets and industry groups that are influenced by common factors.

SUMMARY

While the economic, fundamental and technical factors are crucial to forecasting the trend of bonds and stock, there are some important intermarket relationships that could not be ignored. Crude oil prices, for example, is an important determinant of the direction of inflation, interest rates, and the fixed income market. Those, in turn, affect securities prices and impact the stock market's trend.

Commodity prices could also serve in identifying strength or weakness in industry groups that are sensitive to them. Aluminum companies, for example, could benefit from rising aluminum prices. The same thing could be said about copper stocks and other mining issues.

Interest rate sensitive groups tend to follow developments in the bond market. Gold is a barometer of inflation. It, too, tends to react to interest rate fluctuations in an inverse relationship. Some industry groups are inter-dependent and react to developments in other sectors of the economy. Awareness of these inter-market relationships could enhance both market pricing and stock selection. Without due consideration to those relationships, market analysis would not be complete.

PART 5

Investment Strategies

❏ 12

Tops . . . Bottoms . . . and Trends

*No man has a chance to enjoy permanent success
until he begins to look in a mirror for the real
cause of his mistakes.*

Napoleon Hill

Investment analysis is a great vehicle for making informed decisions. In this study, the tenets of economic analysis and the business indicators have been explained. Their behavior during past cycles has been examined, with emphasis on how they reveal the loss of upward or downward momentum in the economic aggregates near major peaks and troughs. This study, then, focused on the tenets of fundamental analysis. Financial ratios illustrate the progression of a firm's fundamental position over a period of years. Such analysis reveals the fundamental catalyst that propels trends and enables investors to measure a company's intrinsic worth. Past growth records, although not guaranteed to continue, generally display management's ability to deal with business risk and the stability of the company's revenue sources. The quantitative techniques explored help explain the irrational behavior of the market relative to the prevailing investor psychology at any given time. The internal dynamics at work in the marketplace shape the future direction of prices in the investment arena. At times, however, both the economic background and the fundamental environment may fail to explain the market's behavior. A study of the market's internal dynamics may allow better anticipation of such aberrations.

As a discounting mechanism, the market is constantly digesting the flow of information and deciding on the likelihood of its impact on business. Investors, portfolio managers, analysts, brokers, financial consultants, traders, strategists, and financial planners are all involved in the continuous guessing game that shapes the daily, weekly, and monthly movements of both the equities and fixed-income markets. Their opinions, judgments, aspirations, fears and greed are reflected in the pricing of securities. The market trend is the sum total of all economic, fundamental, and quantitative research and thought. The trend is the melting pot and the meeting of the minds in pursuit of profits. There are the positioners and the traders, the speculators and the investors, the informed and the gamblers. The purpose here is to use all the knowledge gained from these well-respected schools of market analysis to project the trend and to understand better the current stage of the cycle. By integrating all the methods studied, investors may stand a better chance of profiting from market opportunities and of achieving their objectives. No one is always right in guessing where the next trend is heading, but in the stock market, investors are dealing with possibilities. A thorough analysis of all the economic, fundamental, and quantitative factors can help improve the odds of success and enhance the decision-making process. In the next few pages are assembled many of the various techniques studied; they are integrated into an analysis of tops, bottoms, and trends.

MARKET CYCLES

Historically, there is a sequence of lead and lag among financial markets, economic policies, and the business cycle. In order to integrate all the market analysis disciplines discussed, the manner in which the different markets interact during the long-term phases of economic expansion and contraction must be clarified. Four important areas will be investigated in light of knowing of the relationships between commodities prices, interest rates, bonds, stocks, and industrial production. Figure 12–1 illustrates a theoretical framework for the typical behavior of economic and financial markets during the business cycle.

Figure 12–1. *The economic cycle.*

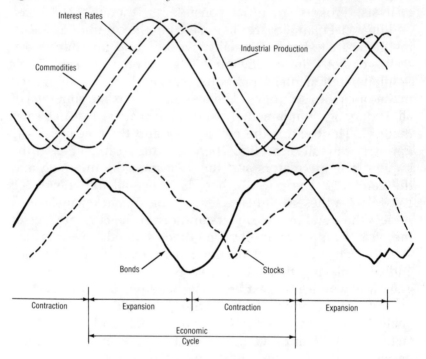

This cycle starts from the juncture at which the economy is emerging from a recession. At this stage, interest rates are likely to be in a downtrend. The slowdown in business activities is expected, at such times, to lead to soft commodities prices and low inflation. The bond market, which is inversely related to both commodities prices and interest rates, rises. Share prices of stocks also rise, in anticipation of an earnings recovery and a broad fundamental improvement in most industrial and consumer sectors. Industrial production shows signs of revival, as it is rebounding from a cyclical trough. As interest rates continue to decline, commodities prices fall, decelerate, and may remain locked in a narrow range. The bond market, now aware of the potential for rising commodities prices, is likely to undergo a similar pattern of fluctuation within a defined trading range; this is likely to be part of a topping process. Then the stock market stampede moderates and is interrupted by an intermediate-term correction. The resumption of the bull market after such interim decline is likely to be selective and characterized by a reduced number of industry groups gaining in prices. Industrial production, meanwhile, accelerates as the business recovery is at full swing, and demand for goods and services is on the rise.

As the economic recovery proceeds, commodities prices begin to rise. The Fed's concerns then shift toward fighting inflation instead of stimulating business and creating job opportunities. As money tightens, interest rates begin to rise. The bond market is likely to start showing early signs of weakness, and a trend reversal may be approaching. The equities market, taking its lead from bonds and interest rates, continues to decelerate its upward momentum and grows even more selective. Industrial production continues to rise, and business conditions improve, backed by healthy consumption and production statistics.

Capacity utilization then reaches dangerous limits, beyond which inflation accelerates. The Fed makes its policy known—that its prime mission is to stop inflation. Commodities prices accelerate as congestion develops in manufacturing, and an imbalance is created between supply and demand. At that stage, the threat of inflation is real. Interest rates rise sharply, and the high cost of money takes its toll on all sectors of the economy. The bond market is in a clear cut downtrend, and the stock market has surpassed its cyclical peak. At this point, many industry groups have led the way down, and the strong issues are declining. Good news may continue to emerge on the earnings front, but the market ignores it. The investing public, which is likely to be influenced by the perceived healthy state of the economy and the preceding market advance, is still buying on decline as hope blinds investors to the future consequences of rising interest rates. Industrial production statistics begin to slow down and hesitate, for consumption is on the decline. Consumers are likely to start belt tightening; they postpone buying decisions concerning expensive items. Housing permits decline as the real estate market begins to feel the pinch of rising mortgage rates.

There comes a point where the rise of interest rates puts a dent in high-flying commodities prices. Then the economy slows down and the outlook for unemployment looks bleak. Consumption wanes, and the upward pressure on prices is removed. Commodities prices begin to decline, and interest rates are close to their cyclical peak. The bond market begins to stage sharp rallies that interrupt its downward path. Some firmness in bond prices develops. The stock market is still in a free fall. The decline is precipitated, for investor capitulation is at its peak—stocks are sold independent of prior value or fundamental worth. Fear replaces greed in the investment arena. Industrial production statistics display subtle weakness, reflecting the slowdown of the economy.

At this point, the recession has already been predicted by economists, as a host of economic aggregates clearly display the contraction of business activities. Commodities prices fall; interest rates peak and reverse their trend as the Fed becomes more concerned with rising unemployment numbers. The discount rate is cut to add liquidity to the banking system and to encourage credit expansion. The bond market bottoms out and begins its advance. The stock market climaxes in a frightening, sharp decline that drives investors to panic selling.

Then the first signs of strength begin to emerge—many blue-chip stocks fail to participate in the decline and resist the wave of negative news. Industrial production shrinks as business continues to slow down. As the momentum of receding economic activities intensifies, interest rates plummet. The bond market then accelerates its advance. The stock market stampedes amid great disbelief from the investing public. The final stage of economic contraction is at hand, and the cycle is about to repeat itself all over again.

The Economic Indicators and the Business Cycle

The most important of all economic indicators is the interest rate trend. Rates have a direct impact on all sectors of the economy, on corporate earnings, on commodities prices, on the housing market, on auto sales, on consumption, on industrial production, on bonds, and on stocks. The economic aggregates fluctuate during the business cycle, driven by the direction of interest rates. When the Fed tightens, the leading indicators weaken. The average weekly hours of production in manufacturing subside as sales lag and inventory accumulates.

With the slowdown in sales and production, companies begin to lay off workers, which begins to show in the average weekly claims for unemployment insurance. As more and more workers are idled, this leading series rises until the Fed eases. As the economy begins to slow down, manufacturers' new orders also decline, and vendor performance worsens. With declining cash flow and sales, contracts for new plant and equipment are either curtailed or canceled outright.

The most sensitive indicator among all the economic aggregates is the number of new private housing units authorized by local building permits. This aggregate is so sensitive to rising interest rates that, in the past, it has led all other leading indicators near major cyclical peaks. It could even serve as a leading indicator to the stock market itself.

In addition to the deterioration of the leading indicators, other signs of weakness can be seen in such other economic statistics as: rising credit risk, higher foreclosure rates, sagging auto sales, falling retail sales, higher bankruptcy rates, increasing downward earnings estimates by industry analysts, decelerating rate of growth of the GNP, rising unemployment, declining commodities prices, declining personal income, rising average duration of unemployment, increasing inventory accumulation, soaring inventory to sales ratio, deteriorating consumer sentiment, sliding help-wanted advertising, a shrinking money supply, decline in consumer and business borrowing and a rise in the savings rate.

Investors have to get a good grasp of the meaning of the economic indicators, what they represent, and what their behavior implies for business at large. Furthermore, it is crucial to digest the indicators' relationship to securities price behavior. There is no one single economic aggregate that tells the whole story. When a number of them is monitored and they all flash the same message, then corresponding strategies should be adopted in order to control the potential risk. For example, when interest rates begin to rise and the Fed announces its

intention to tighten the monetary policy in order to fight inflation, investors should immediately realize that the risk in both
the fixed-income and equities markets from that point on is
likely to rise. It becomes only a matter of time before the high
cost of money causes a broad-based slowdown in both consumption and production activities. This may eventually lead
to a full-fledged recession, rising unemployment, and a decline
in corporate earnings.

Monitoring any single economic indicator may not be the
solution to digesting what is happening in the economy and
what the outlook may be. Instead, a number of indicators
should enable investors to measure the weight of the evidence.
Plural deterioration of a large number of leading indicators
constitutes a strong signal that high rates are causing the slowdown in broad-based industrial sectors.

The Diffusion Index

The diffusion index of the eleven leading indicators is
closely watched by many investors, as it can describe the way
the majority of them are behaving. It is the ratio of improving
or rising leading indicators divided by eleven, which is their
total number. It describes the breadth or extent of improvement or deterioration of those important aggregates. The six-
months rate of change of this indicator describes how well the
diffusion index is faring relative to its performance six months
ago. This indicator tends to lead the stock market near cyclical
peaks and troughs by a number of months that have varied in
the past from one business cycle to another.

Figure 12–2 illustrates the behavior of the diffusion index
compared with the S&P 500. Near market cycle peaks, the
diffusion index has tended to have a long lead time on the S&P
500's final peak. Near stock market cycle lows, however, the
diffusion index has had a shorter lead time. Whenever this
index reached the zero point, major lows in stock prices were
reached within nine months. Like all the other economic indicators, this one does not give absolutely accurate and timely
prediction of turning points. But its value is anticipatory in the
sense that when it reaches an extreme reading, a major change
in the trend's direction cannot be far behind.

Figure 12–2. The diffusion index.

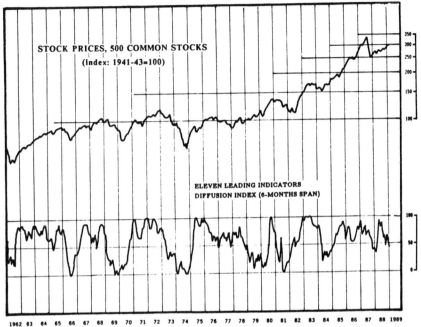

Analysis of Indicators is Key

Analysis of the economic indicators is key to determining the major wave in the cyclical nature of the economy. Such analysis enables investors to anticipate the extent of market risk surrounding the investment environment. Analysis also helps anticipate future deterioration in the fundamental outlook of most industry groups without providing exact indications as to the extent of the risk or its impact on individual industry groups. The leading, lagging, and coincident indicators satisfy the overall analysis aspect of the outlook for the investment environment without giving any precise or accurate estimation of when exactly the slowdown or recovery will occur.

In order to better utilize the signals of the economic indicators, they should be integrated into a model that monitors the internal dynamics. Fundamental analysis of industry groups and individual stocks should then confirm the effect of improving or deteriorating business statistics on the financial position of a broad cross-section of the economy. At this stage of the analysis, it is time to combine all the indicators studied and review their positions during the business cycle.

CHARACTERISTICS OF STOCK MARKET TOPS

Major stock market reversals do not follow set rules; however, when a large number of economic, fundamental, and quantitative factors are monitored, better forecasts can be achieved. Such indicators as interest rates, commodities prices, the bond market, economic indicators, investor psychology, and the stock market are contemplated here, as they demonstrate typical market behavior. In order to organize the analysis, some of these indicators can be separated into categories.

Interest Rates

Near major cyclical peaks, rates have already been on the rise or are beginning to show signs of accelerating upward momentum. Combined with this is the rise in inflationary pressures and the unequivocal intention of the Fed to fight rising prices. Short-term rates are likely to have gone higher and faster than long-term ones. Such a condition leads to an inverted yield curve, which signals the potential for a period of economic contraction ahead. The rise in short-term rates, such as the three-month T-Bonds and the Federal Funds rate, leads the rise in the prime, mortgage, and discount rates. The short-term rate rise's effect rapidly slows down business activities in all sectors of the economy.

Commodities Prices

Raw material prices are likely to be on an upward course because supply is unable to satisfy demand. The rise of commodities prices, especially industrial raw materials, combined with constraints in capacity utilization (usually exceeding 80 percent), is a sign of congestion in production that fuels inflation. When judging the trend of commodities prices, it is important to differentiate between strength in a limited number of them or a widespread rise among industrial, energy, and food items. It is also crucial to analyze the price rise's cause and determine whether it is due to seasonal factors or a surge in consumer demand that existing capacity cannot satisfy. The CRB index's trend should be closely monitored, as it may foretell the future direction of commodities prices and reveal the outlook for inflation.

The Bond Market

The fixed-income sector leads the stock market near major cyclical peaks. As the economy is reaching a mature stage of its expansion, accompanied by rising inflation, bonds are likely to be in a downtrend. The rising rates and advancing commodities prices are not welcome developments for the fixed-income market. The competition from short-term money market alternatives and the inverted yield curve foretell of an impending period of credit risk in the making.

The Economic Indicators

The leading indicators would be showing loss of upward momentum, with the housing permits leading the way on the downside. The other aggregates, while considered to be good barometers of future business conditions, would continue to show only deceleration, without any material deterioration. Other aggregates tend to decline and confirm economic weakness after the stock market has already reversed itself. At that point, unemployment is likely to be the most treacherous indicator. Investors tend to feel assured about the outlook for the economy because of favorable news of declining unemployment. Consumption is typically at its highest, for personal income is rising and jobs appear to be secure. Help-wanted advertising, while decelerating, is still rising as job openings continue to be posted. The work week is likely to be expanding, and capital spending is also increasing. Retail sales statistics are healthy, and corporate profits grow fast and remain promising. Dividends are being increased with announcements of improving results. The coincident indicators are advancing and industrial production is expanding. Consumer borrowing is likely to be rising and savings rates falling. Thus, consumer sentiment is still optimistic given the orderly expansion of the economy and the robust growth in almost all sectors.

Investor Psychology and the Media

Optimism abounds, household finances seem to be in good shape, major newspapers and business magazines are reporting favorable projections in light of recently released statistics. Advisory services are bullish and the "mom and pop" investors are dreaming of a quick killing in the stock market. Takeover activities are on the rise and gurus of the time are giving hundreds of reasons why the market is heading higher.

The Stock Market

Volume is rising and speculative buying of stocks with little or no fundamentals is supported by the view that the economy is expanding and that it is only a matter of time before material improvement gets started. While all of this is happening, the market's breadth is likely to be showing subtle deterioration. Industry group performance is lackluster, the number of stocks making the list of new highs for the year is shrinking. The annual rate of change for the S&P 500 has reversed its position from levels near 30 percent. The percentage of stocks trading above their 200-day moving average is declining. The put-to-call ratio is low. Good news on the earnings front is not met with a corresponding rise in securities prices. Stocks, in general, resist advancing on good news—most likely the news has already been discounted. One or two broad-based averages may have signalled major divergences as they stop confirming the Dow industrial's new highs. The interest-rate sensitive groups, such as the banks, savings and loans, utilities, home building, and insurance companies are likely to be displaying the early signs of weakness that precede the final high. The rally of the averages is likely to be characterized by an advance in a narrow list of stocks, as leadership is missing.

Amid many healthy economic statistics—a great deal of optimism, rising earnings, increasing dividends, a positive job market outlook, and favorable forecast opinion—the stock market slowly makes its highs. In most cases, the form of the topping process is rotational, meaning that some groups will deteriorate while others are still advancing, which gives a false impression of strength.

One way of recognizing the topping action is to review a chart book and see how stock prices are behaving relative to their long-term moving average. It is also important to analyze the reaction of a large number of stocks during market rallies. If the majority of stocks an investor is monitoring fails to participate during market strengths and meanders around the 150-day moving average, and if stocks do not advance on rising earnings reports and increasing dividends, the top of the stock market cycle, as strange as it may sound, is at hand. The early signals of an impending major trend reversal are generated from the market's internal dynamics themselves, long before economic or fundamental statistics reflect them. That is why the efficient market theory is correct. Its followers are most likely relying on the published reports that are well known to any diligent investor. Because very few Wall St. speculators have the depth of knowledge to investigate and to recognize all the internal, as well as external factors, the majority of players fails to see the top as it is occurring.

. . . ONLY HALF THE STORY

Around cyclical peaks, the systematic and unsystematic risk increase substantially. The end of an economic expansion phase can cause extensive damage to the financial position of a stock or an industry group. The market risk is best explained in light of anticipatory shrinkage of consumer demand and the accompanying decline in sales volume. Some industries may be affected more severely than others. Cyclical industries and consumer-sensitive sectors may feel the pinch of household consumption. Machinery and capital spending sectors may suffer from the curtailment of capacity expansion at the corporate end. Technology groups may be dealt a blow, as they may not be able to recapture their research and development costs.

Obsolescence threatens their ability to sell today's technology tomorrow, when the next cycle of business expansion is underway. The unsystematic or security risk also rises near cyclical peaks. The high debt-to-capital ratio makes it difficult for many corporations to service their interest burden. Rising interest rates, typical of the end of a boom cycle, suppress profit margins, which leads to lower earnings. The decline in the general level of consumption, accompanied by the soaring interest charges paid on debt obligations, impairs a company's ability to execute long-term plans. Figure 12–3 illustrates the impact of rising rates on the interest rate burden as a percentage of cash flow. The relationship between the two is direct— the higher rates rise, the larger the percentage of cash flow that is allocated to servicing debt. If the debt-to-capital ratio is excessive, or much higher than the industry standards, the risk of total ruin mounts. Also observe how corporate debt soared in the "roaring eighties." The wave of mergers and acquisitions and the aggressive borrowing during that decade pushed debt levels to excess. Over 25 percent of gross cash flow was paid out to service the interest on companies' obligations. Such high levels should not pass unnoticed, as they increase the credit exposure of many firms during a credit crunch. The trend of corporate debt and the proportion of the cash flow needed to service it should be monitored carefully as the business cycle matures. This can foretell the depth of the ensuing recession. During periods of economic contraction, the debt liquidation process can cause severe damage to the balance sheet and to the overall financial position of a company.

Figure 12–4 illustrates the cyclical dynamics of the rising interest rate burden and its influence on profit margins. As can be seen, margins suffer during periods of rising rates and this, in turn, negatively affects earnings potential. In addition, at such junctures, the possibility of total bankruptcy may affect the credit worthiness of the corporation.

Figure 12–3. Interest rates relative to corporate interest burden.

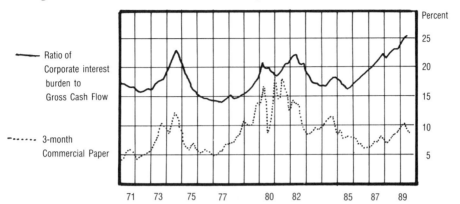

The graph clearly demonstrates the evil of debt. Its impact on profit margins is pronounced during times of rising interest rates. Since the mid-1960s, the corporate interest burden has risen significantly. In turn, profit margins have suffered a secular erosion. Despite the tremendous rise of securities prices in the 1980s, profitability dropped substantially compared to its historic levels. The skyrocketing inflation of the 1970s compelled the Fed to raise interest rates to an excessively high plateau. But the psychology that prevailed at the time convinced all corporate executives that leverage was the way to inflate earnings. The borrowing trend did not abate once inflation subsided. On the contrary, the percentage of interest service continued to rise despite the decline of interest rates. The drop in profit margins in the 1980s should have cautioned investors to reassess the nature of the market's rise. Although securities prices rose substantially, they should have been suspect, as the real profitability had declined.

These two illustrations demonstrate the unsystematic risk that securities face during business recessions. Stocks go down as the prospect for earnings, sales, profit margins, and other financial measures deteriorate. Depending upon how severe the ensuing economic slowdown may be and depending upon the type of industry group, this risk may vary.

Most market timers and portfolio managers are constantly

Figure 12–4. Interest burden and profit margins.

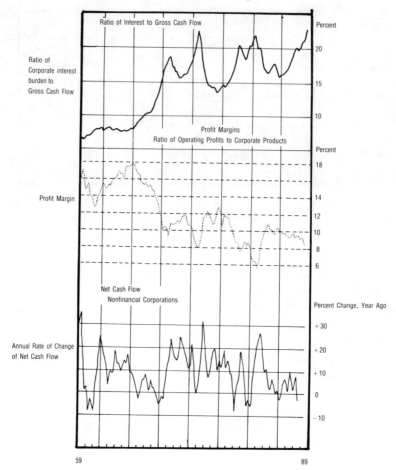

trying to identify major peaks. But cyclical peaks may not necessarily have to affect all the investor's portfolio holdings with the same magnitude. Moreover, even during bear markets, some stocks that possess compelling fundamentals continue to resist the broad market decline and may even succeed to rise to new highs. Identifying a major peak will enable the investor to restructure his or her portfolio appropriately. An increasingly defensive strategy may have to be implemented in order to avoid hefty losses. Reallocation of assets among investment alternatives may also be a good defense against sagging securities prices; raising cash or increasing the portion of the portfolio in low-risk money market alternatives may be the wise thing to do.

The meaning of a major cyclical peak helps only the top-down-oriented investors. While it has validity, stock selection is the best way to reach desired returns and to prevail in the investment arena, even when the market is vulnerable.

When a peak is reached, there are industry groups that still continue to do well. The raw materials sensitive groups and mining stocks tend to gain upward momentum after the cyclical peak in equities has been reached. Energy stocks, in particular, usually fare better than the market in a maturing cycle, when most groups are entering a major downtrend. Stocks that benefit from accelerating inflationary pressures, such as gold, silver, and other precious metal issues, also stage a strong advance in the latter stages of the market cycle.

In addition, growth stocks that are selling at reasonable P/E multiples may resist the broad market decline and prepare themselves for the next big "up" move. Some of the big capitalization companies that are paying relatively high and secure dividends may discover a second wind and buck the downtrend in the early part of a bear market. The Dow Jones Industrial Average tends to fall last during a bear trend. The quality of its components, their high creditworthiness, and their well-established position in their field makes them less vulnerable to market setbacks than small-cap stocks. Last but not least, special situations can also enhance performance at times when the outlook for the market is not constructive. There are always stocks that have a large cash-to-asset ratio and a low debt-to-capital base. Their high liquidity makes them excellent candidates for takeover. In the past, the peak in merger and acquisition activities lasted well after the market reversed its long-term position and entered into a bear phase.

Finally, near major cyclical peaks, an inverted yield curve almost always results whereby short-term rates rise above long-term ones. This causes the risk structure in financial markets to vary depending upon the type of security under consideration. Stocks grow more vulnerable than bonds as the valuation benchmarks of short-term T-Bills to dividends yield ratio favors cash. Such periods suggest a rising demand for high-quality yields. That is why bond returns become more appealing than, and far superior to, stock dividends.

PRIMARY BEAR MARKET CHARACTERISTICS

At this point in the cycle, interest rates have been advancing for some time. The Fed's intention—that its prime mission is to fight rising inflation has been made clear. Stock prices have started their swift decline. Investors who were enthusiastic during the final phase of the bull market advance are "hanging in there" hoping for a final rally that will bail them out. They cite the remnant strength in corporate earnings and the sporadic advances in some issues. But, in general, they prefer not to face up to the fact that the outlook is growing increasingly uncertain and that an economic recession may be in the making. Volume on the securities exchanges sags as more and more investors await the next recovery, which does not materialize any too soon. Bear markets are usually interrupted by sharp rallies that are more likely to be reflected in the market averages than in individual securities. Time is of essence as the bear market wears patience out.

Soon enough, government reports reveal a tapering of economic growth. But as long as interest rates continue to surge on an irregular, sliding course, stock prices work their way down. The cyclical industries usually lead the way on the downside. The high debt and low savings rates lead to retrenchment in household consumption. This is reflected, in particular, in auto stocks, which tend to sell at depressed P/E multiples because the market anticipates further deterioration in sales and margins. During the early phases of a bear market, many analysts and investors try prematurely to predict the lows. Any favorable economic or fundamental news is hailed as the end of the slowdown and the beginning of a recovery—

but the decline continues. Industries with high P/E ratios suffer sharp declines as the market trims lofty future forecasts. The airlines, the high-tech companies, the machinery, the interest-rate sensitive sectors, and many others falter as the market declines. The erosion in prices usually takes the form of a rotation of weakness, whereby a group declines and then stabilizes when another starts to precipitate downward. A third and a fourth group soon weaken. Then the groups that started renew their weakness, and so on and so forth. In a few months, prices have fallen to levels considerably lower than where they had been. Many investors who at one time had great gains witness them evaporating. Those who were emotionally persuaded to buy amid the speculative binge that preceded the final peak are now locked in with big losses, which compels them to hold on to their stocks, only to see them going down further.

Interest Rates

Interest rates, at this stage of the business cycle, are likely to be accelerating upward and the inverted yield curve is declining precipitously. The TED spread is also expected to be slanting upward as the difference between the Treasury Bills and the Eurodollar rate keeps expanding. This interest rate acceleration phase brings about a slowdown in business activities, and toward the end of the bear market the interest rate's cyclical peak is reached.

Commodities Prices

Commodities prices may show some early strength during the accelerating rise of interest rates. As a matter of fact, inflation also speeds up its advance, which causes the Fed to tighten even further. The peak in rates occurs after commodities prices start to lose upward momentum and reverse their trend. Softening commodities prices are a signal that supply is gradually increasing over demand and that the impact of the interest rate rise has finally started to take its toll on the economy.

The Bond Market

The bond market, at this stage of the business cycle, is likely to be in a downtrend. The heating up of the economy triggers fear of further rises in interest rates which, in turn, makes them lose their investment appeal. The interest-rate sensitive groups, such as utilities, banks, insurance companies, and homebuilding groups also usually reflect the possibility of the credit crunch that is about to occur.

The Economic Indicators

Several of the eleven components of the leading indicators show signs of economic weakness led by the housing permits, stock prices, average weekly hours of production, average weekly claims for unemployment insurance, vendor performance, change in sensitive materials prices, money supply, and the index of consumer confidence. The coincident indicators may not necessarily reflect the deterioration in economic activities, but may display loss of upward momentum in the aggregates. The lagging indicators may continue to rise during most of the early stages of an economic slowdown. They camouflage the underlying weakness of the leading indicators and may encourage noneconomists to hope still for a resumption of the economic boom. One of the most treacherous numbers on that front is the unemployment rate, whose rise may not be necessarily reflected in the released statistics.

Meanwhile, consumption may start to decline in earnest as households curtail their expenditures on big-ticket items. Savings rates may also begin to rise, only to reflect the cautious attitude of consumers. Figure 12–5 illustrates the behavior of consumer spending and savings rates during the business cycle.

During this phase of the business cycle, corporate earnings are likely to suffer. Downward revision of previous forecast by industry analysts also increases as the dismal outlook begins to dawn, threatening the fundamental position of most groups. Profit margins erode, sales volume declines, inventories accumulate, the corporate interest burden soars, dividends may be cut, returns on assets shrink, and the P/E multiples suddenly appear inflated given the expected deterioration in a slowing economy.

Investor Psychology and the Media

The latent bullishness resulting from the previous boom, the hefty paper profits on stocks, the favorable unemployment numbers, and the hesitation of investors to acknowledge the possibility of a recession is probably one of the most important characteristics of investor psychology at the onset of an economic contraction. Overwhelming disbelief sets in and the mood is likely to be governed by bullish emotions. Enthusiasm will wear out with time, but complacency surfaces as the major cause for big portfolio losses. The news background is likely to be mixed at that stage. Opinions are often split, and confusion clouds future possibilities.

Figure 12–5. *Consumption spending and savings rates during the business cycle.*

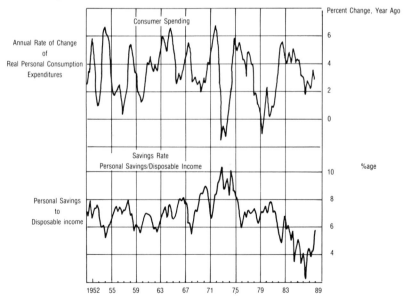

The Stock Market

At such a time, the stock market is declining precipitously with bear market rallies, usually very sharp, interrupting the downward trend. Industry groups are falling in unison. Any negative development is penalized harshly as stocks plummet. Good earnings don't matter as much as bad ones, which for a while would seem to take hold. The price decline is slow but persistent. Shattered hopes soon awaken to reality as the relentless melting of values proceeds. Worries begin to replace optimism, and capitulation is about to take place. The slow decline is now accelerating as several sharp plunges scare even the boldest investors. The cautiousness of investors is only a step away from fear. Often the market goes into a deep tailspin that shakes out the remaining hesitation. Volume is likely to soar as margin liquidation and panic selling intensify. The bear market is by now about to end amid a gloomy economic and fundamental outlook.

The momentum indicators spend most of the time in oversold territories. The annual rate of change is now trending lower, the percentage of stocks trading above their 200-day moving average continues to fall, the advisory services are gradually turning bearish and getting very selective on the market. Their commentaries are likely to be dominated by unclear, hedged statements. The put-to-call ratio usually rises during market declines.

During bear trends, the market, as well as the security risk, rises and real losses may occur. Stocks may take years to double or triple, but weeks if not days to roll back all their gains. Bear markets are vicious and merciless. Even the best fundamentals may not be sufficient to keep a stock from losing ground. Cash is king, at least during the first few months of the bear market, as it may be difficult for many stocks to rebound to their previous cyclical highs.

CHARACTERISTICS OF MAJOR BOTTOMS

Around cyclical lows, the aggregates are clearly reflecting the slowdown, the stock market psychology is plagued by fear, inflation is moderating, unemployment is rising, and most companies are reporting lower earnings and sales figures. In addition, the recession is acknowledged by economists, the consumers are cautious, and investors are disinterested in stocks. This is the juncture of the cycle at which both the market risk and security risk are minimal. The market has already discounted the worst and is beginning to see hope amid despair. Investors are liquidating positions, when they should be buying. While this is easy to write in a book, the truth is that during such times it is difficult to defy the prevailing emotional forces. Remember that the long bear market has slowly but surely inflicted enough pain such that rational behavior mandates preservation of capital strategies.

Interest Rates

Interest rates have spiked sharply and then retreated. The Federal Funds rate and the three-month T-Bills rate lead the way down. Soon after, the discount rate, which is controlled by the Fed, is lowered a notch. Rising unemployment, subdued inflation, and the deteriorating economic aggregates compel the Fed to ease the monetary rein. The clearest sign of that process is the lowering of the discount rate. The TED spread has also spiked and is losing its upward momentum.

Commodities Prices

Typically, at this stage of the business cycle, commodities prices reverse their trend to signal a slowdown in demand for raw materials and an excessive supply of industrial commodities. Precious metals, such as gold, silver, and platinum, are also likely to have started a major downtrend as inflation seems to be waning. Crude oil prices are either stable or falling as the economy is undergoing contraction and consumption is faltering. Food commodities are in abundance as corn and soybeans crops exceed actual market demand. The CRB index is likely to be trending below its long-term moving average.

The Bond Market

Seeing the collapse of commodities prices, the slowing rate of inflation, and the declining interest rates, the bond market starts to advance slowly. Some sporadic setbacks occur and interrupt the advance, but pullbacks from here on are opportunities to add to the portfolio rather than to liquidate. Unfortunately, the truth of the matter is that the negative investor psychology prevents seizing opportunities. The interest-rate sensitive groups are also likely to show some sign of revival. They resist the equities market decline and ignore news of perceived credit risks. At times, utilities stocks lead the broad market when the conditions described come into existence. Insurance companies, which invest a large portion of their portfolios in bonds, begin to display strength relative to other industry groups. The brokerage stocks, which are likely to be the beneficiaries of the forthcoming bull market, may also show strength and lead most other industry groups.

The Economic Indicators

Near stock market troughs, the leading economic indicators have either reached levels of previous cycles' lows or have exceeded them. Housing permits typically have plummeted. Often this indicator leads the stock market lows by a few months. It may even have started to rise when equities were reaching for the final low. But every cycle may be slightly different than the others. The S&P diffusion index has probably reached less than 10 percent and is also rebounding. This indicator leads the stock market at the lows. The money supply may have started to advance and the index of consumer expectations may have reversed its downward trend. The coincident indicators are still trending lower as they continue to confirm the slowdown of the economy. The lagging indicators are falling and the unemployment rate, in particular, should still be rising. The recessionary forces at such a juncture are clearly portrayed in all the economic aggregates. The outlook looks dismal. But a shadow of hope appears as the discount rate is lowered a second and a third time, revealing the Fed's intentions to ease.

Psychology and the News Media

"Apocalypse Now" or "The Death of Equity," or similar headlines are likely to be displayed on the front covers of major newspapers. Analysts are leery of market rallies and the investing public fears further losses. The predominant psychology is that the stock market is a big gamble and extremely dangerous at this stage. The consensus is that the market is going lower, and gurus are urging their customers to get out.

THE STOCK MARKET

The advance/decline, or market breadth, line is more helpful at major cycle peaks as it clearly shows the narrowing participation of stocks in the sporadic market rallies that occur at the top. The divergence that accompanies the market's final highs, just before major trend reversals, is probably one of the strongest warning signals, because it takes place ahead of any other economic or fundamental indicators. However, while the advance/decline line is not as helpful around major troughs, once in a while it does reveal the emerging strength in the broad list of stocks. The typical ending of many cyclical lows is in a climax or violent decline. During that time the advance/decline line is likely to either hesitate and hold its lows or to mark fractional deterioration that is quickly resolved in the stampede shortly to follow.

Several quantitative factors can also help reveal market lows. On market selloffs, the number of new lows stops expanding as it did during the downtrend. The annual rate of change is likely to have moved below the minus-10 percent mark and is about to reverse its course, and the long-term moving averages are approaching the prices of securities of most industry groups. The percentage of stocks above their 200-day moving average is meandering around the 20 percent-, or below, mark. Simultaneously, a large number of stocks has been building a base, or catapult, from which to launch the next advance. They have been spending a number of weeks fluctuating in a narrow range. Volume picks up on the final low as panic selling and fear dominate investors' psychology. The market is about to stage a huge advance and is about to present patient investors with great opportunities. The contrarian investor may vastly outperform all others, for stocks now sell at their wholesale price.

PRIMARY BULL MARKET CHARACTERISTICS

Amid gloomy expectations and a dull market, a stampede in securities prices sets in. All stocks and most industry groups advance aggressively. There is no hesitation—the rise is relentless. Both small-cap and giant firms launch a major, continuing rally. Bull markets are notorious for not providing chances to get in. The winners are the plungers, for a change. The risk of losing during the initial market stampede is minimal, often independent of book value, earnings, or any other fundamental consideration. This condition often prevails for an average of six months. During that time, most of the gains of the bull market are achieved and the strategy is to be fully invested.

Interest Rates

Interest rates then go on a downward slide. The Fed is likely to announce several discount rate cuts. The Federal Funds rate and the three-months T-Bills rate are trending downward, below the discount rate and most other interest rates. The TED spread has also reversed its direction and is heading down. Inflation is under control, and the Fed eases in order to allow a broad economic recovery.

Commodities Prices

In real terms, the economy is still contracting at the early stages of the bull market, and demand for goods is lagging the supply. Commodities prices are declining and inflation is under control. This leaves room for the Fed to accommodate the cyclical expansion of the economy and to fight the rising unemployment that is not politically palatable. Then gold, silver, and other precious metals go into a long-term downtrend that is likely to last for some time. Crude oil prices are stable, if not declining. Food commodities are likely to remain subdued or to be in a declining trend.

The Bond Market

The fixed-income sector advances during that stage and adds fuel to the rising prices in the equities market. The declining interest rates and commodities prices are great news for bonds. In the past, a bull market in stocks has seldom materialized in the absence of a robust bond market. The interest-rate sensitive groups are also likely to be in a strong position and to advance aggressively as the credit risk slowly evaporates.

The Economic Indicators

The leading indicators are likely to have bottomed out at this stage, which indicates the birth of a brand new business cycle. The expansion first takes place in housing starts, which advance aggressively. But, in sync with the bull market, all the coincident indicators also begin to show signs of economic recovery. The Fed continues to ease and consumption picks up. Capacity utilization begins to rise as industrial activities are revived. The unemployment rate stops rising, help-wanted advertising expands, consumer sentiment improves, and industrial production advances. The economic recovery is intact. From here on, it is only a matter of time before the threat of higher inflation compels the Fed to change its policy and start the cycle all over again.

Psychology and the News Media

Good news slowly finds its way back on the front pages of major newspapers and the covers of business magazines. Initially, conservative and controlled reporting of improving business conditions characterizes the early stages of the recovery. Here again, however, enthusiasm will set in shortly as the bull market continues on course.

The Stock Market

The rise in equities prices is healthy and spreads out among all industry groups. The cyclical, the credit-sensitive, the consumer staple growth, the machinery, the transportation and most sectors revive. The annual rate of change of the S&P 500 rebounds sharply, and the number of stocks making new 52-week highs expands. The percentage of stocks trending above their 200-day moving average also increases. The bull market stampede is accompanied by a rising advance/decline line and healthy volume. Earnings are rising and sales are growing. The P/E multiples are quickly expanding from previous depressed levels. The outlook is enticing and the promise of a rosy economic outlook fuels the advance. After some time, signs of a tired bull are likely to emerge. Divergences are likely to occur as they did around the previous bull market top. The investment environment grows selective again, and the fading momentum warns of a replay of the past.

ELEMENTS OF JUNCTURE RECOGNITION

The stages of the business cycle and the behavior of the stock market during their progression cannot be quantified in any precise way. The above discussion is only an approximation of what has happened in the past. Each cycle has differences from those that preceded or followed it. The general behavior of the indicators is a means of unifying the well-known disciplines of market analysis without adhering to the rigidity of a single model. Some cycles are characterized by consumer retrenchment, others by excessive inventory accumulation. Recessions have often been global in scale; at other times, some countries' markets or economies suffer a much larger decline than others. In the 1950s and 1960s, the uptrend in equities prices was secular in nature. Since 1974, equities have again embarked on a secular advance that has briefly been interrupted by setbacks. The indicator characteristics may change over time. The eleven leading indicators were once twelve, and they may change again in the future. No one single indicator is superior to all the others. In the past, the odd-lot theory gained much attention from market analysts as a good measure of sentiment. Over time, it became cheap enough to buy round lots, the theory died, and now its indicators are seldom followed. This study is meant to illustrate market dynamics at important trend junctures. In the future, some variations may be expected, but the general theme is likely to remain the same. The market will continue to fluctuate, and whenever an indicator becomes widely followed, it is time to expect it to stop working as well as it did.

Market analysis is only a step toward taming the risk on Wall Street. But the true survivors in the investment arena are those who determine their objectives early on and formulate strategies to realize them. Dealing with the awesome risk is at all times only a step toward preservation of capital. Gains in the stock market can be wiped out in a relatively short period of time if prudence is abandoned and risk is underestimated. One thing is sure in this business—the market will be there, and opportunities will always emerge. Recognizing junctures at which great profits are possible is the universal dream of those who hope to prosper at buying and selling stocks.

SUMMARY

The foregoing discussion has aimed at integrating the tenets of the multi-disciplinary analysis in order to identify major reversal junctures. The characteristic of cyclical peaks and troughs have been studied in light of the economic, fundamental and quantitative factors that are likely to accompany them.

The study expounds on the status of the economic indicators that tend to develop around important turning points of the business cycle. The momentum of the aggregates at any point in time could enable investors to anticipate the likely new phase of an economic trend.

Earning, sales, and other pertinent fundamental factors tend to lag major peaks and troughs. However, the rate of change of the debt to equity ratio, as well as the interest burden as a percentage of cash flow, have often signalled the state of maturity of the general business conditions. Profit margins, too, are squeezed or expand ahead of the final change in trend direction.

The internal dynamics are extremely important in timing the market reversals. Divergences develop among the averages and the breadth momentum tend to fade away or stampede sharply ahead or in coincidence with tops and bottoms.

Throughout the book, many economic and quantitative techniques have been studied. The interpretation of these indicators is key to the process of controlling the element of market or systematic risk inherent in the investment process. Similarly, the fundamental and qualitative techniques could also be used towards refining the stock selection phase. They could help to further reduce the security or unsystematic risk.

The multi-indicators technique should be applied to both the market averages and industry groups. The final analysis is then to be used in structuring investment portfolios that are suitable for the prevailing business background. Strategic allocation of assets in light of the likely future economic and fundamental forecasts could then enhance final results.

❑ 13

Portfolio Management Dynamics

*There is always a disposition in people's minds to
think that existing conditions will be permanent.
When the market is down and dull, it is hard to
make people believe that this is the prelude to a
period of activity and advance. When the prices are
up and the country is prosperous, it is always said
that while preceding booms have not lasted, there
are circumstances connected with this one which
make it unlike its predecessors and give assurance
of permanency. The one fact pertaining to all
conditions is that they will change.*

Charles H. Dow, 1900

Analyzing market conditions and the economic outlook is key to making informed investment decisions. But success in achieving investment objectives is a function of the strategies chosen to reach those goals. So far, the focus has been on exploring the most effective analysis techniques. Yet, this work would be incomplete if strategy were not touched on.

In order to formulate viable investment decisions, investors need first to identify the suitability of the chosen investment vehicle vis-à-vis desired goals. Profiling and a good understanding of the investor's need is a must in choosing the vehicles by which one hopes to accomplish final objectives. A young investor with modest resources may find aggressive growth stocks suitable, since capital appreciation may be of greater importance than income-producing alternatives. An older investor, however, may wish to avoid stock speculation and may hold a portfolio of high-quality utilities, T-Bonds, and other income-yielding vehicles.

Like goal setting, determining time and duration with respect to investment plans is crucial. The strategy chosen may enable the realization of profits, or it may enable only partial accomplishment of desired goals. One important element of the investment process is that of understanding the constraints and risks associated with it. Effective strategies to dealing with the unknown are focused on portfolio diversification and asset allocation.

Portfolio management, whether passive or active, serves little purpose if not accompanied by a careful review of the results relative to the initial plan. Performance is key to the overall success of investing. If desired results are not realized, then a reevaluation of style and strategies is probably in order.

PORTFOLIO STRUCTURING

There are some important considerations that have to be observed when structuring a portfolio. The most important are diversification, stability of value, asset mix, and inflation hedge. Diversification is probably the most effective measure of controlling risk exposure. A stock portfolio must be positioned in several industry groups, depending upon its size. Diversification can mean either an equal share amount or an equal dollar amount. The equal share amount is likely to dampen the portfolio's volatility but may result in average returns. Equal dollar investing can lead to better results, but returns may suddenly grow somewhat volatile. Small stocks are likely to appreciate at a faster rate than more expensive ones. Yet, when they even incur a modest decline, their effect on the overall performance of the portfolio may be devastating.

Another important consideration when structuring a portfolio is the stability of its value. Diversification between debt and equities investment vehicles is a step closer to achieving that goal. Bonds are less volatile than stocks. Blue-chip stocks are more defensive than new issues or small capitalization issues. A portfolio's volatility depends to a great extent on the desired objectives and the financial makeup of the investor. A moderate-return portfolio invested in utilities, bonds, and Dow component stocks is expected to have a high level of stability; a high return often means increased volatility and increased risk. A portfolio concentrated in emerging growth companies' equities with hefty P/E multiples, however, may be at the mercy of market risk. During periods of economic expansion, it may appreciate severalfold relative to its initial value. During phases of business contraction, the same portfolio may suffer large setbacks as multiples decline.

Varying portions of the portfolio have to be invested in

income-producing securities, depending upon the type of portfolio under consideration. Government bonds present the least
amount of risk exposure among debt securities. However, even
in this category, the longer the bond takes to mature, the more
it will decline when interest rates rise. So, although such securities have little, if any, credit risk, the long-term maturities are
more sensitive to the inflation and interest rate outlook. Corporate bonds have a credit risk attached to them, as the issuer
may fail to pay interest on them or default on the principal
when it matures. The higher the bond's rating, the lower the
interest, and the lower the rating, the higher its yield should
be. Typically, during the latter stages of the business cycle, the
spread between interest paid by investment grade and specula-
tative grade corporate bonds expands. In addition, the spread
between the yield on corporate bonds and Treasury securites
also widens. Finally, utilities stocks can also be considered as a
source of income in the portfolio. They combine the benefit of
high dividends, comparable to money market and bond alternatives, with the potential for capital appreciation. However, it
is important to keep in mind that utilities issues carry the risk of
much wider price fluctuations than do bonds.

When structuring an investment portfolio, the final consideration is that of securing some form of protection against
inflation. One way of achieving this objective is by allocating a
portion of the portfolio to precious metals or asset-rich stocks.
Especially in the latter stages of the business cycle, mining
issues tend to do well. Gold, silver, copper, aluminum, and
energy stocks are late market leaders. They often rise after the
stock market cycle has peaked and when most industry groups
have made their final peak. It is important to note that these
same stocks may underperform the rest of the portfolio during
the early stages of recovery or a new bull market.

PORTFOLIO RISK COMPONENTS

Applied money management has to assess risk exposure
continuously and to secure measures to control it. Although it
is not an easy task to protect investment portfolios at all times,

awareness of the amount of risk during the different stages of the business cycle aids in realizing consistent performance. Among the most common risks are yield volatility, inflation, price gyrations, interest rate cyclical fluctuations, reinvestment, and balance sheet risk.

Yield Volatility

Yield volatility is one type of risk that depends to a large extent upon the nature of the stocks held in the portfolio and their credit rating. The higher the quality or investment-grade issues that the portfolio contains, the less the risk from yield volatility. The same can be said about the fixed-income components used in structuring investment portfolios. Treasury securities have a higher rating than corporate bonds. The longer the date to maturity, the more volatile the yield.

Inflation

The inflation risk is also a key factor in determining the structure of an investment portfolio. When inflation is on the rise, companies that do not have a high asset base, such as technologies, have to demonstrate above-average sales and earnings growth rates in order to qualify for investment. Companies with large corporate real estate holdings and reasonably low debt-to-capital ratios can benefit from rising inflation. In general, portfolio structuring decisions should be based on securing overall value with some sort of hedge against inflation, such as precious metals or mining stocks and asset-rich companies. In a disinflationary environment, more weight in defensive industry groups, such as foods and beverages stocks, can enhance overall portfolio performance.

Price Gyrations

Portfolios that consist of high-grade stocks are less prone to price volatility risk than those positioned in fast growth or secondary securities. The fixed-income portion of a portfolio is also expected to have less exposure to price gyrations than equities portions. Price volatility intensifies during the latter stages of the business cycle. Secondary stocks tend to carry a greater credit and financial risk than blue-chip Dow issues. Bonds, too, while they decline ahead of equities, show a smaller percentage decline than that incurred in equities portfolios generally.

Interest Rate Cycles

Interest rate cyclical behavior constitutes another risk for passive portfolio management. Rising rates have a double impact: the downtrends that are usually propelled by such developments, and the relative loss of investment appeal that accompanies it. The interest-rate sensitive portion of the portfolio can be particularly penalized if the trend of interest rates is secular, as was the case in the inflationary 1970s. The equities market is also influenced by diminishing sales and earnings prospects which result from high interest rates.

Reinvestment

For active portfolios, the reinvestment risk is another factor that demands elaborate analyses of future possibilities and further decisions. With each sell decision, a risk is created from the need to reassess the investment environment before selecting the new vehicle that may achieve predetermined portfolio objectives. Especially in bond portfolios, the callability, maturity, and risk factors complicate the analysis process and result in a reinvestment risk.

Balance Sheet Risk

Balance sheet analysis can be simple or complicated, depending upon the individual security under study. Innovative financial management techniques can be used to enhance earnings results. For example, some companies may use debt-to-equities swaps to retire long-term obligations. In such cases, companies may back all or part of the older, low-coupon bonds at a deep discount and finance the purchase by issuing new common stocks. This technique is likely to inflate earnings for the period under consideration. Nonrecurring earning gains result from the debt-to-equities swap. Another accounting strategy known as last-in/first-out can be used to bolster earnings and draw down inventories.

INVESTMENT MANAGEMENT STYLES

Money management styles fall into one of two categories: passive management and active management. Both styles have their advantages and disadvantages. Passive management is concerned with positioning the portfolio in investment vehicles that have particularly long-term appeal. Such a style of management requires patience. It is based mainly on a thorough analysis of the fundamental position of a particular investment, be it stocks, bonds, real estate, or any other kind of investment. The passive investor is a believer in the long-term potential of the chosen security. With passive investment, the internal dynamics of the market are of little value in the decision-making process. The portfolio manager may even ignore the long-term cyclical behavior of the broad market and focus only on those securities with above-average future potential. Such an investment style is oriented toward the bottom-up approach of investment analysis. Active portfolio management, however, requires an active interest in, and talent for, forecasting and trend analysis. The components of the portfolio can be blue chip, a mixture of big-cap and fast-growing companies, or tilted towards emerging growth stocks, depending upon desired objectives.

Passive Portfolio Management

A passive portfolio management style requires a high level of diversification, low turnover, and, usually, high-quality securities. Because of the nature of passive management, an above-average level of diversification is advised. The objective is geared to the securities' long-term appeal and little is expected to occur before full realization of potential appreciation.

Such portfolios are characterized by low turnover, as patience is key in order to let the investment reach its full potential. From the portfolio risk standpoint, passive management should be positioned mainly in high-quality stocks. Those portfolios that contain fast-growing companies are difficult to manage with this style–overweighting a portfolio with emerging growth stocks can be very risky no matter how well diversified.

Active Portfolio Management

Active portfolio management relies on trading and forecasting both the market and the securities trends. While still based on a fundamental assessment of the financial position of the investment under consideration, market-timing methods are applied to enhance performance. With active portfolio management, the duration of time that any particular security is held is far shorter than it is with the passive investment style. The top-down market analysis method is key to anticipating important reversal points and in timing buy-and-sell decisions. Active management requires less diversification, is research intensive, and relies heavily on market-timing techniques. Its objective is to capitalize on market opportunities while maintaining quality and good fundamental value. High volatility issues necessitate close supervision and monitoring of the overall portfolio at all times. The turnover can be high, as needed. A stock belongs to such portfolios as long as it carries potential for appreciation. The moment it reaches its objective, it should be sold and new opportunities investigated. That is why this style of portfolio management relies on intensive and abundant research materials.

TYPES OF INVESTMENT PORTFOLIOS

Investment portfolios may fall into one of the eight types. Portfolios may be classified as value-, growth-, or income-oriented, or may be indexed, sector, broadly diversified, tilted, or global types. This section examines these types of portfolios.

Value-oriented Portfolios

Value-oriented portfolios consist of stocks believed to be selling below their fair market value. The undervaluation may be due to the fact that a stock is selling below what its ultimate potential may be in light of its fundamental position of expected rate of growth. A stock may also be selling at a discount because of investors' ignorance of its true value. It may have been overlooked for a long time. Typically, such a security may have been dormant, with little relative activity or attention from the media or the research community. Another possibility is that a stock may reach an extremely undervalued position during a sharp market decline or a period of price aberration. Such portfolios are more suitable for the passive portfolio management style as it may take an extended period of time before the stock appreciates to its full valuation point.

Growth-oriented Portfolios

Growth-oriented portfolios focus on emerging growth companies that promise an above-average appreciation potential. Many such securities are issues of small-capitalization companies or undiscovered situations that are positioned in a fast-growing industry. Such portfolios can substantially outperform the market during uptrends but are likely to be penalized during bear markets. The P/E multiples can be high for such securities. This type of portfolio may have an above-average risk and should be highly diversified, as the mortality rate of fast-growing companies is high.

Income-oriented Portfolios

Income-oriented portfolios are positioned in securities that bring in high yields or pay large dividends. Theoretically, income-oriented portfolios should have less volatility than any other type of portfolio as long as the credit risk of its components is low. However, a high-yielding junk bond portfolio may appear to serve income-oriented objectives, but the risk associated with such a portfolio can exceed any other type.

Income portfolios that mix maturities, diversify in quality, and have some utilities for capital appreciation may, over the long term, outperform other portfolios in the same category.

Indexed Portfolios

Indexed portfolios contain a large number of blue chip stocks that are representative of the market averages. For example, a portfolio, without regard to its size, may contain all the Dow stocks. Here, the investor has to differentiate between an equal dollar amount invested in each security compared with an equal number of shares of each stock. The latter is the way such portfolios are usually structured. Their performance will match the performance of the index they are representing. At times, secondary stocks outperform big capitalization stocks. At such times, indexed portfolios geared to represent secondary stocks will probably outperform other portfolios representing the Dow industrials or the S&P 500. Indexed portfolios are often managed passively, without regard to business cycle fluctuations.

Sector Portfolios

Sector portfolios focus on investing assets in a single industry group. The basis of selection is dominated by fundamental considerations. Such portfolios are usually small. This investment style is usually passive unless important fundamental changes emerge. Sector portfolios' performance is dependent upon the strength or weakness of their group and its behavior relative to the market. However, every bull market has its leaders and its favored industry groups—those high performers will not necessarily repeat their performance in subsequent business cycles.

Broadly Diversified Portfolios

Broadly diversified portfolios are usually very large and equally diversified in almost all sectors of the economy. Depending upon such portfolios' size, stock selection plays an important role in determining their ultimate performance.

Large portfolios combine the benefits of both passive and active management. Both the top-down and the bottom-up principles are applied in managing such portfolios.

Tilted Portfolios

Tilted portfolios are broadly based, but overweighted in some sectors. Depending upon the position of industry groups during the business cycle, the percentage allocated to some may be larger than to others in order to enhance the overall performance. Leading industry groups or those that possess favorable fundamental appeal are overweighted in such portfolios.

Global Portfolios

Global portfolios seek a broad level of diversification in order to lower the risk. But many other considerations have to be accounted for when investigating the potential of an enlarged menu of investment choices. The key to global portfolio management is the use of asset allocation strategies that determine the portion of investment positioned in the different sectors. More will be said about global portfolio management later in this chapter.

ASSET ALLOCATION

Asset allocation means diversifying assets among such different investment vehicles as equities, debt securities, cash, gold and precious metals, international investments, and real estate. There is a difference between diversification within the same type of investment, such as holding a diversified stock or bond portfolio, and diversification among different kinds of markets. Asset allocation is concerned with the latter, whereby if stocks and bonds fail to produce results, the total return may be enhanced if the real estate or precious metals portion picks up the slack.

In the 1970s, real estate and precious metals were the stellar performers—since, in an inflationary environment, investing in real assets is the best choice. Over-weighting asset concentration in those two investment vehicles may have more than compensated for the poor performance of stocks and bonds. In the 1980s, real estate portfolios continued to appreciate at above-average rates of return. But stocks also averaged a 17-percent rate of return, from 1982–87. Bonds, for the first time since the 1950s, surged to new highs. Precious metals, meanwhile, proved to be poor performers. In the 1990s, international investment may prove to be the next winner as globalization comes on stream. Also, theme investing may outperform most markets. For example, industry groups in the health-care, nursing home, technology, and waste management sectors may benefit from changing demographics and emerging awareness of environmental hazards.

Diversification

Proper asset diversification serves two purposes—to minimize risk and to stabilize returns. Every market gets the touch of grace once in a while. Given a specific set of fundamental and economic circumstances, the outlook may become favorable for a particular market. A portfolio positioned in several industry groups is likely to do better than those specializing in any single one of them. The decline of the value of some of the assets may be compensated for by the appreciation in the others. The record of the past two decades is the best proof of this. When gold and real estate soared, stocks and bonds fell, or at least lagged. And when inflation subsided, bonds and stocks took off, while gold and other precious metals declined. Moreover, asset allocation strategies enable investors to stabilize their returns as the oscillation of strength and weakness among different markets continues through periods of inflation or disinflation. The returns may be less than those on any single market that happens to be in favor for a certain period of time. But the average return is likely to be consistent with healthy appreciation.

Asset allocation can be devised for a mix of active and passive strategies. Part of the position in a specific sector or market may be passive, while another position may be active.

Objectives are targeted by means of forecasts and expectations. If prices reach expected returns, profits can be locked in by changing to an active management style. Active or passive techniques can be used to maximize returns of both individual sector investing and the broad-asset-allocation model.

Asset allocation can also be attained by using mutual fund switching. A family of mutual funds consisting of fixed-income, money market, real estate investment trusts, precious metals, and global portfolios issues is one way of achieving diversification without sacrificing liquidity. One of mutual fund switching's greatest advantages is that it does not require a large amount of capital.

MANAGING A GLOBAL PORTFOLIO

Asset allocation in a global context must focus on the interdependence among world markets. International economies are governed partly by domestic policies and partly by exogenous or external factors related to trade activities. The extent of influence that internal and external factors exert on the risk associated with global investing differs from one country to another. Four main types of risk are associated with global portfolio management: country economic and political risk, currency risk, and liquidity risk.

Country economic risk is a function of the monetary and fiscal policies used to manage internal inflation, unemployment, and growth prospects. Although the business cycle is universal to free market systems, interest rates tend to move in sync both up and down among most western economies. Rising rates in the United States are often followed by money tightening in Japan, Germany, the United Kingdom, and Canada. The high interest rate in any single country compels others to raise their rates to protect their own currency. If countries let their local currencies depreciate in the foreign exchange markets, they could be importing inflation by means of trade imbalances. In addition, for the past two decades, inflation has become a global issue, which has prompted central banks around the world to take consistent monetary action to control it. Because of the global interdependence, a risk is assured by all nations when a country mismanages its own local economy, interferes in the foreign exchange market to boost the value of its own currency, or adopts an excessively stringent or accommodative monetary policy.

In western economies, the political risk is less than in other parts around the world. Yet, in 1988, the Hong Kong stock market plummet in the wake of the unrest in mainland China is an example of the country risk that could prevail even in progressive and capitalist economies. Protectionism could also be considered as a political risk that depends upon foreign government decisions on how to manage their trade surpluses or deficits. The integration of the European community in 1992 could also be analyzed in terms of political risks. It remains to be seen if the process will evolve into a fortress Europe or another progressive step towards globalization.

All investments carry some kind of risk for investors, but when managing global portfolios, the currency risk is by far the most serious factor that managers have to deal with. The value of investments may appreciate in terms of one currency, but may lose when translated into the base or local currency of the country of origin. The question of how adequately investors are rewarded for taking on the currency risk factor is a complicated issue. Identical portfolios may perform differently in terms of the chosen base currency. Asset allocation in a multicountry portfolio adds further complications to the process of evaluating the final risk/reward ratio.

Thus, with global diversification, currency hedging is an integral part of strategic investment decision. A full hedge is realized by selling futures contracts in an amount equivalent to the portion invested in a certain country. Under such circumstances, the fluctuation of the currency may not be a consideration, and the performance of the portfolio may be solely based on the appreciation or depreciation of the chosen assets. A riskier approach is that of investing in foreign markets without currency hedging. In this case, investors or portfolio managers have to analyze the fundamentals of the type of investment chosen *and* forecast the likely future trend of the base currency under consideration. The results can be outstanding, provided that forecasts are accurate on both scores, but that is difficult to ascertain.

Investors and portfolio managers also have to consider the liquidity factor in their risk assessment of global asset allocation. For example, equities markets around the world are illiquid relative to the United States, Japan, the United Kingdom, and probably France and Canada. The number of issues listed on the stock exchanges in of the other countries are few, and the volume is low. A position of 10,000 shares of a particular security can be sold in minutes in the United States, but in Italy, Sweden, Spain, and other European countries, the exchanges may take a few days, if not weeks. As far as investing in real estate around the world, the markets may be even more illiquid than for equities. Bonds are quite liquid in many countries, especially those issued by the governments. The issue of liquidity, in general, should be seriously considered in any international investment program.

THE ACHILLES HEEL

The term "Achilles' heel" comes from the Greek myth of the great warrior Achilles. According to the myth, when Achilles' mother dipped him in the river Styx to make him invincible, the water washed every part of his body except the heel by which she held him. That one weak spot, his heel, was both the proof of his being human and his potential downfall. Rather than accepting his vulnerability and learning from it, Achilles defiantly sought to prove his invincibility. He repeatedly exposed himself to attack and won several battles before his bitter rival Paris shot a fatal arrow in his heel.

This legend can be applied to the way an investor operates in the market. If mistakes are accepted, and learned from, then an investor's Achilles' heel can be the source of success in the investment process. It is more common, however, for bright individuals who know a great deal about market mechanics to demonstrate their lack of ability to beat the game by being too set in their ways. Then there are other categories of investors who go to Wall Street unprepared. Most of these people are successful in their careers as physicians, accountants, lawyers, or engineers, but they do not spend the time necessary to learn the basic rules of investment analysis. Yet, another type of investor sticks to his or her conviction even when the weight of the evidence suggests a different strategy and then it is too late to repair the financial damage that is eventually incurred.

Everyone has his or her Achilles' heel. The brightest analysts, the most astute strategists, or the wisest decision makers, can have dismal investment results when they fail to consider risk seriously. Successful investors recognize their limitations at an early stage and, thereby, cure themselves from their Achilles' heels.

Never Expect Something for Nothing

The most common investor's Achilles' heel is the expectation of getting something for nothing. Prudent investors make sure that the funds they have invested in the securities markets are not needed for any immediate use. Such people often have a well-conceived financial plan in place. A comprehensive financial plan can only be devised if the amount of risk that can be taken has been determined in light of age and expected future earnings. The older an investor, the less risk he or she should be willing to accept. Cash flow needs should be thoroughly analyzed in order to choose the financial objectives of income or growth. A strong financial plan should be reviewed periodically and modified to accommodate new changes in the investor's profile. Once a plan has been devised, the investor should decide whether he or she has the time, knowledge, and inclination to actively manage his or her portfolio or if the responsibility should be delegated to a professional money manager. The stock market is a humbling business and consistency of outstanding performance is illusive at times. But, for those who take the time, acquire the necessary knowledge of trend determination, and overcome their Achilles' heels, the rewards can be substantial.

Success on Wall Street is the result of the interaction of correct trend identification and capital management. The first step that wise investors take is studying as much as they can about the techniques of sound investment. This is the first and best investment they make. Capital management, for the typical investor, deals with risk on a continuous basis. Discipline and the fight against impulse buying and selling are the cornerstones of capital management. It also requires that the investor control his or her emotions and have a long-term perspective of what is happening. The issue should not be how much is to be made on an investment, but rather how much can be lost. And, while it sounds unpleasant, the possibilities of total financial ruin should always be considered when an investor strays from his or her set capital management formula.

Dealing with Investment Risks

In the investment arena, great rewards entail risk taking. In the hierarchy of risk, two factors have established themselves as the most persistent causes of large losses. They are fighting time and fighting the tape. The first is apparent in the awesome losses often incurred in the futures and options markets. The investor should always remember that the market is patient and that a market move takes a long time to materialize. Time, in this case, is the enemy.

As to fighting the tape, it is the equivalent to wrestling with the trend. Prudent investors concern themselves with the long-term outlook. When conditions warrant a change in strategy, however, action should be quick. Trend analysis lets the investor have an objective for his or her gains. As long as a stock is on target with such expectations, an investor's position should remain the same. The moment the norms are violated, however, a move should be made and the position of the stock should be reassessed on all scores.

Consistency and Diversification

Throughout the book, diversification has been stressed. While all studies of securities market analysis and portfolio management techniques share this view, and while Markowitz portfolio studies proved the inverse relationship between risk and the number of securities in a portfolio, the urge to concentrate one's investment has great appeal. The allure of striking it rich with a stock like Compaq Computers, L.A. Gear, Teledyne, or any other high flyer, drives even the most conservative investor into forgetting the best of investment advice. The spirit of gambling is very hard for anyone, even a professional money manager, to resist, and it often influences investment strategies. Yet, the golden rule in the stock market is consistency in actions. Many who succeed in beating the market with one or two stocks tend to give back most of their gains, or they even lose, by following the same strategy with the same stocks. Consistent diversification allows the investor to balance his or her holdings, achieve regular returns, meet predetermined objectives, control his or her emotions, and rid his or her portfolio from excessive volatility.

Never Say Never

The Crash of 1987 is the best testimony to the extent of risk that is constantly present in the stock market. The U.S. economy was growing healthily. Corporate earnings were on the rise. The real estate market was still enjoying its best bull market of the century. The prospect of globalization and world peace propelled optimism throughout the world. The stock market charged along to a level thought impossible only a few years earlier. Wealth and prosperity abounded and corporate takeover activities were at their peak. Industrial production was on the rise. Interest rates were lower than in the 1970s. The market was perceived as destined to move higher. Even those who saw a crash coming found it unwise to make their predictions known. Bearish opinions were ignored. Business school graduates had their eyes on only one thing—a career on Wall Street. Yet, all of a sudden the unexpected happened and the market capitulated in one single day. Even the Great Crash of 1929 could not match the one of 1987. The damage of a full bear market, which used to take years to materialize, took only one day.

If this painful experience taught any single lesson it was "never say never" in the stock market. Many investors today feel safe investing in giant stocks that have the fundamental strength to ensure that a principal investment is safe and sound. History tells us, however, that similar corporations were listed on the Dow Jones Industrial Average earlier this century and have since disappeared.

Have an Objective and Stick to It

"One more point and I will get out" is a common invest-ment mistake that individual investors, as well as profession-als, make. Guessing where the bottom may be is easy at times and buying a security is easier. But determining when to sell is one of the most difficult tasks in the investment arena. Strate-gies may help control the risk, but the realization of a desired objective can only be achieved by selling and locking in the gains. If an assessment of the potential value of a stock is correct and it moves the projected way, the investor should close the position once his or her expectations have been ful-filled. The Achilles' heel syndrome often takes over at this point because once a stock rises, greed prevails and higher targets and expectations set in. The dreams of unlimited rich-ness replace the logical and quantitative reasoning that were used to select the investment and to time its purchase. The investor should position as much as he or she wants but when it comes to selling he or she should have a trader's mentality. Traders treat investments unemotionally. They detach them-selves from the romance that becomes associated with owning a stock. Streaks of success do not lead them to forget that stocks come down as fast as they go up.

Margin Could Be Disastrous

The market is patient. While it is true that some stocks rise fast and yield hefty gains to their holders, the majority of stocks, no matter how enticing their fundamentals are, move slowly and advance moderately. This is why it is dangerous to tamper with margin. Its cost is high and, in the absence of diversification, a sudden decline (even a temporary one) can work against the speculator and lead to total liquidation. Even when margin strategies are executed carefully, the cost associ-

ated with them—otherwise known as the interest payment—
diminishes part of the gains that could be realized. The records
of commodity traders are good examples of the disasters that
can wipe out the diligent efforts of many years. While it is true
that price volatility of commodity futures markets is the main
culprit behind the staggering losses, the reverse process in the
stock market—the slow and contained advance—is the reason
why margin accounts fail to achieve what seems on paper, to
be a more sensible course of action.

Trade with the Trend

The fundamentals of an investment may portray excellent
potential. The economic environment may be ripe for a healthy
advance. Yet, a stock price may remain dormant for many
years despite all the positive catalysts surrounding it. A stock
that has been advancing for a long time may react violently to
one of the many corrections that interrupt the advance of a bull
market. When its subsequent action is monitored, the stock
shows that as the market recovered, the price either continued
to decline or fluctuated in a narrow trading range and was
unable to regain its upward momentum. Under either scenario,
fighting the tape and adhering to a previous forecast may be
dangerous. There is a difference between a normal correction
and a trend reversal.

An interim decline within an overall long-term upward
trend occurs if the stock is able to recover as soon as the market
resumes its advance. On the other hand, a trend reversal occurs when a stock undergoes what looks like a normal decline
within a favorable uptrend but then fails to rebound when the
market does. Growth prospects and excellent financial position
help little when a stock has reversed its major thrust. A quick
response to the apparent deterioration is the only option an
investor can choose. Good traders know very well that a stock
that declines and fails to come back should be suspect no
matter what its fundamental catalysts are. The market, when
least expected, may be driven by its own internal dynamics,
just as it was during the Crash of 1987.

Have the Patience To Wait for High Reward and Do Not Play Against Time

Investment vehicles that have a limited amount of time could be dangerous. Stock options, index futures, and commodity speculation are all limited by a pre-determined time horizon. The market, on average, advances slowly and orderly and declines quickly. Going long on any investment vehicle that has an expiration date is an invitation to a loss. When an investment decision is made, the investor needs long-term perspective.

A Stock Well Bought Is Half Sold

At the market low of 1974, Boeing and Teledyne sold below $3 per share. In the late 1970s, Sears Roebuck sold below $20, American Airlines was priced below $10, United Airlines could be bought for less than $15, Singer sold at below $7, and Chrysler ticked in at less than $5 per share. In the 1980s, Bethlehem Steel once sold below $5, and Compaq went below $6. This list could go on and on. Yet, its lesson is simple: every stock at one time or another, for one reason or another, sells at wholesale levels. The market always presents the patient investor with great opportunities. Once in a while, well-known stocks, decline to levels that are ridiculous when judged by historical value. These are the times when good buys are made. The patient investors whose strategy is based on the context of diversification can profit the most from these opportunities. It is important to remember that such great opportunities occur regularly during almost every bear market. The recognition of the long-term potential of such deep discounted prices is the only way that a reasonable individual may dare to buy a position in them. While the examples mentioned earlier are extremes, there are other situations when a good stock does not go that low and is still a bargain.

A Final Word

This book is aimed at helping the investor to adopt a cohesive investment strategy that he can live with. By illustrating how the different schools of thought function in the stock market, I have attempted to give each investor the insight he or she needs to make wise decisions. The reader should always remember that the stock market is volatile but that a consistent approach to it that is grounded on sound capital management can lead to exciting and, often fulfilling, experiences.

Bibliography

Ayres, Leonard P. *Turning Points in Business Cycles*, New York: The Macmillan Co., 1939.

Bernhard, Arnold. *"The Evaluation of Common Stocks"*, New York: Simon and Schuster, 1959.

Bishop, George W. *Charles H. Dow and the Dow Theory*. New York: Appleton-Century-Crofts, Inc., 1960.

Bolton, Hamilton A. *The Elliott Wave Principle, A Critical Appraisal.* Bermuda: Bolton-Tremblay Ltd., 1960.

Clarkson, Geoffrey, P. E. *Portfolio Selection: A Simulation of Trust Investment.* Englewood Cliffs, N.J.: Prentice Hall, 1962.

Cootner, Paul. *The Random Character of Stock Market Prices*. M.I.T. Press, 1964.

Crane, Burton. *The Sophisticated Investor*. New York: Simon and Schuster, 1959.

Cohen, Zingbarg, and Ziekel. *Investment Analysis and Portfolio Management.* Homewood, Illinois: Richard D. Irwin, Inc., 1987.

Dewey, Edward R., and Dakin, Edwin R. *Cycles: The Science of Prediction.* New York: Henry Holt and Co., 1947.

Drew, Garfield. *New Methods for Profit in the Stock Market*. Boston, Mass: The Metcalf Press, 1951.

Edwards, Robert, and Magee, John. Technical Analysis of Stock Trends. Encyclopedia of Stock Market Techniques. Larchmont, New York: Investors' Intelligence, Inc., 1963.

Graham, Benjamin. The Intelligent Investor. New York: Harper and Bros., 1949.

Graham, Benjamin and Dodd, David. Security Analysis. New York: McGraw-Hill, 1962.

Granville, Joseph. A Strategy of Daily Stock Market Timing for Maximum. Englewood Cliffs, New Jersey: Prentice-Hall, 1963.

Hamilton, William P. The Stock Market Barometer. New York: Harper Bros., 1922.

Jiler, William. How Charts Can Help You in the Stock Market. New York: Commodity Research Publications, 1963.

Lewis, John P. *"Business Conditions Analysis"*. New York: McGraw-Hill, 1959.

Mackay, Charles. *"Extraordinary Popular Delusions and the Madness of Crowds"*. London, 1841.

Moore, Geoffrey H. Business Cycles, Inflation, and Forcasting. Cambridge, Mass.: Harper & Row, Publishers, Inc.

Murphy, John J. Technical Analysis of the Futures Markets. New York: New York Institute of Finance, 1986.

Nelson, Samuel. The ABC of Stock Speculation. Vol. V: The Wall Street Library. N.Y. S.A. Nelson, 1902.

Pring, Martin. Technical Analysis Explained. 2nd edition. New York: McGraw-Hill, 1985.

Rhea, Robert. The Dow Theory. Binghampton, New York: Vail-Ballou Press, 1932.

Samuelson, Paul A. *"Economics."* 5th edition. New York: McGraw-Hill Book Co., Inc., 1961.

Schultz, John. The Intelligent Chartist. New York: WRSM Financial Services Corp., 1962.

Schumpeter, Joseph A. *"Business Cycles"*. Two Volumes. New York: McGraw-Hill Book Co., Inc., 1939.

Schumpeter, Joseph A. *"History of Economic Analysis."* New York: Oxford University Press, 1954.

Smith, Edgar L. Common Stocks as Long Term Investments. New York: The Macmillan Co., 1924.

Stigum, Marcia. The Money Market. Homewood, Illinois: Dow Jones-Irwin, 1983.

Business Periodicals

ABA Banking Journal
Across the Board
Advertising Age
Algemene Bank of Nederland—ABN Economic Review
American Banker
American Demographics
American Express Bank—The Amex Bank Review
American Gas Association Washington Letter
Asiabanking
Asian Finance
Asian Wall Street Journal
Audit's Realty Stock Review
Aviation Week & Space Review
Aviation Week & Space Technology
Banca Commerciale Italiana—The Italian Economy
Banca D'Italia Bolletino Statistico
Banca D'Italia Economic Bulletin
Banco Central De Reserva Del Peru—Bulletin
Banco Central De Reserva Del Peru—Economic Review
Banco Central De Venezuela—Monthly Bulletin
Banco Exterior De Espana—Extebank Monthly Economic
    Report
Banco Nacional De Mexico—Review of the Economic
    Situation of Mexico
Bank & Quotation Record
Bank Dagong Negaraeconomic Review (Malaysia)
Bank Expansion Quarterly
Bank Hapoalim Bulletin (Israel)
Bank Letter

Bank of Canada Review
Bank of England—Quarterly Bulletin
Bank of Finland Monthly Bulletin
Bank of Greece—Monthly Statistical Bulletin
Bank of Israel—Recent Economic Developments
Bank of Japan Economic Statistics—Monthly
Bank of Korea—Monthly Economic Statistics
Bank of Korea Monthly Statistical Bulletin
Bank of Korea Principal Economic Indicators
Bank of Korea Quarterly Economic Review
Bank of New Zealand—New Zealand Business Indicators
Bank of Papua New Guinea—Quarterly Economic Review
Bank of Tokio Financial Review
Banker
Bankers Magazine
Banking Expansion Reporter
Barclays Review
Barron's
Berliner Handels Und Frankfurter Bank—Economic Review
Best's Review—Life/Health Insurance
Best's Review—Property/Casualty
Biotechnology
Biotechnology Newswatch
Bond Buyer
Bond Week
Brookings Papers on Economic Activity
Business Conditions Digest
Business Korea
Business Month (Dun's)
Business Tokyo
Business Week
Canadian Business Review
Central Bank of Ireland—Economic Statistics Quarterly
Central Bank of Kuwait—Monthly Monetary Review
Central Bank of Kuwait—Quarterly Statistical Bulletin
Central Bank of Trinidad and Tobago—Monthly Statistical
    Digest
Central Bank of Trinidad and Tobago—Quarterly Economic
    Bulletin

Central Bank of Trinidad and Tobago—Quarterly Statistical
    Digest
Central Bureau of Statistics of Norway—Monthly Bulletin of
    Statistics
Central Statistical Office of Finland—Bulletin of Statistics
Chain Store Age—General Merchandise
Chase Manhattan Economic Week
Citicorp Investment Bank—Economic Week
Citizens Investment Trust Management Co.—Korea
    Investment Review
Communications News
Conference Board Statistical Bulletin
Construction Review
Copenhagen Handlesbank—Denmark Quarterly Review
Corporate Finance
Coporate Financing Week
Country Report
Credit Suisse Bulletin
Creditanstalt Ca Quarterly—Facts and Figures on Austria's
    Economy
Daewoo Securities Monthly (Korea)
Dai Ichi Kangyo Bank—DKB Economic Report (Japan)
Daishin Securities Co.—Daishin Express (Korea)
Daiwa Securities Co. Ltd.—The Daiwa Economic &
    Industrial Indicators (Japan)
Danmarks Nationalbank—Monetary Review
Danmark Statistik—Monthly Review of Statistics
Database
DE Nederlandsche Bank N.V.—Quarterly Bulletin
Deutsche Bank International DM Bonds
Deutsche Bundesbank Monthly Report
    —Statistical Supplement Series 3: Balance of Payments
        Statistics
    —Statistical Supplement Series 4: Seasonally Adjusted
        Economic Data
Direction of Trade Statistics
Donoghue's Money Fund Report
Dresdner Bank Economic Quarterly
Economic Indicators

Economic Week
Economist
Edward D. Jones Natural Gas Industry
Electric Utility Week
Electrical World
Electronic News
Employee Benefits Journal
ENR (Engineering News Record)
Eoro Week
Eurobond Letter
Euromarket Letter
Euromarket Report
Euromoney
Euromoney Capital Markets Guide
Euromoney Corporate Finance
Export/Import Bank of Korea—Quarterly Exim Bulletin
Far Eastern Economic Review
FDIC Economic Outlook
FED Fortnightly
Federal Home Loan Bank Board Outlook
Federal Register
Federal Reserve Bank/Atlanta—Economic Review
Federal Reserve Bank/Boston—New England Economic
    Indicators
Federal Reserve Bank/Boston—New England Economic
    Review
Federal Reserve Bank/Chicago—Economic Perspectives
Federal Reserve Bank/Chicago—International Letter
Federal Reserve Bank/Cleveland—Economic Trends
Federal Reserve Bank/Dallas—Economic Review
Federal Reserve Bank/Kansas City—Economic Review
Federal Reserve Bank/Minneapolis District—Economic
    Conditions
Federal Reserve Bank/New York—Quarterly Review
Federal Reserve Bank/Philadelphia—Business Review
Federal Reserve Bank/Richmond—Economic Review
Federal Reserve Bank/St. Louis—International Economic
    Conditions
Federal Reserve Bank/St. Louis—Monetary Trends
Federal Reserve Bank/St. Louis—Review

Federal Reserve Bank/St. Louis—U.S. Financial Data
Federal Reserve Bulletin
Federal Reserve Historical Chartbook
Federal Reserve Statistical Release Country Exposure
    Lending Survey
Federal Reserve Statistical Release Foreign Exchange Rates
    —Daily
    —Annual Averages
    —Monthly Tabs
    —Year End Tabs
Federal Reserve Statistical Release Selected Interest Rates
Financial Analyst Journal
Financial Post/Canada
Financial Times of London
Financial World
Financier
Flow of Funds
Forbes
Foreign Affairs
Fortune
Fuji Bank Bulletin
Global Investor
Going Public: The IPO Reporter
Harvard Business Review
Hawaii Business
High Technology
Hydro Review
IMF Balance of Payments Statistics
IMF Survey
Inc.
Industrial Bank of Japan—Quarterly Survey Japanese
    Finance and Industry
Information Week
Infoworld
Inside EPA Weekly
Institutional Investor
Institutional Investor International
International Commercial Bank of China
    —Economic Review
    —Monthly Economic Survey

International Insider
International Financial Law Review
International Financial Statistics
International Financing Review
Investment Dealers' Digest
Investment Decisions
Japan Economic Journal
Journal of Accountancy
Journal of Commerce
Journal of Corporate Taxation
Journal of Finance
Journal of Financial and Quantitative Analysis
Journal of Financial Economics
Journal of Financial Research
Journal of Partnership Taxation
Journal of Portfolio Management
Journal of Taxation of Investments
Kansallis Banking Group—Investment Newsletter (Finnish
    Economy & Stock Market)
Kansallis Osaki Pankki—Economic Review (Finland)
Kiplinger Washington Letter
Korea Development Bank—KDB Report
Korea Investment Trust News—Capital Market Trends
Korea Investment Trust News
    —Company Note
    —Economic Review
Landerbank Report—Report on the Austrian Economy
Landibanki Islands—Iceland Economic Outlook
Latin American Times
Leumi Review Israel Macroperspectives
Manhattan, Inc.
Mergers & Acquisitions
Mergers & Corporate Policy
Midland Bank Review
Monthly Energy Review
Monthly Labor Review
Morgan Guaranty Trust Co.—Morgan Economic Quarterly
Morgan Stamley Capital International Perspective (Monthly
    + Quarterly)

Mortgage-Backed Securities Letter
Municipal Finance Journal
Mutual Fund Forecaster
National Bank of Hungary Quarterly Review
National Bank of Yugoslavia
    —Economic Scene of Yugoslavia
    —Quarterly Bulletin
National Journal
National Real Estate Investor
National Underwriter
    —Life/Health
    —Property/Casualty
National Westminster Bank—Quarterly Review
National Thrift News
New York Times (+ Sunday Edition)
New York Stock Exchange Weekly Bulletin
Norges Bank Economic Bulletin
Le Nouvel Economiste
Novick's Income Property Report
OECD Publications
    —Economic Outlook
    —Financial Market Trends
    —Financial Statistics
    —Main Economic Indicators
    —Quarterly National Accounts Bulletin
Oesterreichische Nationalbank—Austria's Monetary Situation
Offshore
Oil and Gas Journal
Oil Industry Comparative Appraisals
Online
Paris Stock Exchange Charts
Paris Stock Exchange Monthly Statistics
PC Magazine
PC World
Pension World
Pensions & Investment Age
Personal Computing
Petroleum Outlook
Platt's Oilgram News

Privatbanken—Danish Economic Review
Private Placement Letter
Producer Prices & Price Indexes
Public Utilities Fortnightly
Quarterly Financial Report for Manufacturing Corporations
Real Estate Finance Today
Real Estate Forum
Real Estate Review
Reserve Bank of Australia Bulletin
Reserve Bank of New Zealand Bulletin
Royal Bank of Scotland—UK Business Conditions
Sales and Marketing Management
SEC Docket
SEC Monthly Statistical Review
SEC Official Summary
SEC Today
Securities Industry Association (SIA) Foreign Activity
Securities Industry Trends
Securities Regulation Law Journal
Securities Regulation Law Report
Securities Week
Singapore Stock Exchange Journal
SRC RED Book of 5-Trend Security Charts
Stanger Register
Statistics Sweden—Monthly Digest of Swedish Statistics
Stock Charts—Daily Action
Stock Exchange of Singapore—Companies Handbook
Stock Exchange of Singapore—Listing Manual & Corporate
   Policy
Disclosure
Stock Exchange of Singapore—Rules, By-Laws &
   Requirements
Survey of Current Business
Sveriges Riksbank—Quarterly Review (Sweden)
Swiss Bank Corporation—Economic and Financial Prospects
Telecommunications Reports
Telephony
Tokai Bank Ltd.—Tokai Monthly Economic Letter (Japan)
Tokyo Business Today

Toronto Stock Exchange Monthly Review
Treasury Bulletin
Union Bank of Finland—Unitas Economic Quarterly Review
Union Bank of Norway—Stock Market Newsletter
U.S. Banker
Venture
Venture Capital Journal
Wall Street Computer Review
Wall Street Journal
Wall Street Letter
Wall Street Transcript
Washington Post
Wiesenberger Mutual Funds Investment Report
World Financial Markets
Zentralsparkasse Und Kommerzialbank—Austria's Econony
    in Brief

Index